HOMILIES FOR SPECIAL OCCASIONS

HOMILIES
FOR
SPECIAL OCCASIONS

Edited by

CATHAL O'FLANAGAN, O.F.M.

Costello Publishing Company, Inc.

Library of Congress Catalog Card Number: 78-62371
International Standard Book Number: 0-918344-06-9

Printed in the United States of America

CONTENTS

Introduction

Cathal O'Flanagan O.F.M.

Since the publication of the Lectionary in 1970 a great deal has been written to help the homilist break the bread of God's Word for the people. The quarterly *Scripture in Church* has provided commentaries on the readings for Sundays and weekdays. However, comment on the weekday readings is being phased out of *Scripture in Church,* and the *Scripture in Church* editors and contributors have produced *Making the Most of the Weekday Readings,* containing commentary on the week-day readings for the entire year. *Saints in Season* comments on the readings in the Proper of the Saints and the Common Masses. This present volume aims to open up the least known sections of the Lection-ary: the Ritual Masses, the Masses for Various Occasions and Votive Masses. It also includes commentaries on the many readings assigned to Penance and the Anointing of the Sick — two sacraments that have been renewed since the Lectionary first appeared.

So great was the number of readings to be covered that some select-ion had to be made. All the Ritual Masses have been included apart from those concerned with religious profession and the blessing of an abbot or abbess. The more common interests have been selected from the Masses for various occasions: vocations, Christian unity, evangeli-sation, peace and justice, work, world hunger, refugees and exiles, thanksgiving. Among the Votive Masses, only the readings for the Sacred Heart have been included as these are the only ones likely to be used on a regular basis.

Each chapter is divided into two or sometimes three sections. An Introduction gives the background to the readings provided in the Lectionary — the new emphases in the theology of each sacrament; the reasons why Masses for vocations, Christian unity etc. have taken on a new importance. The second section provides a commentary on each reading and in almost all cases on the responsorial psalms too. In some chapters a third section contains suggestions for grouping particular readings and psalms so as to highlight one aspect of the general theme.

The contributors are drawn from a wide variety of background. Many are professional theologians and exegetes. Many are men with great practical experience in their subject: work for peace, involvement

with exiles, first-hand knowledge of world hunger. The aim throughout
has been to relate the scripture readings to the liturgical setting and to
the world in which the listeners live. May this volume help to promote
that "warm and living love for scripture" which is the necessary foundation of any lasting renewal in the celebration of the sacraments and
other liturical rites of the Church. (Cf. Liturgy Constitution of Vatican
II, n. 24).

*   *   *   *   *

Publications referred to above, all published by Costello Publishing Co.,
P.O. Box 9, Northport, N. Y. 11768

Scripture in Church, General Editor: Martin McNamara, M.S.C. $18.95
per year. Quarterly.

Saints in Season, Editor: Austin Flannery, O.P. , 229 pages, paperback,
$5.95
Homilies for Weekdays of the Year, Editor: Martin McNamara, M.S.C.,
267 pages, paperback $6.95
Companion to the New Breviary, Editor: Austin Flannery, O.P., 171
pages, paperback, $3.95

*These books are available at your local Church Goods dealer or
Catholic bookstore.*

Baptism and Catechumenate

Sean Collins, O.F.M.

I INTRODUCTION

The Constitution on the Liturgy of the Second Vatican Council directed that the catechumenate for adults be restored, so that 'the time of the catechumenate, which is intended as a period of suitable instruction, may be sanctified by sacred rites to be celebrated at successive intervals of time' (*Sacrosanctum Concilium*, n. 64). That this provision was not a radically new departure is indicated by the fact that the Congregation of Rites had already, in the previous year (April 16, 1962), promulgated an adapted Ritual for adult baptism which was envisaged as an introduction in stages to the sacrament itself. What is of greater interest in the Council's statement is the manner in which it seems to envisage the juxtaposition of instruction with sanctifying rite. Before commenting on this, it may be possible to clarify what we mean by quoting the 1972 Order of the Christian Initiation of Adults on what the catechumenate is seen to be.

In no. 4 of the Introduction to this Order we read: 'The initiation of catechumens is achieved progressively in the ambient of the community of the faithful. The latter join with the catechumens in dwelling on the riches of the Paschal Mystery, and thus renew their own conversion and simultaneously stimulate the catechumens by their example to open themselves more generously to the Holy Spirit'. One notices immediately the shift in emphasis. The Council speaks in terms that are extrinsecist and static: instruction is 'given' to the candidate, and this imparting of instruction is punctuated by 'sacred rites' — which are indicated as a means of 'sanctifying' the process. These rites do not arise from the inner logic of the catechumenate, but constitute a stand-by apparatus which may be manipulated in order to achieve the desired result. The Order, on the other hand, uses a personalist-relational language which places the emphasis on the dynamic of reciprocity between community of believers and catechumens, and regards the 'sacred rite' as precisely this shared mediatation on the love of God as manifested in the Christ-event (in theological jargon the 'Paschal Mystery') in reading and in

9

prayer, leading to conversion and docility to the Holy Spirit.

It will be argued that a difference of language cannot be all that important: after all, is it not still true that the same catechumenal process will admit of description in either language? The answer must undoubtedly be Yes, but this cannot be taken to mean that it is a matter of complete indifference which kind of language one adopts. We are free to choose our linguistic models, but once chosen they tend to condition our thought, even our perception. The great mistake is to think that any rite is a thing 'in itself', outside of our involvement in it. (The teaching on intention and attention, if nothing else, tells us that.) One can describe, from the outside, what appears to be 'going on' in a Christian celebration; one cannot 'know' what is going on except by being part of it, by sharing in it with faith and commitment. Therefore, while the extrinsic-descriptive kind of language is capable of giving an account, on one level, of what is happening, it is inadequate to convey the faith-experience in its full human richness and depth. The personalist-relational language, while it can never coincide with the vital experience, makes a much better attempt to convey the human texture of the celebrations. The basic reason for the long introductions to all the new sacramental rites is to present them as experiences of encounter between Christ and his people, in the context of faith and community, in the hope that they will be approached and celebrated as such — and not as 'grace machines' that can be turned on and off by using the appropriate magic passwords.

This perspective is particularly important with regard to Baptism, which is the 'sacrament of faith' par excellence: so much so that the sacrament was for a long time administered by the credal interrogation and immersion. In Baptism we are made partakers in the death and resurrection of Christ, and are thus placed, objectively and irrevocably, in the sphere of Christ's victory over sin and death. This is our context: and it is the context of faith, the context of the believing community, the context of the assembly. Faith and sacrament, faith and community, these are correlative terms. The option of faith is fundamentally the decision to accept Jesus Christ as the focus and key to our existence, and this automatically involves community as the end and purpose of what Christ gave himself for and as the locus of his presence in today's world. It also involves the sacraments as the covenanted signs and celebrations of his activity in the Spirit. A faith which could exclude this structure could not be a properly Christian faith.

The renewal of the sacrament of Baptism has as its fundamental thrust the restoration of the vital context of faith and community to sacrament, and their meshing anew into an ecclesial experience. The dislocation of this experience — in practice if not in theory — has in the new rites an opportunity of realising a new articulation and coherence, if the rites are properly understood and utilised. This basic aim, which may be seen in both rites, that for the Christian Initiation of Adults, and that for the Baptism of Infants, is the nucleus of the renewal and its best interpretative key. We shall examine the rites successively with these ideas in mind. Since the Baptism of Adults represents the typical form of this sacrament (though *de facto* in very many countries Baptism is normally conferred on infants) and is the only legitimate starting-point for the theology of the sacrament (theologies of Baptism which begin with God's paternal care for infants who are helpless, etc., can scarcely be taken seriously, even though infant Baptism does high-light God's gracious and unmerited initiative in Baptism), we think it best to begin with the new Order for the Christian Initiation of Adults.

The Christian Initiation of Adults

The new Order, first promulgated in 1972, has provoked some startling-ly different reactions. The most usual is that the entire ritual structure of adult initiation (the typical edition is a bulky volume of 185 pages) is scarcely more than an exercise in archaeologism, the meaningless resuscitation of ancient forms. This is to overlook completely the fact that the new forms are presented as a framework which may be adapted and telescoped as necessary. No. 5 of the Order states unequivocally that 'the Order of initiation is adapted to the spiritual itinerary of adults. This itinerary varies according to the grace of God, which mani-fests itself in so many ways. It depends also on the free cooperation of the candidates, on the degree of activity on the Church's part, and on the various circumstances of place and time'. No. 20 includes the state-ment — truly startling when one considers the normal tenour of this kind of document — that 'nothing can be laid down formally *a priori*'. All this is an effort to offer guidelines without constraining the parti-cular community to follow a rigid pattern which it may find artifical, or which may not correspond to the authenticity of the relational situation. The forms suggested guarantee a minimum skeleton for a progressive faith-encounter between the catechumens and the com-munity in an ecclesial setting: but, as we have stressed above, this can remain a set of dry bones unless the community which is fostering the candidate appreciates the meaning of the process.

Many pastors react to the new Order like the woman in the West of Ireland, who, on the introduction of decimal currency, remained con-vinced that it was perhaps all right for Dublin but would never 'catch on down here'. The basic reason for regarding it as impracticable is that it demands a genuine Christian community to implement it. The days of liturgy confined to the clergy are finished. The catechumenate demands that a community, not only 'sacramentalised' but also 'evangelised', be there to accept and sustain the candidate in his or her initiation; Christian initiation *is* initiation to community. Thus a vicious circle immediately presents itself: a community that is made up of merely sociological Christians, people who regard their coming together on Sunday as at best a token of obedience to the Will of God and at worst a grudging compliance with an arbitrary Law of the Church, a community that is no more than the juxtaposition of devout people, cannot possibly support the catechumenate as it is presented. This gives rise to a ritualistic initiation ('instruction' and 'sacred rites') which in turn leads to another generation of Christians who are initiated sacramentally but not communitarily. How is this circle broken? How are we to restore faith from its artificial vacuum of notional 'instruction' to its connatural setting in community adherence to Christ and celebration of his Lordship? These agonising problems are at the basis of the 'Evangelisation and Sacraments' programmes under way in many countries today. One interesting development is the so-called 'neo-catechumenate', which gathers Christians into groups or communities which try to live out an experience of Christian life and prayer. They use the name 'neo-catechumenate' because they feel they have been baptised (generally in infancy) without being evangelised, and they feel the need to recover the experience of vital Christianity. No doubt this venture is attended by the risks of elitism and even a crypto-Donatism, but hardly more so than religious life. It is at least an attempt to promote a community of faith which experiences itself and constantly feels the need (rather than just heeding the precept) to experience itself as such.

This is the kind of community envisaged by the new Order for the fostering of catechumens. Broadly speaking, the process of initiation is articulated in four stages (but, as we have noted, the guidelines are quite fluid). The first is the precatechumenate, where the interested outsider meets informally with Christians and feels the attraction of the Christian way of life. Eventually the sympathiser is presented to the community and asks to be admitted to the catechumenate. The community prays with him and he hears the Word of God, calling him to conversion and faith. He is signed with the sign of the cross. He now belongs to the household of the faith: it he marries, he is married in church, and if he should die, he receives Christian burial.

With this first public encounter with the community the catechumenate proper beings. It varies in length, depending 'on the grace of God and on the various circumstances' (no. 20) — such as the number of catechumens in a group, the number and quality of catechists available, the cooperation of the community, etc. The catechumens gain a familiarity with the life-style of the community. Their catechesis is to adapt itself to the liturgical year and to be sustained by celebrations of the Word of God. They should be gradually familiarised with the Church's rhythms of prayer, with the help and friendly cooperation of the community. The Church shows her concern for their welfare by praying with them and blessing their efforts.

After suitable consultation between pastors, sponsors and the community, the candidates are admitted to the third stage of initiation, which normally coincides with the Lent before their Baptism. The Rite of Enrolment or Election of Catechumens normally takes place on the first Sunday of Lent, and is conducted, if possible, by the Bishop, who is the one who focuses the unity of the entire local Church. This last period before the sacraments is one of quiet contemplation rather than instruction: 'it is orientated towards the purification of mind and heart by a searching examination of conscience and penance, and the illumination of the candidate through a deeper knowledge of Christ our Saviour' (no. 25). The entire community adapts itself to this progressive development of the catechumens by recalling the graces of Baptism together with them in the Lenten liturgy. In this way all are preparing to celebrate Easter together 'in sincerity and truth'. On the third, fourth and fifth Sundays of Lent there are rites anciently called 'Scrutinies' or rites of discernment: these centre on the three Johannine Gospels of Year A (the Samaritan Woman, the Man Born Blind, and the Raising of Lazarus), and are meant to present Christ as Living Water, the Light of the World, and the Resurrection and the Life. Prayers of purification accompany these Gospel passages. The candidates are also solemnly entrusted with the Creed and the Lord's Prayer, 'the precious documents which have been regarded from antiquity as the quintessence of the faith and prayer of the Church' (no. 181).

Finally, on Holy Saturday night, after the Service of the Word in which God's love for man is set forth, and the unfolding of his plan of salvation, the candidates are baptised, confirmed and communicated. Their faith, which has been growing and maturing in the community, is ratified and sealed by the sacraments of faith. They become a new creation in Christ, are anointed with the Holy Spirit, and become sharers in the one Body of Christ as a 'living sacrifice of praise' in the Holy Eucharist, which is at the summit of the entire process of initiation. Therefore the sacraments are not seen as momentary events, atomised and apart. An excessive validism had torn them out of their natural context, so that 'preparation' was one reality and the 'sacrament' another, on a different plain. If the entire process of initiation is seen from the beginning as the development and intensification of the mutual relationship between the candidate, within the community, and

Christ, then the sacraments will be seen as privileged moments, certainly, and as moments which hear a special convenanted promise, but which are nevertheless on the same vector of growth in intimacy as what has gone before.

The sacraments are normally followed, for a time, by a period of 'mystagogy' — which simply is a deepening of the neophytes' appreciation of the mystery of Christ, by further meditation on the Gospel, and particularly by an assiduous frequenting of the Eucharist. It is recommended that the newly baptised deepen their links with the faithful, and even 'afford them a new vision of things and a new impulse' in their own Christian life (no. 40).

So we have been given an entire programme which, while it may be extensively modified to meet particular circumstances, should, if engaged in wholeheartedly, renew the entire Church. At the moment it may not be used very much in our countries, but this state of affairs can scarcely last very much longer. With the demise of 'Christendom' the ecclesial community no longer automatically coincides with the state, and faith becomes a very personal option. And Baptism must be, and be seen to be, the sacramental consecration of this faith-option. Which brings us to the question of Infant Baptism.

The Baptism of Infants

The new rite provided for infants is a single service, but a preparation is required for the parents and sponsors of the child. This is to ensure that the child will, in so far as we can foresee, be brought up as a member of the Church, and thus 'fulfil the meaning of the sacrament' (Introduction, no. 3). Adults are admitted to the sacraments, as we have seen, after their faith has matured in the community. In the case of infants, the fact that they are born in a Christian household is taken as a sign that God wishes to save this child through the Church. But we must have some assurance that the child will in fact become an active member of the community as it develops into a member of society, otherwise the authenticity of the sacrament as a sacrament of faith is compromised.

The infant is said to be baptised 'in the faith of the Church'. This cannot mean that the Church substitutes for the child's faith. It means that the believing community celebrating the baptism constitutes it as a true sign of God's saving love, and that the infant is received into this community of faith. 'That is why the Church believes it is her most basic and necessary duty to inspire all, whether catechumens, parents of children to be baptised, and godparents, to that true and living faith by which they adhere to Christ and enter into or confirm their commitment to the new covenant' (General Introduction, no. 3).

In the old rite, which was a telescoped version of the rite for the baptism of adults, the infant was directly addressed and questioned, and his sponsor answered for him. The artificiality of this procedure, and the impression it gave that the faith of one could substitute for that of the other (cf. 'standing for' somebody), caused it to be revised in the present rite. At no stage in this rite does anybody 'ventriloquise' for the infant. The parents and sponsors answer for themselves, and profess their own faith. They will constitute the most immediate ecclesial context for this infant (particularly the parents: a fact acknowledged for the first time in this rite), guaranteeing the authenticity of the Church's action in baptising the child. Therefore their faith is of the utmost importance. It must incidentally be an unconscious throwback to the old idea when the English translations of the rite of Confirmation, in rendering the bishop's address, speak of the faith 'which your parents or god-parents acknowledged *on your behalf*' (Interim English version), 'made *for you*' (ICEL), when the Latin text says nothing of the kind.

The faith of the parents and god-parents is fostered by the readings proposed for infant baptism. The infants themselves may be carried to a separate place (presumably because they may become obstreperous!) during the Liturgy of the Word. This must be borne in mind when we examine the Readings for this rite. It is also stressed that, even though formal rites have not been provided for the meetings with parents and sponsors prior to the child's baptism, 'it is important that the instruction should be supported by prayer and religious rites. The various elements provided in the rite of baptism for the celebration of the Word of God will prove helpful' (no. 27). One might also adapt some of the elements from the catechumenate for adults.

It has become customary in the case of infants in the Western Church to separate Baptism from Confirmation and the Eucharist. This means that the catechesis which would normally, in the case of an adult, precede Baptism is imparted, to some extent, before Confirmation and the Eucharist—though these latter are normally also inverted. Traditional preparation for first Communion concentrated almost exclusively on the Real Presence, very little on the Eucharist as the celebration of the Christian community. And preparation for Confirmation consisted of an intensive Religious Knowledge course. Perhaps, if those in charge see fit to retain as normal the practice of infant baptism, though it becomes more problematic—practically, not theoretically—every day, it might be useful to study the elements of the catechumenate for adults, and particularly the vision it contains of the relationship between faith, community and sacrament, and apply them in a modified way to the completion of the initiation of children and young people. In this way the impression may be avoided that the religious upbringing of children consists, unhappily, in doses of 'instruction' punctuated by 'sacred rites' (Eucharist and Confirmation).

II COMMENTARY ON READINGS

CATECHUMENATE AND BAPTISM OF ADULTS

Enrolment of a Catechumen

This is the celebration in which the candidate and the Christian community meet publicly for the first time. The candidate manifests his desire to become a Christian, and the community accepts him and blesses his intentions. The candidate has already, in the 'pre-catechumenal' stage, conceived an initial faith and a desire for conversion, with the help of his Christian friends. The first reading (Gen 12:1-4), describing the call of Abraham, stresses that even the beginning of faith is God's gift, an answer to his gracious call. At this very first moment, the dialogical nature of the whole Christian life is highlighted. The Christian has no ultimate security other than his loving trust in the fidelity of the God who has called him. This concept is further underlined by the Responsorial Psalm (Ps 32): those whom God has chosen for his own are sure of his love, as they place their entire trust in him, because 'the word of the Lord is faithful'.

The Gospel (Jn 1:35-42) presents a sketch of conversion. The witness of John leads the disciples to approach Jesus, and to accompany him, at his invitation, to his house. The result of their prolonged visit is a personal conviction about him; and the enthusiasm of this conviction results in their bringing others to the Lord. It is also possible that the episode of the renaming of Simon, mentioned here, was chosen on account of the imposition of the new Christian name which may be performed at this rite (cf. *Ordo* no. 88).

The essence of the celebration is well illustrated in the Liturgy of the Word and in the prayers for the candidates; the other anxiliary rites — signing with the sign of the cross, presentation of a copy of the Gospels etc., together with 'other gestures which seem locally suitable for signifying the welcome of the community for the newcomer' (*Ordo* no. 89), flesh out this nucleus and express it plastically: thus the acceptance of a catechumen is never to a faceless or simply bureaucratic 'Church', but always to this specific faith-community.

Nomination of Candidates for Baptism

This celebration normally takes place on the First Sunday of Lent. The readings suggested are simply those of the current year. The reason for this lies in the renewal of the Lenten liturgy itself. The final stages of the preparation of the catechumens is no longer something which takes place alongside and parallel to the Lenten liturgy. Lent has been more consciously restored as a time of conversion and baptismal orientation; the entire community meditates on the Paschal Mystery and plunges itself more deeply into its actualisation. Catechumens and faithful assist each other in progressive conversion — to be crowned with the Sacraments of Initiation in the case of the catechumens, and with sacramental reconciliation and the Paschal Eucharist in the case of the faithful. Thus the Lenten themes proposed in the Lectionary are of vital importance for the catechumens too.

The celebrant's introduction to the 'Intercession for the Candidates' is instructive: 'Dear friends in Christ, today we have set out on our Lenten journey, in preparation for the saving mysteries of the Lord's passion and resurrection. Those who have been chosen to prepare with us for the Easter sacraments expect from us the example of our renewal. Let us therefore pray to the Lord on their behalf, and on our own behalf, that, moved by mutal example and support, we may become worthy of the graces of Easter'.

The Scrutinies or Discernment Rites

The three celebrations of the Scrutinies take place — normally — on the third, fourth and fifth Sundays of Lent. 'The purpose of the Scrutinies' — according to the *Ordo* no. 154 — 'is to purify the minds and hearts of the catechumens, to strengthen them against temptation, to bring about a greater change of heart and strength of purpose in following Christ more closely, and to foster the love of God in their lives.' The celebrations hinge on the three Gospels of Year A for these Sundays: on the Samaritan Woman (Jn 4), the Man Born Blind (Jn 9) and the Raising of Lazarus (Jn 11). On each Sunday the Church unfolds before the candidates an encounter of Jesus with a stylised character from the Gospel, revealing how inadequate men's understanding of Christ can be, and how he can and will satisfy the deepest longings of our hearts.

This concrete approach with its immediate impact (the Gospels can easily be dramatised or read by various 'voices') is a good example of the pedagogy of the Liturgy. Rather than give notional definitions of the nature and effects of Baptism, the Church leads her catechumens, by the hand as it were, to the living Christ. She does not seek to programme the encounter — each person is unique. The evocation through the Gospel episodes of what it must be to come to Jesus and to experience him more and more profoundly as the meaning and justification of one's life — this is the significance of the scrutiny Gospels. And their impact is reinforced by the prayers of Exorcism, which recall in each case the specific episode narrated in the Gospel.

In the *first Scrutiny* (Third Sunday) Jesus is encountered in the Gospel (Jn 4:5-42) as the one who gives 'living water' — the new economy of the Spirit, which is 'a spring welling up to eternal life'. The one who has faith in Christ has within him a radically new source of life; he is in communion with reality, beyond the deceptive and evanescent appearance of everyday affairs. He is the 'true worshipper', because his relationship with the Father is rooted in Jesus (who is the 'truth' of man before God: the obedient son) and is realised in the Spirit. It is the Spirit that is poured into our hearts to make us sons in Christ, thus constituting us as polarised towards the Father.

This Trinitarian relationship is sketched for us by St Paul in the second reading (Rom 5:1-2, 5-8). Another emphasis in both readings is the initiative of God in Christ with regard to our conversion and salvation. Christ died for us while we were still estranged from God; he waits by the well for the Samaritan woman. Both concepts are expressed beautifully in Thomas of Celano's verse—

> Quaerens me sedisti lassus,
> Redemisti crucem passus —
> Tantus labor non sit cassus.

The first reading is simply an account of a water-shortage among the Israelites in the desert (Ex 17:3-7). They took lack of water to be a sign of God's disinterest, its presence to be a sign of his fatherly care. The living water of life in the Spirit, as a permanent and abundant gift of the Father, excludes lack of trust on our part — if we have really 'known the gift of God'.

The *second Scrutiny* (Fourth Sunday) centres on the symbol of light, especially as experienced in the gift of sight (Jn 9:1-41). The contrast between the leaders, who might have been expected to 'see' but are blind, and the blind man who does have sight, carries along the narrative. The leaders are convinced they know all about Jesus just because they can slot him into their own categories. There is no openness towards encounter. The beggar finds these categories completely irrelevant ('whether he is a sinner or not I don't know'); he has encountered Jesus, and the encounter carries its own authentication ('I know I was blind and now I can see'). Here is the point. Only a personal meeting with Jesus, so intimate that I know and can see that he has an ultimate claim on me, is of value for faith — and this meeting is Jesus' own gift. It can shortcircuit all the theological arguments and categories, and without it there can be no faith. The prayers appointed for the Scrutiny emphasise this insight, which is so important for the catechumens, especially where the catechumenate is seen as a series of doses of 'instruction'.

The second reading is a parenetic section from Ephesians (5:8-14) on the theme of light and darkness (in a different key, therefore, from the Gospel). But it embodies a snatch of an early hymn—possibly baptismal—which gives it a relevance here. Life before one encounters Jesus is the same as sleep or even death; the baptismal encounter is an enlightenment (a favourite term of the Greek Fathers in referring to the sacrament of 'Illumination') — not in the rationalistic sense that we act thereafter in a more 'enlightened' way, but in the sense that we are utterly recreated from within, and equipped to see the splendour of all God's creation in a fresh way, as centred on the 'New Man', Jesus Christ.

The first reading (1 Sam 16:1, 6-7, 10-13) on the divine election of David and his anointing by Samuel, is not related intimately enough to the other readings to be very useful for our purpose.

The *third Scrutiny* (Fifth Sunday) brings to a climax the existential understanding of Jesus which has been developing in the previous Sundays. The giver of living water, the one whom we have embraced as the Light of the World, is now shown as the very principle of our existence, our very Life (Jn 11:1-45). All the images which have tried desperately, pushing against the edges of language and imagination, to convey what God has prepared for those that love him — i.e. Christ in us, our hope of glory — now culminate in the supreme affirmation of Jesus as the resurrection and the life. This is the final moment of discernment in these 'Rites of Discernment', the final orientation towards the moment of sacramental encounter itself. The growing faith of the catechumens now enables them to 'see' the final sign of Jesus, the raising of Lazarus, as a paradigm of their own relationship with him. Each one of them is the 'one whom Jesus loves' and calls to life.

The other readings prepare for this moment of discernment. The first (Ezek 37:12-14) is the ending of Ezekiel's parable of the dry bones: God's promise of new life. This will come, not as the result of a completely fresh start from chaos, but through the renewal and re-creation of a remnant (the 'bones'). Note that it is in this act of resurrection that the Lord is known as Lord—not so much by the bystanders as by those directly affected. This dovetails with the Scrutiny Gospels: the hurler on the ditch can remain indifferent to what Jesus does. Acknowledging him as the Christ comes only with allowing oneself to be engaged by him, and ultimately transformed.

The second reading (Rom 8:8-11) returns once again to the Spirit as the principle of risen life in the followers of Jesus.

The Giving of the Creed

The solemn presentation of the Creed, which normally takes place during the week after the first Scrutiny, is intended to 'fill the candidates with faith and joy in the contemplation of God's wonderful deeds on our behalf' (*Ordo*, no. 25). The Creed is, as it were, a synopsis of salvation history, 'starting out from the fact that God made all things very good, and continuing down to the present period of Church history' (St Augustine). Therefore it has the nature of confession-praise as well as profession. Rather than being simply a shibboleth to identify the orthodox, it is the expression of a commitment to the loving Father who, 'for us men and for our salvation' sent his Son to bring us abundance of life, and continues through the Spirit in the Church to inaugurate the new humanity.

The readings underline this approach. The Old Testament reading (Deut 6:1-7) voices the supreme conviction of Israel: all-consuming love for the Lord God who creates and saves must be the mainspring of life and activity. Commandments and ordinances must be seen in this light; threfore we must have God always before our eyes. For the Christian, and for the Catechumen, the Creed must never become a sterile formula, but serve as a memorial of what God's love has achieved for sinful man. The Responsorial Psalm (18:8-11) links praise of the Law with Peter's confession after the Bread of Life discourse: 'You have the message of eternal life, O Lord'.

Two epistles are suggested: Rom 10:8-13 or 1 Cor 15:1-8. The first emphasises that salvation is not something arduous to be won by one's own efforts, but has been given to us as a free gift in Christ. Our part lies in grasping that salvation through a lively faith in Christ, whom God has raised from the dead for us, a faith which has its expression in the baptismal profession 'Jesus is Lord'. Confessing the faith with one's lips is seen as the natural concomitant of faith in the heart. The second epistle is a rehearsal of the primitive tradition by Paul, just as he had received it: fidelity to the Good News as it was handed on is essential for salvation. What is in question here is the central nucleus of the faith: the death and resurrection of Jesus.

There are also two Gospels: Mt 16:13-18 and Jn 12:44-50. Peter's confession of faith in Jesus at Caesarea Philippi is a gift from the Father; it is not the result of his own effort or personal interpretation of events. And it is in this gift of God that Jesus' followers are gathered together. Their profession of faith in Jesus' personal status and his relationship to the Father grounds them firmly against attack and renders them victorious even over death. The alternative passage is a resumé of Jesus' preaching at the end of the first twelve chapters of John. The themes are: Jesus as the Father's 'apostle'; Jesus as the Light of the world; condemnation as coming, not from Jesus, but from man's own refusal to accept the word of Jesus. The Father is the source of the word of life which is manifested in Jesus. Those who accept and embrace this word have eternal life. Those who refuse stand condemned already by the very wilfulness of their rejection of Jesus.

The Giving of the Lord's Prayer

This is celebrated during the week after the third Scrutiny. The Lord's Prayer, which Tertullian called 'breviarium totius Evangelii' (compendium of the entire Gospel), 'is the special prayer of those who have received the Spirit of Adoption of Sons in Baptism, the prayer which will be recited for the first time by the newly baptised in the midst of the faithful, during the Eucharist of Easter Night' (*Ordo,* no. 188). It is often assumed that the 'Our Father' is a prayer that anybody 'who believes in anything' could join in: this is not the attitude of the Church. Rather, it is the prayer of those who have become sons by their sharing in the Spirit of Christ and can say, with and in him, 'Abba' to the Father.

The first reading (Hos 11:1, 3-4, 8-9) is an expression of the tender love of God for his covenant people. It is unfortunately somewhat mangled as it stands in the Lectionary. What is clear is the warm compassion of God, which is not lessened by the disobedience of his child. The novelty of the New Testament will be that God's Son will reciprocate the Father's Love, and will extend to all who believe in him the power to share in his loving obedience to the Father.

Two responsorial psalms are proposed. Psalm 22 uses the imagery of pastoral life to express the complete confidence of the psalmist in God. This trusting repose in the knowledge of the Lord's continuing care extends even to moments of darkness and trial. Psalm 102 rejoices in the thought that the awesome Lord of heaven and earth shows his might in compassion and tender love. This has been experienced in the life of the covenant people, and the psalmist makes it his own: his ecstatic call to 'his soul' to praise the Lord can readily be shared by the Christian who is aware of God's grace and pardon in a degree never dreamt of by the Old Testament.

For the second reading, there is a choice between the two famous Pauline 'Abba' passages, Rom 8:14-17, 26-27 and Gal 4:4-7. It is the Spirit of the Son, sent by the Father into our hearts, which cries out in us (Galatians), or which makes us cry out (Romans) 'Abba'—'Father'. The use of the original word, with its Greek translation, shows us how vitally important it was regarded. The new relationship through the Son with the Father is the quintessential reality of the Christian life, and it is the mission of the Spirit precisely to bring about this 'new creation'. The catechumens, in hearing the Lord's Prayer in the context of these readings, are introduced to what they are fully to experience in the Sacraments of Initiation. The passage from Romans adds a later section (8:26-27) on the aid we receive from the Spirit 'when we cannot choose words in order to pray properly'. Our intentions fail, not simply because we haven't the strength to fulfil them, but because they are not 'according to God'. The continual assistance of the Spirit is not merely the suggestion of prayers (even the Lord's Prayer), since the outward forms can conceal a self-centered mind, but the direction of our deepest selves towards wating what God wants: he 'pleads for God's own people in God's own way' (NEB). The 'Our Father' is fundamentally the embodiment of the community's concern for the hastening of the manifestation of God's rule—but even this prayer falls short on our lips if we do not allow the Spirit to articulate it in the depths of our hearts.

The Gospel proposed in the Lectionary is the version of the Lord's Prayer according to Luke, the shorter one (Lk 11:1-2). Whereas in the *Ordo* the version offered is that according to Matthew—the ecclesiastical version (Mt 6:9-13). It is preceded by the deacon's invitation: 'Let those who are to receive the Lord's Prayer come forward'. And the celebrant tells them: 'Listen now to how the Lord taught his disciples to pray'. The deacon then continues with the Gospel. It would seem more sensible to use the version which is in fact being used in the community when it prays—normally the version of Matthew. Luke's version, normally regarded as 'the oldest form with respect to *length*', whereas 'the Matthaean text is more original with regard to *wording*' (Jeremias), has the advantage of using the familiar address of Jesus, 'Father', without any adornment. But the Matthaean form, already found prescribed for formal prayer in the Didache, is more balanced and better adapted for public recitation.

Preparatory Ceremony

This is an optional ceremony, which may take place on the morning of Holy Saturday. It may contain the recitation of the Creed by the catechumens, the choosing of a Christian name for the candidate (if he hasn't already got one), and the rite of *'Ephphatha'*, 'which, by its symbolism, stresses the necessity of grace for the proper hearing and the saving confession of the Word of God' (*Ordo*, no. 200). The idea comes from Mark (7:31-37) where the cure of the deaf mute is accomplished by Jesus with the command 'be opened' ('ephphatha'). The celebrant reads this Gospel passage and explains it briefly. It is important to emphasise that the 'business' connected with the cure is not the essential point: the word of Jesus heals the afflicted man. (Though retained in the Gospel as a foreign word—possibly Christian healers used it—it is a simple command on Jesus' lips, in his own tongue.) The crowds acclaim Jesus as the one who 'has done all things well'. He is the one who heals and restores man integrally. Not just in his physical afflictions, but in making him a 'new creation' from within, restoring his faculties in their essential harmony. This is why the Church can use this episode as expressing the gift of Christ by which a man is reorientated towards God and made sensitive to hear and proclaim his word. After the Gospel the celebrant touches the ears and lips of the catechumens, saying:

> 'Ephphatha, which is, "be opened",
> to profess the faith, which you have received by hearing,
> to the praise and glory of God.'

Baptism during the Easter Vigil

The Orthodox theologian Alexander Schmemann has recently written on the disastrous consequences for the Church of having divorced Easter from the mystery of Baptism, 'a mystery for which the Church prepared herself by forty days of fasting and which constituted the very essence of her paschal joy'. The relegation of baptism to quasi-private celebrations went hand in hand with a reduction of its meaning to a 'wiping out' of original sin and a membership-card of the Church, which was necessary to present to the heavenly doorkeeper eventually. Baptism as the new creation, as a participation in the death and resurrection of Christ, was forgotten, and the Christian's life became an 'upper storey' built on top of 'normal' life and running on grace. Whereas by Baptism we are placed in an utterly new relationship with everything; we are still the same, yet wholly new. Baptism is not something on a certificate *entitling* me to certain benefits, it is my re-creation, the establishment of my truest self, in the risen life of Christ.

When Baptism is celebrated in the course of the Easter Vigil—which is the normal time for baptising adults—the readings appointed for the Vigil find their fullest application. The collects which follow each of the Old Testament lessons are the Church's own reading of the Old Testament in the light of Christ, symbolised here by the Paschal Candle, and of the life of the Church. As Augustine says, 'for no other reason were all the things that we read in the Scripture written before our Lord's coming than to announce his coming and to prefigure the Church to be, that is to say, the people of God throughout all the nations. . .' As we ponder the wonderful deeds of God in the past, we see them as the anticipation and inauguration of the baptismal mystery: 'even today we see the wonders of the miracles you worked long ago'

(Prayer of Third Reading); 'by the preaching of the prophets you proclaimed the mysteries we are celebrating tonight' (Prayer of Fifth Reading). The Blessing of the baptismal water also highlights the Old Testament types of Baptism.

What is more important than a detailed commentary on the various readings is a grasp of the underlying spirit of the celebration. This is well expressed by Danielou when he says that 'In the Exodus, in the death and resurrection of Christ, and in Baptism, it is the same redeeming action which is accomplished on different levels of history—that of the figure, of the reality, and of the sacrament'. The broad sweep of salvation history: how 'all things were created in wonderful beauty and order', and 'how still more wonderful is the new creation by which, in the fulness of time, you redeemed your people through the sacrifice of our Passover, Jesus Christ', the unity of God's saving plan, the essentially forward orientation of the entire celebration—all these make of this liturgical event the most intense experience of what Christianity *is*. In it we are given the possibility of overcoming the false dichotomy between doctrine (what we hold to be true *about* God and Christ and man) and life (our encounter with God in Christ and our experience of them *in* the Spirit). For too long liturgy has been something to be *performed*, while we nourish our Christian vision on the latest trendy theologians. The spirit of the Paschal Vigil, if we immerse ourselves in it, is not only a splendid presentation, in word and gesture and colour and music, of the kernel of the Christian reality, but it is a profound *experience* of what it presents: the victorious presence of the risen Lord, forming in the Spirit the new humanity of free and selfless people, moulding them to be for the Father a 'living sacrifice of praise'. At this point Baptism and Easter are one.

Baptism of Adults outside the Easter Vigil

Adults may be initiated outside of the Paschal Vigil 'on account of extraordinary circumstances, if pastoral considerations demand it' (*Ordo,* no. 58). The Lectionary offers a long series of readings to be chosen ad libitum for this eventuality. They emphasise different aspects of the sacrament, and should be carefully chosen to meet the needs of the particular celebration, according to the needs of the candidates, surrounding circumstances, etc. The idea of leaving the choice of readings to the last minute, and then to have it done solely by the candidate, is not a very responsible attitude. It may be a good idea to go through all, or most, of the proposed readings in the course of the catechetical sessions, and then choose, by general agreement and on an informed basis, the readings to be used for the celebration. The readings of the Paschal Vigil are always the ideal form of the celebration, and should be borne in mind as a model.

A. OLD TESTAMENT READINGS

1. *Gen 15:1-6, 18.* Abram, 'our father in faith', put his trust in God's promise. Even though, humanly speaking, all his goods would pass into the hands of outsiders—since he was old and had no son—he stood firm, against all the evidence, in the hope that the word spoken to him would be fulfilled, and God reckoned him as righteous on that account. The final verse (the account of the mysterious alliance ceremony is omitted here) connects the theme of the promised land with Abram's faith. Baptism is the sealing of the response of faith to the God who has addressed a man inwardly and led him to the Christian community. In the ancient baptismal rites the interrogatory confession of faith in the Father, the Son and the Holy Spirit—i.e. in God as creating, redeeming and sanctifying us—was the 'form' of the sacrament. This option of faith, which must resolutely be distinguished from mere conformism, has no other basis than the fidelity of God to his promises. The extreme expression of this faith is found in the second reading of the Paschal Vigil—the sacrifice of Isaac. Both these lessons stress the essential truth: faith, upon which baptism and justification are based, is a divine gift. It is utterly remote from human calculation, and finds its source and principle only in the 'opening of the heart which comes from the Holy Spirit' (*Ordo*, no. 9).

2. *Gen 17:1-8.* God grants a covenant to Abram. He reveals his name ('God of the Mountains'?), and bestows a new name on the patriarch: Abraham. The covenant changes Abram's life and very being—he is now in a new relationship with God. The names express the depths of this relationship. Abram, now become Abraham, must 'walk blamelessly before' God: he must never forget his close bond of obedience to him. This hieratic priestly account emphasises the essential passivity of Abram's role—God takes a sovereign initiative; man bows in acceptance.

3. *Gen 35:1-4, 6-7.* The renunciation of cult-objects recounted here, whether they pertain to the worship of other gods, or were superstitiously used in the worship of Jacob's own God ('the God who appeared to you'), is scarcely very relevant in the modern baptismal context (except perhaps in certain cultural settings) unless one transposes it to the plane of the renunciation of 'all that is not God'. The Fathers, in their catechetical instructions, stress the importance of the renunciation of Satan and confession of adherence to Christ, and urge their hearers remain faithful to their promise. 'From you he receives only words, yet he entrusts to you realities, a great treasure. He forgets your past ingratitude; he remebers nothing of your past; he is content with these few words' (John Chrysostom). This reading might be used—though with careful explanation—to inculcate the absolute fidelity to Christ implied in baptism.

4. *Deut 30:15-20*. The existential choice between obeying and ignoring God is presented in this reading and in the next one. The discourse, put into the mouth of Moses, is directed to the people in exile: the repetition of the word 'today' underlines the actuality of the hearing of the word—it placed each one unequivocally before a choice. And ultimate happiness or destruction depend on this freely entered decision. While we might regard the system of reward and retribution proposed in the Deuteronomic works as simplistic, the basic message is vigorously presented and rings true: obedience to God means life, disobedience means death. 'Life' for the exiles meant in the last analysis a return to their homeland: for us it may mean something like rich and fulfilling relationships, meaningful goal realisation, etc. There is nothing we can legitimately desire that fidelity to God does not enrich immeasurably.

The early sections of the Didaché, before the account of how baptism is conferred, treat of 'the Way of Life' and 'the Way of Death', and probably represent a primitive catechetical presentation of the moral aspects of Christianity. They are the best Christian commentary on the present lesson.

5. *Josh 24:1-2, 15-25*. The account of the covenant-renewal assembly at Shechem would seem to be envisaged as fulfilling the same function in the baptismal liturgy as the previous reading. Both the people's freedom of choice and the gravity of the decision are stressed as in no other text. Unfortunately the motivation for the choice, the mighty deeds of God in favour of his people, is not included in the present pericope. It must always be stressed that our adherence to God is always a response to his gracious gift. Certainly the extreme difficulty of fidelity is underlined here ('You cannot serve the Lord, because he is a holy God. . .'); the Christian is continually aware of the fact that it is only through God's own gift that he can persevere in God's love.

6. *2 Kings 5:9-15*. The cure of Naaman is one of a cluster of stories which circulated about the figure of Elisha. Since it is effected by water it is connected with baptism in church tradition. The contrast between the spectacular display expected by Naaman and the actual means used by Elisha (who doesn't even bother to come out to receive him) is instructive. What matters is faith and obedience—God's power doesn't need external fanfare. 'There is absolutely nothing which makes men's minds more obdurate than the simplicity of the divine works which are visible in the act, when compared with the grandeur which is promised thereto in the effects; so that from the very fact, that with so great simplicity, without pomp, without any considerable novelty of preparation, finally, without expense, a man is dipped in water, and amid the utterance of some few words, is sprinkled, and then rises again, not

much (or not at all) the cleaner, the consequent attainment of eternity is esteemed the more incredible' (Tertullian). There is a pastoral-liturgical lesson here: we must continually verify whether our celebrations have not become overlaid with useless incidentals so that the essential simplicty of the sacramental action is obscured. An injudicious and slavish application of the letter of the baptismal *Ordo* (which is more complicated than it was in Tertullian's time!) could lead to this imbalance. We must constantly stress faith and its encounter with Christ in the covenanted sign of his death and resurrection.

7. *Is 44:1-3.* The fidelity of God to the people he has chosen with special love is again proclaimed. The promised new manifestation of God's predilection is accompanied by the phrase, 'Do not be afraid', which is often connected with theophanies. The reassurance is based on the fact that the Lord is present in love and compassion. Water in the desert is something which has to be seen as pure gift—it is so patently beyond the power of man himself to provide it. God will satisfy his people with every good thing, including a renewal of life ('my spirit').

8. *Jer 31:31-34.* The famous passage on the new covenant has had an immense influence on Christian thought. The Church draws her very origin from the 'new covenant' sealed in the blood of Christ. The covenant is new because it will be an interior relationship, one of trust and intimacy, between the people and God. The Law, being an external ordinance, could be broken; the new covenant will consist essentially in a direct experience of the forgiving and faithful Lord. Jeremiah had experienced the reform of Josiah, which had been a decreed 'clean-up' of religion, but which had failed in the long run because it was based on externals: 'Judah did not return to me with her whole heart, but in pretence' (Jer 3:10). The Christian covenant is based on the sacrifice of Christ; with him there is no question of 'Yes and No—with him it is always Yes' (2 Cor 1:19). We have the possibilty of sharing in this steadfast obedience, this intimate knowledge of the Lord, offered us in baptism. In him we too become sharers in the new covenant. We cannot count on our own strength, but we can draw on his. The Holy Spirit, poured into our hearts, equips us to 'know the Lord', so that he is our God, and we are his people.

9. *Ezek 36:24-28.* The promise of a new and intimate relationship in sincere love and fidelity is again stressed in this remarkable passage from the priest-prophet, Ezekiel. His imagery very often hinges on concepts of purification from defilement. The 'rite' by which the Lord will invisibly purify his people will have an efficacy unparalleled in the history of the nation. Its effects will penetrate to the very depths of men's hearts and bring about a change in feelings and outlook. By

implication, the hollowness of merely external purification rites is insinuated. The use of water-imagery here is purely figurative: no water, even in a ritual context, could do what God promises to do here— change the deep-seated sinfulness of man. In the same way, there is no proportion between the water used in baptism and the wonderful change it effects in a man; nevertheless the water, as symbol, in conjunction with the word of God and as its covenanted embodiment, sets us in the context of salvation which is the Church of Christ. 'Withdraw the word, and what is water but simply water? The word combines with the element, and it becomes a sacrament' (Augustine).

Note that the Old Testament readings which refer to water (nos 6, 7 and 9) treat it as a cleansing agent (6 and 9) or as refreshment (7). The primary symbolism of water in Christian baptism is that of death and life, destruction and creation. The primary type is the crossing of the Red Sea. The Israelites crossed over dry-shod (hence they didn't even touch the water, so there can be no question of washing or purification!) and escaped the threat of destruction 'through the water'; the pursuing Egyptians were drowned in the same water. The Fathers saw the waters of baptism as the drowning of the 'old man' and the birth of the new. 'It is the nature of water to receive men who are alive and cast them up dead. The water of baptism, however, receives dead men and casts them up alive' (Zeno of Verona). It is unfortunate that none of the proposed Old Testament readings portray this water-symbolism: the notions of washing and of quenching thirst are simply too restricted to depict the radical change which is effected by baptism. Of course it always remains possible to take the Exodus reading from the Easter Vigil. In any case, it is important to avoid a tritely moralistic approach to the sacrament.

B. NEW TESTAMENT READINGS

1. *Acts 2:14, 36-42.* A stylised presentation of the entire initiation process: kerygma (rather stunted here!), conversion-response, baptism, fellowship, eucharist. Without teasing out any of the various elements, it shows their dynamism and inner relationship. Repentance and faith in Jesus lead to baptism and forgiveness of sins, and the gift of the Spirit. The Spirit keeps men in communion with the living faith of the Church and its eucharistic expression. This reading could prove very useful when—as is normally the case—the three sacraments of Initiation are celebrated together in a community context.

2. *Acts 8:26-38.* The account of the baptism of the Ethiopian eunuch is part of a composite picture, showing that membership of the Church is not confined within the limits of the old rules. Philip is seen converting Samaritans in the first part of this chapter; here he accepts one who is a

foreigner and legally an outcast. The Ethiopian seems to have been a sympathiser; he is returning from a pilgrimage to Jerusalem and is reading the prophet Isaiah. Philip begins from the man's immediate preoccupation, and in this way explains the Good News to him. Verse 37, which is included in the Lectionary, is an early addition to the text (found in the Western text). It is a baptismal profession of faith: 'I believe that Jesus Christ is the Son of God'.

3. *Rom 6:3-11*. The fact that this passage is the most extended on baptism in the writings of St Paul causes us to forget at times that it is not an ex-professo treatment of baptism. Paul here is concerned to refute the (false) inference from his previous chapter that, since where sin abounded grace abounded all the more, we should continue sinning so as to give grace greater scope. Paul's answer is that we cannot do this, since as far as sin is concerned we are dead. Being 'baptised into Christ' means being baptised 'into his death': Paul seems to be thinking of the descent into the water and subsequent re-emergence. Baptism is not just an external application to us of the value of what Christ did in dying, being buried, and rising on the third day. It is, for Paul, being grafted onto the likeness of his death and resurrection. And this proves his point and refutes the objection: since we have died to sin 'with Christ' and now live for God, sin has no more claims on us. Our task is to be what we are, to display the baptismal reality into which we have been plunged. This passage, which is also the Epistle for the Easter Vigil, is a splendid presentation of baptism as a sharing in the mystery of Christ.

4. *Rom 8:28-32, 35, 37-39*. Our sublime vocation in Christ, which God has planned from long ago, is the ultimate gift. God gave up his own Son in order to win us for himself. He will not now refuse us anything that can help us on our way. Paul enumerates the trials of his apostolic ministry: all these cannot upset him, sustained as he is by Christ's love. The upshot of it all is that God will never fail us—only our own sinfulness can hinder God's plan for us. Baptism is a victorious gift: symbolised by the white garment which the neophyte is to 'bring unstained to the judgement seat of our Lord Jesus Christ' (*Ordo*, no. 225), the baptismal newness of life can be lost only through our own non-correspondence with grace.

5. *1 Cor 12:12-13*. We have become one body through our one baptism. Though functions may be different in the community, the fundamental dignity of all the members is that of being part of the body of Christ and possessing a share in the same Spirit. In the faction-ridden Church of Corinth Paul's concern is to point out that it is an utter contradiction to set the gifts of the Spirit against one another—just as he has

pointed out in Chapter 11 that coming together to celebrate the Lord's Supper is vitiated by making it the occasion of divisions. Rivalry concerning spiritual manifestations betrays a total misunderstanding concerning the nature of these gifts. To explain this, Paul uses the image of the body—necessary unity amid differing functions, with each part concerned for the others. The Spirit has made us into the one body of Christ, and the gifts of the Spirit are for the harmonious progress of the entire body. All that we are and all that we do for the good of our community flows from our baptism in the Holy Spirit.

6. *Gal 3:26-28.* This reading stresses another facet of our baptismal unity in Christ. Now that we have 'covered ourselves' in Christ, the various accidental distinctions which might have come between us are of minor moment. Not that our nationality, social condition, sex, etc., are suppressed: but, compared with the overwhelming reality of our being a 'new creation' in Christ, they are scarcely noticeable. What unites us is infinitely stronger and more intimate than what might have divided us. 'Putting on' Christ means becoming identified with him in outlook and behaviour. And in this passage Paul sees the substance of this identification in our new sonship of God in Christ. Under the Law, the children of Abraham were in its custody: now, under grace, all men have the possibility of receiving adoption as grown sons through Jesus. The result is that the Law has now fulfilled its pedagogical function—it's now obsolete, because it has been surpassed.

7. *Eph 1:3-10, 13-14.* This reading is a blessing of God, on the Jewish model, its chief motivation being the revelation of the 'mystery' of God's will—the gathering of Jews and Gentiles, of all creation in fact, under Christ as its head. The unification of humanity in Christ takes place through its sealing with the Holy Spirit: the sign that Christ possesses us, and at the same time a guarantee to us of the eventual full possession of our inheritance as sons. The baptised have been chosen by God to be a brotherhood from the beginning, they have been redeemed and have had their sins forgiven, 'to the praise of his glory'—i.e. so that they may consciously bless (as the author does here) the wonderful manifestations of his splendid power and love. This they do chiefly by being 'holy and undefiled before him'. The words have sacrificial overtones: the Christian, by his life of identification with Christ and by walking 'in the good works which God prepared beforehand' (2:10), becomes a living sacrifice to the Father. For this he is set aside by baptism.

8. *Eph 4:1-6.* This passage represents the beginning of the long parenetic or exhortatory section of Ephesians. The phrase which crystallises the thrust of the section is in v. 1: 'lead a life worthy of the calling to

which you have been called'. The first three chapters have expounded the nature of the Christian call: the Father's planned unification of all men in Christ by baptism and the gift of the Spirit which is the unifying principle. Now Christians are exhorted to preserve this unity (which isn't just an ornament or an optional extra!) by avoiding bickering and disputes on secondary matters. Verses 4-6 consists of an enumeration of the chief things which unite us: the one God and Father has called us all with one call to the one faith in the one Lord Jesus through the one Spirit, so that we now form the one body, the one Church. This passage should bring out, as perhaps no other, that baptism can never be an individualistic affair between me and God alone—at the risk of falsify-its entire nature. Baptism is, above all, incorporation into a community. This teaching could do with some underlining, in order the better to offset the 'private' emphasis which has come about over the centuries through almost exclusive infant baptism.

9. *Col. 3:9-17.* In order to understand this exhortation in a baptismal context, it is necessary to look back a little and examine the Christian realities which motivate it. These are, fundamentally, Christ as first-born of creation and Saviour of men by his death, inaugurator of new life for us in his resurrection. Christ's is the only power and leadership the Christian can acknowledge, since it is through and in Christ that he is alive. This means that his activity in this world must be the manifest-ation of his new status. The exhortation given here, therefore, is not so much a listing of what the Christian must do in order to earn heaven, as a series of characteristics of the life that the Christian already possesses, since already, in Christ, his life is 'hidden with Christ in God'. The splendour of the 'new nature, which is being renewed' is expressed, not in spectacular feats of asceticism or in the extravagance of exotic cult-practices (as were being inculcated by some, apparently) but in the beauty of a life lived simply and unpretentiously with Christ.

10. *Tit 3:4-7.* This short extract indicates the importance attributed in the early Church to the water-bath of baptism: it is mentioned here as the means of our salvation. Since it is 'in the Holy Spirit' and 'through Jesus Christ our Saviour', it has attributed to it the sanctifying power of the blood of Christ. The primary effect of this washing is 'regeneration and renewal' in the Spirit. Man becomes an entirely new creation, some-thing changes objectively in him, so that living a life of holiness (as re-commended in 3:1-2) is no longer a matter of diligent striving by our own power, but becomes a real possibility through the new life-principle which has been planted in us 'in virtue of his own mercy'. It should also be noted that, even though a definite instrumental efficacy is attributed to the water-bath, the ultimate reason for the 'regeneration

and renewal' of baptism is the merciful will of God, which expresses itself in the covenanted sign of baptism. There can be absolutely no question of magic, or even of an arid validism.

11. *Heb 10:22-25.* An exhortation to steadfastness, based on the one, all-sufficient sacrifice of Christ which replaced the entire apparatus of Old Testament worship. Access to God has been opened for us once and for all, but we must actively appropriate its possibility by personally 'drawing near'. We can do this without qualms, since Christ's blood has purified us, and we have been washed in the pure water of baptism. We must cling to the hope we embraced at baptism—a hope which is not merely to be professed, but also expressed in a life of moral integrity and mutual upbuilding. The Assembly has the function of providing a framework for this progress, and must be frequented assiduously.

12. *1 Pet 2:4-5, 9-10.* This short section is set in the part of 1 Peter which is normally considered a baptismal exhortation (1:3-4:11). Having begun with a hymn of blessing for the gift of new life in Christ, and then exhorted the baptised to live in holiness during their exile (the symbolism of the Exodus is prevalent throughout this section), and to love one another, in the verses proposed here the author urges them to become intimately part of the true Temple of God—Christ. His is the only 'place' where true worship is offered to the Father, and by becoming part of him the baptised can offer acceptable sacrifices to God, sacrifices of a holy life and of working for the Gospel. For they are in fact the new holy, priestly and royal people of God, and this through God's own mercy. Their task now is to declare, before all men, the wonders of God's great mercy, in words and deeds, so as to extend the privilege of God's people to all men.

13. *Rev 19:1, 5-9.* The heavenly canticle of praise to God and the Lamb centres on the marriage between Christ and his Church—a symbol (already used in the Old Testament) of the intimacy of the relationship between the Lord and his faithful people. The Lord has himself enabled his bride to deck herself in splendour for her wedding-feast, since her ornaments consist of the holy lives and witness of the faithful. This celebration of the escatological kingdom is given its counterpoint on earth in the post-baptismal clothing of the neophytes in the white robes which signify their recreation in Christ. The Byzantine prayer which accompanies this gesture is significant: 'Grant unto me the garment of light, O thou who clothest thyself with light as with a robe, Christ, our God, plenteous in mercy'. This garment of justice goes to enrich the dazzling splendour of the Church: it is therefore the serious duty of the baptised to 'bring it unstained to the judgement seat of our Lord Jesus Christ' (*Ordo*, no. 225), so that all the elect may rejoice together at the wedding-feast of the Lamb.

C. RESPONSORIAL PSALMS

In very many cases the verses of the various psalms are just a fraction of the entire composition: from our point of view it is best simply to take them as they are proposed, and to examine them specifically in the light of the proposed antiphons.

1. *Ps 8.* A hymn to the infinite grandeur of God, as manifested in creation. The most astounding fact of all is that man should be considered worthy to be ruler of all this splendour. Man is 'crowned with glory and honour' from his creation—and this is pure gift or grace. When the Church uses this Psalm she reads it, as does the New Testament on occasion, in terms of Christ, the New Man. Jesus, because of his obedience, was 'crowned with glory and honour' by the Father. Saint John Chrysostom says that Adam was crowned with honour before his fall; and now we, who have sinned, are crowned, in Christ, with even greater honour—we are called 'friends'. The second proposed antiphon (the snippet of a hymn from Eph 5:14) reads the psalm in this key: the Christian is enlightened by Christ and shares in his dignity.

2. *Ps 22.* The image of the Shepherd appears very often in catacomb art, and was prominent in the minds of the early Christians. The various tokens of the care of the shepherd were interpreted as foreshadowing the Christian sacraments—especially the sacraments of initiation. Gregory of Nyssa says: 'You must first become a sheep of the Good Shepherd. The catechumenate guides you towards the pasture. Then you are buried with him in death, through baptism, which is the shadow and image of death. Finally, he prepares the sacramental table, and signs you with the seal of the Spirit...' This psalm expresses, as does no other, the intimacy of the relationship of loving trust between the new Christian and his Lord. This relationship is sealed by the sacraments of Initiation: this new covenant will endure 'all the days of my life'.

3. *Ps 26.* The trust expressed in this psalm, based on God's goodness in the past, causes the author to beg for a more complete manifestation of the Lord's face—i.e. a direct experience of encounter with God. Beyond all assistance from above, more than proofs of mercy, what man yearns for is the immediate presence of God. Baptism is the 'illumination' ('the Lord is my light') which reveals God's face in Christ. The second antiphon—again it is Eph 5:14—focuses on the theme of baptismal enlightenment, which is the quickening encounter with Christ in his sacraments.

4. *Ps 31.* This psalm calls to mind a theme not very much stressed in the new *Ordo*—the remission of sins in Baptism. This is no morbid preoccupation with guilt, but the exultant joy in God's loving kindness which comes from the consciousness of being reconciled with God, with one's fellow man, and—not least!—with oneself. The man who

refuses to face up to his guilt, who seeks to escape it, allows it to fester within him. Candid acknowledgement of sin leads to healing and peace.

5. *Ps 33*. This psalm, which the Church normally associates with the Eucharist, has also baptismal overtones, as the antiphons chosen ('Look towards him and be radiant') indicates. In any case, baptism and the Eucharist are normally administered together to adults. The experience of God's support in trials causes the psalmist to invite his hearers to complete trust in the Lord. God's goodness is so overwhelming, so patent, that one can 'taste and see that the Lord is good'.

6. *Ps 41*. The song of those to be baptised *par excellence*. It was sung during their procession to the baptistery. 'Fly with the ardour and swiftness of the deer to the life-giving stream of the baptismal font' exclaims Zeno of Verona in an Easter Night exhortation to the catechumens. Longing for union with God, characteristics of the preparation for baptism, coalesces with the motif of the water of life to form a baptismal ensemble of striking intensity. This is, all in all, one of the most apt of the proposed psalms.

7. *Ps 50*. The theme of purification and forgiveness is fused, through the second proposed response (Ezek 36:26): 'I shall give you a new heart, and put a new spirit in you', with the theme of the renewal in the spirit presented in the ninth Old Testament reading. Perhaps this psalm is too associated in people's minds with penance for it to be fully suitable here.

8. *Ps 62*. The faithful soul longs for the moment of encounter with God, whose 'love is better than life'. Total fulfilment comes only in the possession of God, in rejoicing 'in the shadow of his wings'.

9. *Ps 65*. The Exodus theme is peculiarly fitting for the baptismal context. God is not just the creator of the world, remote in majesty—though this already is a motive for adoration. He also intervenes in history to save his people. The last strophe offered here (verses 16-17) are from a personal thanksgiving, set in the context of the mighty deeds of salvation. In the same way, the catechumen on the threshold of baptism can set God's mercy to himself in the context of the salvation won by Christ and shared by the entire community.

10. *Ps 88*. These verses form only a small part of the psalm. They avoid the contradiction which is laid bare by verses 38-51 between the promises and the actuality. The present section underlines principally the free and undeserved choosing of David by God. It puts on the lips of the catechumens a response to this loving condescension: 'I will sing for ever of your love, O Lord'. But it is possible that the particularised reference to the Davidic covenant, unprepared by a previous reading (David does not figure in the baptismal imagery to any great degree),

may cause more confusion than otherwise. For this reason, and because the extracts offered here do not adequately mirror the thought of the whole psalm, its use in the baptismal liturgy is to be discouraged.

11. *Ps 125.* This is a psalm of wonder at God's power and love ('it seemed like a dream'), experienced in the past and felt as a guarantee for present distress. The prayer for deliverance is made calmly and trustingly: as sure as joyful harvest follows sombre seed-time, God will once more 'work marvels for us' and gladden our hearts. As is evident from the response, the emphasis here is on the memory of past deeds of God as a guarantee for the present and future. Just as God raised Jesus from death, so he makes us alive, now, together with him (cf. Col. 2:12-13).

D. GOSPELS

1. *Mt 16:24-27.* The criterion of discipleship, of being a follower of Jesus, is radical dedication to him: putting him first, no matter what the cost. This can entail even death—but for the follower of Jesus life is bound up completely with Jesus, so that clinging to him assures ultimate survival. The one who goes down into the water of baptism comes up living the life of Jesus, and this life can never be snuffed out—except by our own infidelity.

2. *Mt 28:18-20.* The post-resurrection commissioning of the apostles for their universal mission expresses the Church's understanding of her own legitimation and purpose. Their action in the name of Jesus assures his continued presence with those he has sent. Baptism 'in the name' of the Trinity means the plunging of the individual into the reality of the Trinity, placing him in the ambient of the saving love now fully revealed in Jesus and communicated by the Spirit. The 'disciple' is the one who is marked as belonging to the Father, Son and Spirit, and who follows Jesus in his pattern of life ('observing all I have commanded you'): one without the other is a falsification. The one who is about to be baptised is first asked to commit himself to Christ by renouncing for ever the attractions of sin and the tyranny of Satan.

3. *Mk 1:9-11.* John baptised in view of the coming Messianic fulfilment. Jesus, by accepting baptism himself, dedicated himself—and was anointed by the Father with the Spirit for this purpose—to the accomplishment of salvation by his obedient life and death. This vicarious baptism of Jesus, foreshadowed in the Jordan and completed on Calvary is extended to the Church at Pentecost, and to each individual Christian in the water-bath of the sacrament. This 'stereoscopic' view of the sacrament of baptism (as T. F. Torrance so aptly calls it) is vital if we are to avoid a magical approach to the sacrament. Baptism, what happens here and now, is grounded in the life, death and resurrection of

Jesus, and operates in his Holy Spirit.

4. *Mk 10:13-16.* This reading (which might appear more naturally in the Readings for Infant baptism) is offered here on account of verse 15. The point of comparison is that the child is receptive: it is fully aware that it cannot fend for itself and therefore is prepared to accept everything, simply and without complexes. The Kingdom of God must be received in this way: to strive to 'deserve' admittance, or to 'pay back' the favour, is to nullify the gift. Those who come, simply and trustingly, are not to be 'hindered' (this was probably a ritual phrase before baptism in the very early Church: cf. Acts 8:36; 10:47, etc.). Conversely, one who has engaged in a long period of catechumenal preparation is never to claim baptism as a right for which one has laboured!

5. *Mk 16:15-16, 19-20.* This passage is taken from the canonical appendix to Mark. It has more or less the same function as the second reading proposed: to authenticate the universal mission of the community ('to every creature'), and to show the 'Lord Jesus' (the only time in the Gospels that this locution is used) as active in the propagation of the Good News, from his glorified position with the Father. Belief and baptism are seen as natural coordinates: baptism is the form taken by a mature and dynamic faith.

6. *Lk 24:44-53.* The passion and resurrection of Jesus, foretold in the Jewish scriptures, have a relevance for all men of all times. The apostolic message of reconciliation radiated from Jerusalem, under the direction and the power of the Spirit (see the explicitation of this in Acts). It consists of 'repentance', that is a change of heart and mind, and 'forgivneness of sins', which is the fruit of a man's opening himself to the power of the good news of Jesus and accepting baptism. The result of the communication of this magnificent design, and of the glorification of Jesus, is a sustained atmosphere of praise to the Father, and of Christian joy.

7. *Jn 1:1-5, 9-14, 16-18.* The prologue of the fourth Gospel culminates in the affirmation that 'the Word was made flesh, and lived among us': the Word which was from 'the beginning' and through whom all things were made is become incarnate and is now the agent of a new creation. Those who accept him, who have glimpsed his glory, are given power by him to become sons of God. His fulness is poured out on the catechumens in the sacrament of baptism, which is the 'bath of regeneration and renewal' (Tit 3:5). Thus they receive 'grace and truth'—the love of God as shown in the one who is the genuine image of God, who is 'nearest to the Father's heart'.

8. *Jn 1:29-34.* John's witness to Jesus, which comes as the result of a revelation. The difficult phrase 'lamb of God' could be a reference to

the Servant of the Lord of Deutero-Isaiah, or to the victorious Messiah. John pales into insignificance before this One who existed before him. His baptism, which was but a preparation and a promise, fades before the Spirit-baptism imparted by Jesus, the One on whom the Spirit permanently rests. Even though the act of baptism remains the same, it is now charged with the Spirit of the Messianic age and imparts a communion of life with God.

9. *Jn 3:1-6*. This is one of the most famous of the baptismal passages of the New Testament. Jesus declares to Nicodemus, one of the most representative and at the same time favourably disposed of the Jewish leaders, that entry into the sphere of authentic relationship with God is achieved only by a new birth from above. When Nicodemus mis-understands this, Jesus adds that this birth is not material but 'of water and the Spirit'. Natural birth is subject to the laws of nature; birth from the Spirit (in baptism) is subject to, and is apprehended by, the Spirit. New birth means an utterly fresh set of relationships and a new prin-ciple of life: only these can equip us for 'the kingdom of God'.

10. *Jn 3:16-21*. God's great act of love for the world, his offer of his own life, takes place in the Christ-event. God's reality is life: those who adhere in faith to Jesus have life already. It is eternal life because, con-sisting in a share of the immutable life of God, it cannot change or be threatened. Those who refuse to accept Jesus, who 'prefer darkness to the light', cut themselves off from this life-relationship, and thus place themselves in the sphere of death. The option for Christ, matured during the catechumenate and solemnly sealed in baptism, is an assur-ance of divine acceptance and of eternal life.

11. *Jn 12:44-50*. This passage is a resumé, in the light of the entire public life of Jesus, of what men have been confronted with by him. It contains more or less the same ideas as the last passage. A man shows exactly where he stands by his reaction to Jesus. The urgency of the choice is based on the significance of Jesus himself: being the envoy of the Father and speaking his word, Jesus confronts men with ultimate reality and its inexorable demands. A man's salvation or perdition hinges on how he accepts Jesus.

12. *Jn 15:1-11*. The relationship of the Christian to Jesus is compared to that of the branches to the vine which supports and nourishes them. Without the vine, the branches wither; if the branches are once in con-tact with the vine, they cannot live without bearing fruit. The fruit of obedience to the Father and the extension of the love-relationship between Father and Son depend on our remaining linked with Jesus. If we desert the outlook and mind of Jesus we are fruitless—since the fruit is nothing other than the propagation of these in the world. The use of

the image of the vine recalls the failure of Israel to correspond with God's gifts, and, in the context of the Last Supper, could be a reference to the wine of the blessing cup, a parallel with the 'bread of life' discourse of John chapter 6.

BAPTISM OF INFANTS

A. OLD TESTAMENT READINGS

Three readings are proposed. The second is the same as no. 9 in the Rite of Baptism for Adults, and is treated above. The first and third deal with the Old Testament concept of water as a gift from God and a sign of life and plenitude.

1. *Ex 17:3-7.* The connection with baptism is tenuous, apart from the reference to water. Saint Cyprian once wrote: 'Every time there is a mention of water in the Scriptures, baptism is foretold'. This, however, can be pushed too far! The story seems to be simply another instance of the fickleness of the Israelites in the desert being met with the loving care of God. God brought his people out of Egypt 'with outstretched arm': would he now desert them? Rabbinic commentary held that this rock followed the people in their wanderings, since their need for water was constant. St Paul (1 Cor 10:4) interprets this rock as Christ—from whom flow the living waters of the Spirit 'springing up to eternal life' (Jn 4:14). On the whole, this reading strikes one as being too abstruse to serve as a starting-point for a baptismal catechesis—which in the case of infant baptism is directed to the parents and godparents primarily. It might serve a similar purpose, though, at the pre-baptismal encounters with the parents.

3. *Ezek 47:1-9, 12.* This is the kind of reading people take to—it has a good story structure, and the very direct symbolism of the great river which sustains fish and fruit-trees is appealing. It also lends itself to visual-aid treatment. There is also less danger of the 'detergent' notion of baptism ('washing off original sin') becoming unduly prominent: baptism is not so much washing as new life out of death, a much more radical idea. The water which flows from 'the right side of the Temple' (the Fathers saw here the water from the side of Jesus on the cross) enables life to germinate and flourish where before there was desolation. The reference to the fish which teem in this river reminds one of the very famous statement of Tertullian: 'We, the little fishes, after the example of our *ichthys*, Jesus Christ, are born in water, and our only salvation lies in remaining in the water'. The waters of baptism introduce even little infants into the circumambient reality of the life of the Spirit, even though they are unaware of it—just as they are unaware of their dependence on the air they breathe for their natural existence.

B. NEW TESTAMENT READINGS

All of these readings are already proposed for the Baptism of Adults—
though in some cases the pericopes presented here are somewhat
shorter. The readings from the Acts of the Apostles are not reproduced
here—no doubt because they depict baptism as following upon the conversion and profession of faith of adults, which does not correspond
with the present situation. Still, the readings are not for the benefit of
the infants (they need not even be present: *Ordo*, no. 43) but for the
congregation. 'The liturgy of the word is directed toward stirring up
the faith of the parents, godparents, and congregation, and praying in
common for the fruits of baptism before the sacrament itself'.(*Ordo*,
no. 17). For this reason, the readings from Acts could, in certain
circumstances, profitably be employed to inculcate what the attitude
of the baptised Christian should be. The parents and godparents would
then profess their faith with more commitment, and more readily
understand and embrace their duty of providing the conditions in
which the 'fulfilment' of the meaning of the sacrament which the
infants have received (*Ordo*, no. 3) is assured.

The individual readings have been introduced above. They are all
pithy expressions of the mystery of baptism—and thus suited to the
situation, where a certain brevity is necessary due to the health of the
infant and the limited attention-span of the congregation, particularly
noticeable on occasions such as this. In fact, if the baptism is celebrated
outside of Mass, the celebrant is wisely given a lot of discretion in the
matter of readings. He may read just the Gospel, or even, rather than
precede it with an Old Testament reading or an Epistle, pick two
Gospel passages. The essential criterion is that the readings, and the
homily which follows, are intended 'to lead to a deeper understanding
of the mystery of baptism and to encourage the parents and godparents
to a ready acceptance of the responsibilities which arise from the sacrament' (*Ordo*, no. 45). In order to achieve this, the celebrant is even
allowed to choose passages which do not feature at all in the proposed
selection, but which 'better meet the needs or wishes of the parents'
(*Ordo*, no. 44).

All the readings have, naturally, a bearing on the baptism of infants.
If one were to suggest the particular aptitude of one rather than
another, then one might mention the second, from Romans 8. This
refers to the prevenient call and predestination of the faithful by God,
and his sovereign initiative in the conforming of men and women to
Christ. This is appropriate to the situation of infants. Here God shows,
by the circumstance of the birth of the infants in a Christian ambient,
that it is his will that they be given the inestimable gift of union with
Christ in baptism. This gift in no way depends on the infants being

aware of it or preparing it. Their part—as also that of adult nephytes—is to accept the gift in faith and 'walk in good works . . . which God has prepared for us beforehand' (Eph 2:10). This response is more gradual in the case of infants—it keeps pace with their growth into human society and relationships—but the principle remains the same. Taken in conjunction with another reading which would stress, for instance, the specific nature of baptism, this section from Romans 8 could provide a springboard for a valuable catechesis on infant baptism.

C. RESPONSORIAL PSALMS

The three proposed psalms (Pss 22, 26, 33) have already been dealt with (see above, pp. 33-34). Naturally, one is not confined to these: Psalm 130, for instance, might stress valuable aspects of God's care of his creatures ('like a weaned child on its mother's breast, even so is my soul') which are especially appealing on an occasion like this. One should beware, however, of sentimentalising the occasion to the detriment of solid catechesis.

D. GOSPEL READINGS

Quite a number of the Gospel passages have already been dealt with in the Rite for Adults. In the celebration of infant baptism outside of Mass, special prominence is given to the following Gospels: Jn 3:1-6; Mt 28:18-20; Mk 1:9-11; Mk 10:13-16. These have all been already dealt with. The other passages suggested in the Lectionary deal with the themes of the double commandment of love (nos 1 and 5), and with some of the Johannine readings which in the Initiation of Adults are used during the Scrutinies (nos 7 and 10).

1. *Mt 22:35-40*. The great commandment of love. The answer of Jesus, rather than singling out one of the 613 commandments of the Law as being more binding than the others, or more important, goes to the heart of what the Law was all about. Love of God, which is a response for all that God has done for me, and love of neighbour, as sharing in the love of God and being its most direct manifestation, are not only the most 'important' commandments, academically speaking: they are the soul of the Law—and also of the Prophets. In short, of all God's revelation and man's response. Once a man is situated in the sphere of God's self-communication—which is salvation—his whole being must become a response of love, and a reflection of love. Baptism is the inauguration of a relationship which must gradually unfold in this direction.

2. *Mt 28:18-20*. See Gospel 2 of Adult Baptism, p. 35.

3. *Mk 1:9-11*. See Gospel 3 of Adult Baptism, p. 35.

4. *Mk 10:13-16.* See Gospel 4 of Adult Baptism, p. 36. One should, perhaps, draw attention to the gesture of blessing used by Jesus. Some see here one of the complementary rites of baptism in the early Church, or at least a reference to such. But to infer from this passage that Jesus favoured infant baptism is a very big leap indeed. One can say that he rebuked those who would keep the children from him, and he declared that they, too, have a share in the eschatological kingdom together with adults.

5. *Mk 12:28-34.* The message is the same as that of Mt 22:35-40 above (no. 1). The passage is characterised by the feeling of amity between Jesus and the scribe, who repeats—and amplifies a little—the answer of Jesus. Jesus in turn approves the position of the scribe. The continuity of Jesus with the best in Judaism is here underlined, in the very moment of the widening rift between him and the leaders.

6. *Jn 3:1-6.* See Gospel 9 of Adult Baptism, p. 37.

7. *Jn 4:5-14.* This is the first section of the encounter of Jesus with the woman of Samaria, which is one of the most important Lenten Gospels (being used for the first scrutiny on the Third Sunday of Lent, see above p. 18). Evidently the point that is being emphasised in this short section is the gift which Jesus brings to meet the thirst of man—a thirst for meaning in life, for fulfilment, for happiness. This gift is the gift of the life of the Spirit—which 'wells up to eternal life'. This is real life, satisfying life, because it consists in a personal relationship with the Father, the ground of all existence and in whom all reality ultimately finds its meaning. It is the Spirit, poured upon us, which makes us cry out 'Abba' (Father). When our relationship with God is right, then everything else falls into place.

8. *Jn 6:44-47.* A tiny section detached from the 'Bread of Life' discourse. The only source of faith in Jesus is the Father's gracious and unmerited call. Those who are called, and respond by believing in Jesus, have eternal life. The reason for this is the unique position of Jesus, as the only one who has really 'seen' the Father (i.e. knows experimentally who the Father is). 'To hear the teaching of the Father' in the depths of one's heart is to come to Jesus, to share his life of loving obedience to the Father. And this is what eternal life consists in. Its seed is already planted in baptism, and must grow and flourish in a life which is intensely evangelical.

9. *Jn 7:37-39.* Again, a reference to the living waters of the Spirit, given to those who believe in Jesus. The Spirit was not yet poured out, John adds, because Jesus was not yet glorified. When he was 'raised up', fulfilling the 'baptism' for which he had been designated by the Father, the Spirit was imparted as 'his first gift to those who believe' (Eucharist-

ic Prayer IV). The task of the Spirit is to conform men and women to the likeness of Christ: the obedient Son who expressed his obedience primarily in his death on Calvary. Thus the Spirit makes us—and is now making those who are baptised into the death of Jesus—Sons with Jesus, so that we can say 'Abba! Father!'

10. *Jn 9:1-7*. The first verses of the episode of the Man Born Blind (read in full at the second scrutiny, Fourth Sunday of Lent, see above p. 18) give the impression, when read in isolation, that this is a simple miracle-story. This unfortunate mutilation is perhaps necessary on account of the brevity necessary on this occasion, but if used, it will have to be explained in the light of the entire chapter. From the reading, one can glean that Jesus, who is the light of the world (theme continued from the previous chapter), can give sight to those who have never been able to see. This entirely new faculty of perception is paralleled by the gift of faith, which in the baptismal context was called 'enlightenment'.

11. *Jn 15:1-11*. See Gospel 12 of Adult Baptism, p. 37.

12. *Jn 19:31-35*. This highly symbolic—and highly involved—passage of the Passion narrative is scarcely comprehensible to the average congregation without special preparation. It is a fine expression of the Christian economy of grace, but should be used only if the baptismal congregation consists of well-informed Christians. The glorification of Jesus, which consists in his 'raising up' on the Cross to draw all men to himself, is marked by the sign of blood and water from his side. The Fathers saw here the birth of the new Eve, the Church, from the side of the new Adam, Jesus, as he slept in death. It is clear, from the insistence that the witness is truthful, that great importance is to be attached to the phenomenon. The blood and water probably refer to the two constituent sacraments of the Church, those which give her birth and sustain her in existence as the Church: baptism (water) and the eucharist (blood). In any case, that is certainly the significance attached to them here, in the context of baptism. All men can become 'Church' (assembly) by sharing, through the sacraments, in the glorification of Jesus.

Confirmation

Thomas Marsh

I INTRODUCTION

To understand the significance of Confirmation in our current sacramental practice requires two things: 1) to see the meaning of Christian initiation as a whole and the respective roles of Baptism and Confirmation as parts of the one whole; 2) to see what application the concept of Confirmation which emerges from this study can have in our present practice.

The Meaning of Christian Initiation

Christian initiation means the formal ceremony whereby one becomes a member of the Christian community, the Church of Christ. This ceremony thus expresses the essential values which characterise this community and its individual members. The Church is the Spirit-filled community of the disciples of Christ. It is such because it was brought into existence by two distinct though intimately related events, which by way of shorthand we may call the event of Christ and the event of the Spirit. The members of the original community were the personal associates of Jesus of Nazareth during his public ministry who, on the basis of their experience of the risen Christ, assembled together again as a community after Easter. They existed at this stage as *the community of the disciples of Christ.* This is what is meant here by the event of Christ.

But they now experienced a second foundation event: at Pentecost they were filled and transformed by the Spirit of God. This is the event of the Spirit. This group now and henceforward exists as the *Spirit-filled* community of the disciples of Christ.

When this young community came to admit new members to its ranks, it repeated sacramentally in respect of them these historical events which made the community what it was, viz. the event of Christ —Baptism; the event of the Spirit—imposition of hands or Confirmation. To enter this community meant to participate in the on-going character of these events and this participation was given visible, sacramental expression in these two sacraments of Christian initiation. Becoming a

Christian thus involved a complex ceremony of initiation consisting of the two sacraments of Baptism and Confirmation.

Yet, though two distinct sacraments were involved here, the reality they referred to and expressed was one—becoming a Christian. Personal union with Jesus Christ, which discipleship of him involves and which baptism refers to and effects, also implies sharing in the Spirit of Christ, which is the special reference of Confirmation. Both sacraments simply express different *aspects* of the one reality, discipleship of Jesus Christ, becoming a Christian.

In the early and patristic Church these two sacraments were celebrated together in the one liturgical ceremony at the Easter Vigil and so the question of their distinction did not arise. They were seen and presented as component parts of the complex unity of Christian initiation serving to express the different basic aspects of this unity, union with Christ in the Spirit. But when in the practice of the western Church from the end of the fourth century on Christian initiation began to be broken up into these component elements and Baptism and Confirmation came to be separated by an interval of some years, the question of their distinction, how they stood over against one another, bluntly arose. Thus arose the 'problem' of Confirmation.

Confirmation today

The natural inclination in answering this question was to parcel out the different aspects of Christian initiation as distinct effects of the two sacraments, Baptism effecting union with Christ, Confirmation conferring the Spirit. But this solution, in any of the many forms in which it has been presented, will not work. One cannot in this way dissociate Christ and his Spirit. One cannot be united with Christ in Baptism without also sharing in the Spirit of Christ. One cannot become a member of the Church in Baptism without also sharing in the Spirit which fills and animates the Church.

The solution must be to once again see Christian initiation as a complex unity and relate the two sacraments in their present situation concretely to this unity. This requires that we make a distinction between Christian initiation as a static and juridical reality, a question of formal status in the Church, and Christian initiation as a dynamic process developing our discipleship of Christ in his community. Initiation as a juridical reality is totally conferred in the one formal moment and is valid even for infants. But as a dynamic process Christian initiation follows the rhythm of life and in the case of the child and the youth develops with their developing personality. The process has its starting-point, its *terminus a quo*, in infant baptism. It has its end-point or *terminus ad quem* when the young person begins to separate himself or herself from the tutelage of parents and other guardians and begins taking personal direction of his or her own life, begins to be a personally mature Christian and member of the Church. At this significant stage it is fitting that the young person personally appropriate the faith and Christian status in which he or she has until now been nurtured. It is further appropriate that this be done precisely in the context of *Christian initiation*, since there is question now of a climactic moment in the process of initiation. And further again it is appropriate that this takes place in terms of that aspect of Christian initiation we call the gift of the Spirit.

Since the Church recognises in its current practice that baptism even of infants makes one a Christian and a member of the Church, one must insist that the Spirit is 'given' from this moment. But viewing Christian initiation as a dynamic process, as growth, one must further recognise that it is eminently fitting that at the completion of this initiation process the young person should enter on his or her mature Christian life through a personal appreciation of and submission to the Spirit of God in the Church of Christ. For this is the Spirit of life, the Spirit who gives life and leads us ever more fully into life, even eternal life. St Paul's words come to mind: 'Since we live by the Spirit, let us also be led by the Spirit' (Gal 5:25). The aspect of Christian initiation which we call the gift of the Spirit has indeed a vital significance at this stage of the young Christian's life.

Conclusion

Presentation of Confirmation today should concentrate on two basic points:
1. Initiation into mature Christian life and personality in the Church;
2. The role of the Spirit of God in leading us ever more fully into this life in Christ.

The biblical theme of the Spirit will help to bring out different emphases and applications of this concept.

II COMMENTARY ON READINGS

A. OLD TESTAMENT READINGS

1. *Is 11:1-4a*. This is the famous passage in the Bible which mentions the seven gifts of the Holy Spirit. In point of fact the Hebrew Bible mentions only six gifts but the LXX by translating 'fear of the Lord' twice added 'piety' to make seven. The passage is a prophecy of God's

endowment of the future Messiah with his Spirit for his mission and the gifts refer to those personal qualities of the Messiah in which this presence of the Spirit will especially manifest itself. The gifts represent the outstanding virtues of the Messiah's ancestors in Israel—the wisdom and insight of Solomon, the heroism and prudence of David, the knowledge and fear of God of Moses. As the final fulfilment of God's promises to Israel the Messiah will reproduce and surpass what was best in the history of God's people.

This prophecy was fulfilled in Jesus Christ who was born of the Holy Spirit (Lk 2:35-36) and who, from the coming of the Spirit upon him after his baptism in the Jordan, performed his public ministry 'in the power of the Spirit' (Lk 4:14). After Christ's exaltation (Resurrection and Ascension) the Father through him gives this same Spirit to the community of Christ's followers at Pentecost and from this moment on the Church shares in the Spirit of Christ. Those who become new members of this community receive in their Chritian initiation this same Spirit of God and of Christ and thus participate in the continuing event of Pentecost. This is the reality which is celebrated in the sacrament of Confirmation.

Since the fourth century the prayer for the giving of the Spirit in the Roman liturgy of Confirmation (the true 'form' of the sacrament) has been expressed in the words of this prophecy of Isaiah, a prayer for the sevenfold Spirit.

2. *Is 42:1-3*. This passage speaks of the Servant of God, the future Messiah, and of his endowment with the Spirit of God to enable him to accomplish the messianic redemption. The New Testament sees this prophecy fulfilled in Jesus, especially in the coming of the Spirit upon him after his baptism in the Jordan. At Pentecost the Church is endowed with this Spirit of God and now shares in the Spirit of Christ. New members receive this gift in their initiation into the Christian community and Confirmation is the sacrament of initiation which especially celebrates this event.

3. *Is 6:1-3, 6, 8-9*. This text refers to the Messiah and his work of redemption, a work of liberation of man from the forces of evil and the restoration of the joy and peace of God's original creation. Truly a Gospel, a Good News.

It is God who accomplishes this salvation through the gift of his Spirit in the Messiah. 'Anointing' signifies the strengthening power of God's Spirit which will enable the Messiah to announce and to accomplish this final revelation and saving word of God.

In his address in the synagogue at Nazareth, as reported by St Luke 4:16-22, Jesus deliberately selects and reads this passage from Isaiah and then claims that he personally is the fulfilment of this prophecy. By placing this event here at the very beginning of the public ministry, and immediately after the descent of the Spirit upon Jesus at the Jordan, St Luke emphasises that this descent of the Spirit upon him marks the fulfilment of this prophecy and that the whole subsequent ministry of Jesus is accomplished in the power of the Spirit he then receives.

Through the event of Pentecost the Church participates in this Spirit of Christ and thus constituted a redeemed and liberated people in Christ. In Christian initiation the Church shares this gift of the Spirit with its new members.

4. *Ezek 36:24-28.* This prophecy describes the abiding renewal of God's people in the messianic age. The renewal is described in terms of stages which the Church applies to Christian initiation. There is first the cleansing from impurities and the giving of a new heart: the effects of Baptism. There then follows the crowning gift, the gift of God's Spirit which will enable the people to *abide* in the renewal, to remain faithful: Confirmation.

5. *Joel 2:23, 26–3:3.* God, who gave his Spirit intermittingly to chosen persons in the history of Israel, here promises the Spirit to the whole messianic people irrespective of age, sex or social condition. This out-pouring of the Spirit will be the sign that the new age has dawned. As an act of God it will herald itself in signs and wonders worked by the Spirit.

St Peter saw this prophecy fulfilled at Pentecost (Acts 2:16) and this fulfilment continues in the Church in the abiding presence of the Spirit of Pentecost. In their Christian initiation new members of the Church receive this Spirit.

B. NEW TESTAMENT READINGS

1. *Acts 1:3-8.* This passage is St Luke's real introduction to his second volume, the Acts of the Apostles. As such it states the theme of this work and links it with the first, the third Gospel. The link is the Risen Christ who is the climax of the Gospel and who here now inaugurates the Church with its mission to bear witness to him, to preach and proclaim him and his Gospel of salvation throughout the world and to lead the world to faith in him. To accomplish this mission the Church will be endowed with the power of the Spirit of God who will be an abiding presence in her. The Church shares her gift of the Spirit with her new members in their Christian initiation in which this commission of Christ is now addressed to them calling them to participate personally in this mission of the Church in the power of the Spirit they here receive.

2. *Acts 2:1-6, 14, 22-23, 32-33.* The gift of the Spirit to the messianic people promised by God through the prophets and again through Christ himself was bestowed on this community at Pentecost. This, the last act of salvation history before Christ's Second Coming, is described here in this passage from Acts.

The phenomena heralding and manifesting this event, the mighty wind, the tongues of fire, are typical biblical signs of an act of God, in this case the giving of the Spirit. The early, pre-Pauline concept of the Spirit, which St Luke still has, presents him as the prophetic Spirit giving power to preach God's message. So the first, direct result of this gift of Pentecost is ability to proclaim the Gospel in the power of the Spirit. As this gift is given to *all* members of the Church, all are called to preach the Gospel of Christ to the world by the witness of their Christian lives through the power of the Spirit working in them and through them. In receiving new members the Church shares with them in their initiation this mission and enabling gift. Confirmation is the initiation sacrament which specifically expresses and celebrates the extension of the Spirit of Pentecost to new members and thus focuses special attention on the missionary aspect of being a Christian.

3. *Acts 8:1, 4, 14-17.* After Pentecost the early Christian community remained in Jerusalem under the Apostles and did not immediately go out on mission. The event which occasioned the first missionary endeavour outside Jerusalem was the beginning of persecution, which at first probably only affected the Hellenists, i.e. the Greek-speaking Christians (cf. Acts 8:1, 4; 11:19-20). These now left Jerusalem and scattered through Judaea and Samaria preaching the Gospel. The first report of a successful mission to reach the Apostles in Jerusalem was that of Philip in Samaria. Peter and John, the leaders and representatives of the Jerusalem community, go down to express visibly the union and full fellowship of this new community with the mother Church of Jerusalem by sharing with them the gift of the Spirit. The rite of imposition of hands used to express this entry into full fellowship by sharing the Spirit shows that this was the rite which the early Jerusalem community was itself using to give the Spirit to new converts in Christian initiation. As the account here shows, it was a post-baptismal rite. Philip was not able to perform this rite because apparently he was not sufficiently high up as a leader of the Jerusalem community to be able to formally act as its representative in giving or sharing the Spirit. He could evangelise and therefore perform the act which was the climax of evangelisation, baptism. The completion of the Christian initiation begun in baptism was reserved to the community leaders, in this case the Apostles. Hence, until Peter and John arrived the Samaritans 'had only been baptised in the name of the Lord Jesus' (v. 16).

We can see here the way the early Christian community saw initiation into the Church. It involved two aspects: personal union with Christ—Baptism; the giving of the Spirit—Confirmation.

4. *Acts 10:1, 33-34, 37-44*. The episode described here has been called the Pentecost of the Gentiles. Cornelius and his household were pagans, not Jews, though they were also 'God-fearers', i.e., pagans who without formally becoming Jews believed in the God of Israel. Until this time the Church had confined its preaching to Jews, or at most to those half-Jews, the Samaritans. So when Peter receives the request of Cornelius to explain the Gospel he has to be directed by God to comply (Acts 10: 28-29). While he is preaching the Spirit comes upon these pagans and Peter recognises from the signs that this is the same Spirit which the Church had received at Pentecost. Peter understands the event as a sign that God wishes pagans too to be directly evangelised and converted. The giving of the Spirit here does not mean that the Spirit is given independently of the Church but that the Spirit is here leading Cornelius and his household to faith and membership of the Church and as a sign to Peter to receive them. The conclusion of the episode therefore is the Christian initiation of this group of pagans.

The programme of the Church's mission which Luke set forth in Acts 1:8—Jerusalem, Samaria, the ends of the earth—here enters its third and final phase, the evanglisation of the pagan world as represented by Cornelius. We have here a good example of the theme St Luke delights in, the Holy Spirit as the directing force of the Church's mission.

5. *Acts 19:1-6*. St Paul's conversion and initiation of the disciples of John whom he met in Ephesus shows the liturgical structure of Christian initiation in the early Church. Following evangelisation and instruction in the faith, initiation consisted in baptism 'in the name of the Lord Jesus' (v. 5) and then imposition of hands for the gift of the Spirit. This initiation signified entry into membership of the Christian community which was formally the *Spirit-filled* community of the disciples of *Christ*. Of the two references which make up this description, Christ and the Spirit, baptism refers to Christ and discipleship of him and imposition (confirmation) to the gift of the Holy Spirit.

6. *Rom 5:1-2, 5-8*. St Paul, a much deeper thinker than St Luke, emphasises the inner, transforming power of the Spirit in the Christian and the Church. He understands the Spirit of God not only as the prophetic Spirit (the consistent concept of Luke as it was the classic though not the exclusive concept of the Spirit in the Old Testament) but also as the life-giving Spirit, that is, the creative power of God which gives and develops life. For Paul the highest and ultimate form of

life is that revealed in the Risen Christ. The Christian shares in this life of Christ through the love of God given to him, transforming him and enabling him to live after the manner of Christ. This creative love of God in the Christian giving and developing his life in Christ is the Holy Spirit, the love of God poured into our hearts (v. 5). the Holy Spirit is thus the source from which the Christian and the Christian Church live.

7. *Rom 8:14-17.* As the life-giving power of God the Holy Spirit leads and directs the life of the Christian. He is the Spirit of Jesus Christ and in him the Christian is united with Christ and shares in his life. In receiving the Spirit and being so united with Christ the Christian is adopted as it were by God, becoming the adopted son of God in Christ. It is through the Spirit of Christ, then, that the Christian is able to approach God and call him Father and it is through this Spirit that he will one day come to share fully as God's son in the glory of Christ.

8. *Rom 8:26-27.* Man, conscious of his own weakness and nothingness and of the distance which separates him from God, is, left to himself, afraid of God and afraid to approach God. He feels himself 'a stranger and afraid in a world I never made'. But God himself has removed this distance and this weakness by himself approaching man through Christ in the Spirit which he gives. God is now present to man through Christ in the Spirit and man can now turn to God with the confidence of being his accepted and understood child.

9. *1 Cor 12:4-13.* Charismatic gifts exhibiting extraordinary powers or phenomena were a feature of the life of the early Christian communities. In the community of Corinth, however, these gifts became divisive as one group sought precedence over another on the basis that its gift was greater. In chapters 12–13 of this letter St Paul deals with this problem and seeks to restore harmony by stressing unity. These gifts have all but one source which is the one God and his one Spirit which he has given to the Church and its members and from this one source they are meant to develop the one life of the one body, the Church of Christ. The Spirit is thus the endowment of the *community* and exists and operates in *all* its members, even those who do not exhibit extraordinary gifts. The life of the community is a work of the Spirit who manifests himself in each member for the good of the whole. Each and every member of the community is therefore a charismatic, endowed with the gift of the Spirit and through his presence and power helping to build up the body of Christ, the Church.

In chapter 13 Paul goes on to point out that the basis of all these gifts is simply Christian charity which is thus the supreme manifestation and gift of the Spirit (cf. Rom 5:5) and one given to all Christians and to which all Christians are called and in living which all help to build up the life and health of the body of Christ.

10. *Gal 5:16-17, 22-23, 24-25.* Christian life is the work of the life-giving Spirit of God operating in the Christian. For the Christian therefore the Spirit replaces the law as the guide of life. Mere and external duty gives way to charity arising from within (cf. Sermon on the Mount). This Christian life in the Spirit expresses itself in virtues which are the fruits of the Spirit, the results he brings to harvest in us, the ways in which he expresses himself in us: love, joy, peace, patience, kindness, generosity, faithfulness, gentleness, self-control. 'Against such there is no law' (v. 23). Hence follows St Paul's supreme moral principle: 'Since we live by the Spirit, let us also be directed by the Spirit'.

This is the gift of the Spirit which we receive in Christian initiation and which Confirmation especially expresses, calling us to be docile to this Spirit of God as he leads us in these ways into life.

11. *Eph 1:3, 4, 13-19.* The Spirit which God has given the Church and which we receive in becoming members of the Church is the eschatological gift of the Spirit, God's final and abiding gift. This means that for the Church the Spirit is not a transient phenomenon as was the case with Israel of the Old Testament but an ever-present and abiding reality. This gift is God's seal on us marking us forever as his own. As such, this presence of the Holy Spirit in us is already the beginning of our eternal life with God, 'the pledge (*arrabōn*) of our inheritance until we acquire possession of it' (v. 14). The term *arrabōn* used here belongs to traders' terminology and means the down-payment given as a pledge and guarantee of full payment in the future. Cardinal Newman's words come to mind: 'Grace is glory in exile; glory is grace at home'. For St Paul grace and the Holy Spirit are practically synomymous.

12. *Eph 4:1-6.* The Church of Christ is one. This unity has an external principle in the visible community and its structures. But this visible community existence is only the visible expression of the Church's internal principle of unity, the Spirit of God which animates it as the source of its existence and life and continually brings it together enabling it to express its unity in communal peace and harmony. Every Christian should seek to be a willing instrument of the Spirit in promoting this Christian unity: 'Do all you can to preserve the unity of the Spirit by the peace that binds you together' (v. 3).

C. RESPONSORIAL PSALMS

1. *Ps 21.* Recalling all the good things God has given us and especially the gift of his Spirit, we seek to share our thankful joy with others.

2. *Ps 22.* Our life is lived in the presence and under the care of God through his Spirit given to us.

3. *Ps 95.* Through his Spirit which he has given us we praise God for his greatness and goodness.

4. *Ps 103*. We praise God who continuously gives life to the whole of creation through his life-giving Spirit.

5. *Ps 116*. Joyfully we proclaim to the world the goodness of God.

6. *Ps 144*. We praise God for all that he is and all that he has done.

D. GOSPELS

1. *Mt 5:1-12*. This is the opening of the Sermon on the Mount, Matthew 5—7. Matthew here presents Jesus as the New Moses delivering the New Law of the New Covenant, the Kingdom of God. In contrast to the legalistic framework of the Mosaic Law, the New Law places greater emphasis on interior dispositions. It opens with the Beatitudes which describe the spirit which should animate and characterise the disciples of Jesus, the children of the Kingdom. As St Paul will emphasise, the Holy Spirit is the source from which the Christian lives and he it is who enables the Christian to adopt and live these Christ-like qualities.

2. *Mt 16:24-27*. There are here and there in the four Gospels individual verses which sum up the whole ethic and spirit of the Gospel of Christ. Matthew 16:25 is one such: 'For whoever would save his life will lose it, and whoever loses his life for my sake will find it'. Man's natural inclination is to think that he will find his true self, his real security and ultimate destiny in material possessions and acquisitions, in 'saving his life'. Jesus states the opposite. Man does not find himself, his security or his destiny in thus turning towards himself, in making himself the centre of the world, but in precisely the opposite, in going out from himself, completely spending himself in the service of God and his fellowman—like Jesus himself. By so 'losing his life' man paradoxically will find it and save it. This is the spirit of the Gospel, the following and imitation of Jesus of Nazareth. Man of himself is not capable of this dedicated selflessness. This is a gift of God through his Spirit who acting within us seeks to mould us in the likeness of Christ.

3. *Mt 25:14-30*. The early Church saw a number of meanings in the parable of the talents. As spoken by Jesus himself the parable was a criticism of the scribes, the learned teachers of Israel who, entrusted with the responsibility of teaching God's revealtion, had failed in their duty to God and the people. The early Church, for whom this original reference had now ceased to have any relevance, saw in the parable a call to Christians to be aware of the gifts they had received from God and to use them well and as a reminder that one day they would have to give an account of them before God.

The Holy Spirit is the primary gift of God to the Christian, the source in him of all other gifts. Seen in this light the parable is above all a call to Christians to respond to the direction of the Spirit in their life.

Or, as St Paul puts it: 'Since we live by the Spirit, let us also be directed by the Spirit' (Gal 5:25).

4. *Mk 1:9-11.* The prophets of the Old Testament had foretold that God would endow the future Messiah and the messianic people with a new and final gift of his Spirit. In the centuries immediately before Christ Judaism had come to believe that God had withdrawn his prophetic Spirit from Israel on account of the sins of the people. This was the doctrine of the quenched Spirit. The return of the Spirit would therefore mean the appearance of the Messiah and the dawn of the messianic age. The public ministry of Jesus opens with his baptism by John. The coming of the Spirit upon him after the baptism is this return of the quenched Spirit marking the appearance of the Messiah and the dawning of the messianic age, the fulfilment of these Old Testament prophecies. During his life Jesus promises that after his glorification the community of his followers will also receive this gift of the Spirit (cf. Jn 7:39). Pentecost is the fulfilment of this promise.

These are the events of salvation history which underlie and determine the sacramental structure of Christian initiation, Baptism and Confirmation. Baptism refers to our personal union with Jesus Christ, Confirmation to our participation in the Spirit of Christ. These two component sacraments of Christian initiation have their original model in the events at the Jordan, the baptism of Jesus and then the coming of the Holy Spirit upon him.

5. *Lk 4:16-22.* The public ministry of Jesus opens with his baptism by John and the coming of the Spirit upon him. This is God's endowment of the Messiah with the promised Spirit as foretold by the prophets. St Luke carefully selects as the first act of Jesus' ministry his address in the synagogue at Nazareth where Jesus interprets the coming of the Spirit upon him. This is the fulfilment of Isaiah 61:1-2, one of the Old Testament passages which foretells the gift of the Spirit to the Messiah. The subsequent ministry of Jesus will be accomplished 'in the power of the Spirit' (Lk 4:14).

Christian initiation follows this pattern of the inauguration of Jesus' ministry, Baptism and the gift of the Spirit (Confirmation). In being united to Jesus Christ and taking his name, the Christian comes to share also in his endowment with the Spirit of God. The Spirit of God which we receive is the Spirit of Christ, the Spirit which came upon him after his baptism, which he acknowledged and proclaimed at Nazareth, promised to his followers and which came upon the Church at Pentecost.

6. *Lk 8:4-10.* As spoken by Jesus this is a parable of the Kingdom, an announcement of the Kingdom as an act of God which is certain. The seed is the Kingdom which, despite the poor character of the soil

(representing weak humanity), God will bring to harvest. Later in the preaching of the Church the parable was adapted to apply to man's varying responses and lack of response to the Good News of his salvation. Emphasis was now placed on the seed as the word, the Gospel, and faith in it. For us, then, this parable speaks of the Gospel as the announcement of God's salvation of man in Christ and calls for our total acceptance of and adherence to this message and its object, Jesus Christ, for our fidelity in the faith. But we are not left to our own meagre resources in making our response of faith and maintaining fidelity. Faith and fidelity are both gifts of God which come to us through the Holy Spirit of God which he has given us. The Spirit it is who constantly makes us faithful, gives us faith and fidelity. This parable calls us to triumph over the false allurements of the world and temptations against faith by opening ourselves to this influence of the Spirit of God.

7. *Lk 10:21-24.* Jesus was conscious of his special relationship with God, his Father. It is through his Son that God approaches man and most intimately reveals himself to him. Likewise, it is through Christ that man can approach God and be united with him. Jesus shares with men his relationship with the Father. Through Christ man becomes the adopted Son of God. As the New Testament elsewhere informs us, it is in the Spirit of God given to him that man is united with Christ and through Christ with the Father. 'The proof that you are sons is that God has sent the Spirit of his Son into our hearts' (Gal 4:6); 'through him we have access in one Spirit to the Father' (Eph 2:18).

8. *Jn 7:37-39.* These words were spoken by Jesus in the Temple in Jerusalem during the Feast of Tabernacles. This was the autumn harvest festival and the most popular of Jewish feasts. It had a messianic significance which centred on the theme of Jerusalem, the Holy City, as a source of living waters, waters that would give new life (cf. Ezek 47: 1-12; Zech 14:8). Jesus here applies this theme to himself and presents himself as the fulfilment of the prophecy. In him the true meaning and reference of the feast is fulfilled. He is the source of the new, redeemed life and those who would receive this life must come to him, as the thirsty man must go to the spring. The way to make this saving contact with Jesus is through faith in him. It is the man 'who believes in me' who comes and drinks from this saving source.

In v. 39 the Evangelist adds an explanatory note: the new life which 'those who believed in him' were to receive is the Spirit of God, the Spirit of life. This Spirit would be given after and because of Jesus' glorification. It means for man a sharing in the new risen life of Christ. In the Spirit we are united to the risen Christ and share his life.

9. *Jn 14:15-17.* Jesus speaks here of the future life of his disciples, of those who love him and keep his commandments (v. 15). These will receive from God through Jesus—'I shall ask the Father'—the gift of God's Spirit who will henceforward remain with them and in them. He is 'the Spirit of truth', which means both that he reveals the true meaning of Jesus through the gift of faith and also helps believers to live this faith, to *be* true followers of Jesus Christ, true *Christians.*

The gift of the Spirit is thus an effect of Christian initiation where we become disciples of Jesus Christ by joining the community of his disciples, the Church, and receive his Spirit who now becomes in us the source of our new life, our Christian life.

10. *Jn 14:23-26.* Those who love Jesus and live this love in their lives, who keep his word, i.e., his true disciples, these through their union with Christ are also united to the Father. The Father loves them and they live in union with Christ and the Father.

But how are those who come after the time of Christ and so cannot know him in the flesh, how are they to meet him and come to know him? They will meet him and be taught about him through the Spirit of God whom the Father will send in Jesus' name. The Spirit of God is the Spirit of Christ and sharing in this Spirit the believer is united to Christ and led to a true understanding of him. The gift of the Spirit is thus an essential part of Christian initiation. This is the gift which Confirmation expresses and celebrates and calls us to appreciate.

11. *Jn 15:18-21, 26-27.* Jesus here speaks about what discipleship of him means and involves. It means sharing with Christ his separation from the 'world' and his persecution by the 'world', 'world' meaning here the active power of evil. Jesus bears witness before this evil world to the truth, i.e. to God, and thereby condemns this world. This witness of Christ will be continued through history by his followers, by Christians. The Christian will accomplish this witness of Christ through the power of the Spirit given to him and active in him. Christ thus lives on in history in his faithful followers and continues to speak to men and to bear witness to the truth through his Spirit given to them. This is the gift of the Spirit which Confirmation celebrates and in this Sacrament we are thus called to a life of witness to Christ among men in the power of the Spirit.

12. *Jn 16:5-7, 12-13.* Jesus here prepares his disciples for his departure from the world. He assures them that this departure does not mean an abandonment of them. He is going to greater things, to new life, to the Father and from there he will remain present to them in a new way. This new way is the Spirit of God which the Father will give in Jesus' name. The Spirit will lead them to 'complete truth', to see the true

meaning and significance of Jesus and the events of his life which they cannot now understand. Christ thus remains united with his followers in the Spirit and in the Spirit they can grow in union with him and understanding of him. This is the gift of the Spirit which we celebrate in the sacrament of Confirmation.

III THEMATIC GROUPINGS

1. a) Old Testament 3 — Isaiah 61.
   b) New Testament 2 — Acts 2.
   c) Responsorial Psalm 3 — Psalm 95.
   d) Gospel 5 — Luke 4.

2. a) Old Testament 1 — Isaiah 11, or 2 — Isaiah 42.
   b) New Testament 4 — Acts 10.
   c) Responsorial Psalm 1 — Psalm 21.
   d) Gospel 4 — Mark 1.

3. a) Old Testament 4 — Ezek 36.
   b) New Testament 6 — Romans 5.
   c) Responsorial Psalm 4 — Psalm 103.
   d) Gospel 8 — John 7.

4. a) Old Testament 5 — Joel 2; 3.
   b) New Testament 2 — Acts 2.
   c) Responsorial Psalm 5 — Psalm 116.
   d) Gospel 12 — John 16.

5. a) Old Testament 1 — Isaiah 61.
   b) New Testament 10 — Galatians 5.
   c) Responsorial Psalm 2 — Psalm 22.
   d) Gospel 1 — Matthew 5.

6. a) Old Testament 5 — Joel 2; 3.
   b) New Testament 1 — Acts 1.
   c) Responsorial Psalm 5 — Psalm 116.
   d) Gospel 11 — John 15.

7. a) Old Testament 1 — Isaiah 11.
   b) New Testament 9 — 1 Corinthians 12.
   c) Responsorial Psalm 6 — Psalm 144.
   d) Gospel 5 — Luke 8.

Children's First Communion

Eltin Griffin, O. Carm.

I INTRODUCTION

Preparing the child for first Holy Communion should mean a great deal more than preparing for the actual rite of receiving or alerting the child to the real presence. The word initiation would seem to be much more appropriate than preparation. Here we are concerned more with the initiation of the child into the Eucharist which will mean its fuller incorporation into the mystery of Christ and into the life of the Christian community. There is a great deal more involved in such a process than the passing on of a body of religious knowledge to the unsuspecting mind of the child. Along with teaching there should be experience of celebration related to life and identification with the religious values and example of the adults concerned.

The parents must play a leading part since they are the first heralds of the Good News of the Gospel with their children. Parents should be actively involved with what is happening in parish and in school, so that they will not seem like strangers to the feast when the great day arrives. The parents fulfil a role which no other person can take on no matter how well trained.

The Mass for the first Holy Communion day will be a celebration with which children, parents, priests and teachers are familiar beforehand. Ideally the celebration should involve a significant sector of the local community which is going to welcome this growing member further into its ranks. This is more easily achieved where the custom of having a family Mass on a Sunday has grown up and where children receive First Communion individually rather than *en masse* when they are judged to be ready for it.

Since the First Communion Mass is obviously a Mass with children guidelines can be taken from the *Directory on Children's Masses.* Pastorally this is the most significant document on liturgy that has appeared since the Liturgy Constitution. It stresses very much the environment that should be created for a celebration. Suitable banners or paintings done by the children themselves can create a festive atmosphere. The procession of ministers into the assembly accompanied by the children along with their parents and teachers sets the right tone.

The liturgy will come alive on such a day if one of the children is assigned to do a reading. The child's clear voice following on the more gruff voice of the celebrant can have an electrifying effect on a congregation. So can a homily which is addressed to the children and to their parents. The priest should not be afraid to engage the children in dialogue. This is the most successful form of preaching. It can have a deep effect on those who are lax in the practice of their faith. So can children at the microphone announcing the bidding prayers while two other children hold up a collage or painting depicting the particular intention. All this will grow out of the school situation especially if the children have had experience of class Masses. The fact that they do not receive Communion at such Masses is no reason for not holding them.

Make the fullest use of the procession with the gifts. It can be very impressive to see the children, especially the girls, who are so often prevented from appearing in the sanctuary, prepare the altar for the Eucharist itself, putting on the cloth, etc. This is one day in their lives when the children should be persuaded to bring gifts to the altar for distribution to poorer children. It will give them a deeper appreciation of what Communion is all about. Use the children's Eucharistic Prayers with the sung acclamations if possible. A First Communion Mass without music is unthinkable.

II CHOICE OF READINGS

Concerning the choice of readings: if the celebration is on a Sunday it would seem pastorally advisable to make use of the Sunday readings, though reduced and simplified (*Directory*, no. 45). For ordinary days there is a very wide choice of readings available in the Lectionary, either from the Christian Initiation of Adults (cf. above pp. 16-38) or from the votive Masses of the Eucharist. It is permissable to have only a Gospel reading (*Directory*, no. 42). The selection of Gospel passages given for votive Masses of the Eucharist have to do with the bread miracle (Lk 9:11-17), with the institution of the Eucharist (Mk 14:12-16; Lk 24:13-35), or provide various sections of the promise of the Bread of Life (Jn 6).

The bread miracle reading is a good one for children. Indeed it could be mimed on occasions. It could be introduced by saying that the picnnic can be the family at its best, especially when everything comes off well. The celebration of the Holy Eucharist is the family of God's Church at its best. Or one could point to the fourfold action of Jesus in taking the bread, blessing it, breaking it and giving it as he does in the Eucharist. The Lucan account of the institution is the richest one we have, perhaps too rich a diet for children. A few short sentences from John 6 might be the most suitable form of Gospel for the occasion of First Holy Communion of children. One could introduce a very short reading like John 6:35, 51 by saying that it is taken from St John's story of the Good News. It happened the very day after Jesus had fed the hungry people with the loaves and fish. A big crowd began to follow Jesus. He knew what they wanted very well. More free bread. But he wanted to tell them all about the Bread of Life.

For Forgiveness of Sins

Sean Fagan S.M.

I INTRODUCTION

The Church has become more aware in recent years of the liturgical poverty of our present form of the sacrament of penance. It is 'administered' so privately and hurriedly that it is seldom experienced as a 'celebration' of reconciliation and of God's forgiveness. Vatican II was conscious of the deficiencies in our present practice when it decreed that 'the rite and formulas for the sacrament of penance are to be revised so that they give more luminous expression to both the nature and effect of the sacrament'. Over the years we had lost sight of the fact that the pedagogical aspect of sacramental celebration is important in stirring up the faith-dispositions of those taking part. During the controversies of the Reformation period, the phrase *ex opere operato* was used to emphasise that Christ's power is at work in the sacraments independently of the personal sanctity of the individual minister. This is a very consoling truth for the recipient. But for various reasons it was more and more understood to mean that a sacrament produces its effect almost automatically, as long as the recipient poses no obstacles. In practice, this often led to mere mechanical reception and an almost magical approach to the sacraments. An important insight of the liturgical revival is that the actual celebration of sacraments should so bring out the inner meaning of what is taking place that those taking part can enter more fully into the experience. In this way, not only is the sacrament an expression of faith, an external sign of the supernatural happening, but it is a generative sign which deepens the life of faith and so intensifies the happening.

Though still meaningful and fruitful for many people, our current practice of the sacrament of penance poses problems. There is a falling off in the number of those going to confession. There are various reasons for this. Since many of the disciplinary regulations of the Church have been relaxed, people feel that they have less to confess. With more emphasis on personal conscience, people are less inclined to look for guidance from a confessor. A greater awareness of the theological pluralism in today's church causes confusion among penitents insofar as they are more inclined to 'shop around' in search of a confessor to suit them. The publicity given to Vatican II debates and the discussions that have arisen since the Council have encouraged people to question many of the things they previously took for granted. Reflecting on their experience of the sacrament of penance, they ask 'Why does confession not change my life?' or 'What is the point of the same list of sins every time, hardly changed since my first confession?' or 'Why confess to a priest?'

For the majority of penitents, their understanding of the sacrament has never gone beyond the rather inadequate preparation they were given for their early confessions. At an age when they were probably incapable of committing serious sin, they were formed to a preoccupation with mortal sin for which hell for all eternity was the punishment. The sacrament of penance was presented mainly as a preparation for communion, with little reference to encounter with Christ and reconciliation with the community. The disciplinary law imposed by the Council of Trent with regard to annual confession and the listing of all mortal sins according to number and kind was so emphasised that it became the norm even for frequent confession of devotion. Confession, which was once the special occasion for forgiveness, gradually became the ordinary and regular means of pardon. Thus, the idea of penance as reconciliation was obscured by the equating of obligatory and devotional confession, since it is difficult to speak of reconciliation with the Church in the case of minor daily sins. Confession and communion were so closely related that when communion was rare, confession was a real and necessary preparation for it. But when the practice of frequent communion developed confession lost some of its impact.

The defects of our current practice are largely the result of historical circumstances. One of these is a shift of emphasis in the Church's self-awareness. In the early centuries the Christian community was aware of itself as a community of faith and love, a close-knit group of people supporting each other and responsible for each other. The sinner, by his action, cut himself off from the group, ex-communicated himself, but the community still felt responsible for him, prayed for him and helped him to return. His public penance was medicinal, and his reconciliation a welcoming home. After Constantine, the Church became more conscious of itself as a legal organisation, and in many ways modelled itself on the state, with its various instruments of power and control. Confession could easily be experienced as such an instrument. Besides, with the loss of community awareness, sin became more a private matter between the individual and God, and the priest was seen more as the representative of God, dispensing divine forgiveness. This meant that in terms of actual experience both confession and absolution bypassed the community, and the sacrament became not only private but individualistic. This individualistic approach was closely linked to the *ex opere operato* understanding of absolution, so that a penitent could feel forgiven by God without any real effort at basic conversion in terms of effective reconciliation with those members of the community harmed by his sin.

Furthermore, many people find the confession of personal faults somewhat irrelevant to the bigger evils in the world: poverty, discrimination, prejudice, war. Confessing to a list of easily measured mortal and venial sins, with all the details of number and kind, can leave whole areas of sinfulness untouched. Devout Catholics who are conscious of their collective responsibility for things like prejudice and social injustice feel that our current practice deals only with sins, but does not go beyond to the deeper and more mysterious reality of *sinfulness*. Confession takes care of personal guilt, but more and more people are looking for ways of coping with *communal* responsiblity for the evils in our world. Our centuries-old concern with the measurement of sin created the impression that since communal responsibility cannot be accurately measured or traced to specific individuals, it need not pre-occupy us.

Too much emphasis on the priest's role as judge can give the impression of a criminal court where every last ounce of guilt must be accurately measure and ultimately paid for. This creates the image of a vengeful less-than-Christian God. It can also encourage people to think that in 'making satisfaction' or carrying out their penance, they are somehow *earning* God's forgiveness. This runs counter to the gospel message that, although conversion is necessary, and a real change of heart is required, nevertheless God's forgiveness is total gift, unearned, unmerited. The sacrament ought to be experienced as a *celebration* of the tremendous gift that is God's pardon.

The new rites are an attempt to make penance more meaningful. They provide for three forms of the sacrament: 1) for individual penitents, 2) for several penitents with individual confession and absolution, and 3) for several penitents with general confession and general absolution. Penitential services with generic confession but no absolution are recommended, but are not recognised as forms of the sacrament in the strict sense. The new rites are really only a slight modification of the post-Tridentine private confession, and the official introduction to them is merely a brief synthesis of traditional teaching and practice, with little reference to more recent theological developments. They are a major change insofar as there has been no modification in practice for centuries, but they are slight when compared with the development of the sacrament from early times.

The changes must be seen in the light of the developing theology of sin and forgiveness and the variety of forms in which the Church's ministry of pardon was exercised. Jesus spent much of his time with sinners and the outcasts of society. He consoled and healed them with his love. He gave the same power of forgiveness to the community of his followers. He taught them how to cope with sin: admit it in yourself and ask for pardon; forgive it in your brothers; build up a community of faith and love to mediate God's forgiveness. Reconciliation with the community is at the same time reconciliation with God, and it is in the power of the Spirit of Jesus that this ministry is exercised: 'Receive the Holy Spirit; whose sins you shall forgive, they are forgiven'. But he did not specify in detail the ways in which Christians would experience this sacrament of forgiveness. In fact, the community discovered a variety of forms corresponding to their needs down through the centuries. Baptism was the great sacrament of forgiveness, when converts turned their back on the past to join the community of grace. But they soon discovered that conversion did not confirm them in grace and they needed forgiveness for later sins. Prayer, fasting, almsgiving, and the living of the Christian life were the traditional forms of penance to overcome the harm done by sin. Prayer restores our relationship with God; fasting and self-denial heal the disintegration within ourselves, and genuine reaching out to others restores us to the communion of our fellows, reconciles us to the community. But for more grievous sins something special is required. In the early centuries there was excommunication, public penance and a public reconciliation. A stage was reached when Church legislation restricted this to once in a lifetime. Fortunately, with the Irish monks the practice of repeated confession spread from the sixth century onwards, and from the thirteenth century the law prescribed confession at least once a year. Our present practice of weekly or monthly confession is less than a century old.

There were gains and losses in the course of this development. The shift to private confession meant less awareness of the community dimension of sin and reconciliation, but it provided the opporutnity for more personal spiritual guidance. Greater frequency of confession was a boon to delicate consciences who recognised it as a special encounter with Christ, but for many it became a mechanical routine. The new rites will not solve all the problems of this sacrament, and no doubt there will be further developments. But if properly utilised, these rites may help people towards a deeper understanding of sin, conversion, penance, reconciliation and God's healing gift of pardon.

An element common to all the new forms is the celebration of the word. Since it is the word of God, it has its own sacramentality. If proclaimed and heard in a spirit of faith, it calls to judgment, consoles and heals, and it sets the tone and provides the context for the words of absolution. In the second and third forms, and in penitential services, the homily gives an opportunity for development of a penitential theme, a theological explanation of sin, conversion, forgiveness, with the possibility of a collective examination of conscience. In these forms too there can be more emphasis on communal acceptance of guilt for sinful structures in the world. An important part of these celebrations is the overcoming of the separation between 'religionised sins' and the real experiences of *sinfulness* which do not easily fall into the categories of mortal and venial, nameable and numerable actions. These communal celebrations are particularly helpful to children, to lead them beyond the experience of rule-breaking and the childish notion of sin as defilement. If properly celebrated, they help to bring home to penitents the basic truth that the Church is meant to be a community of reconciliation. The eucharist makes this point, but it is experienced in a special way in communal celebrations of penance. In the course of the homily, and indeed from the whole experience of these communal celebrations, it should come home to those taking part that every group of Christians, but particularly the family, should reflect the Church's ministry of forgiveness and reconciliation.

Another new element common to all forms is the praise and thanksgiving prior to the dismissal. This emphasises the joy of reconciliation and celebrates the fact that God's forgiveness is a gift, and not simply a reward for good behaviour.

The renewed theology and liturgy of the eucharist stresses the various presences of Christ: in the assembled community, in the proclaimed word, in the ordained minister as well as the special presence under the appearance of bread and wine. This prevents the consecration being isolated from the celebration as a whole. In the same way, the extended manner in which penance is celebrated in the new rites should remind us that the essence of the sacrament is not to be reduced to confession and absolution. Just as sin is not simply an isolated action, but a process of weakening and final break in our relationship with God, self and neighbour, so reconciliation is a gradual return over a period of time. What is 'celebrated' is the sacramental moment in the process, the high point or peak moment, which of course will have no meaning apart from the continuing process of conversion as worked out in daily life.

To avoid the danger of mechanical routine in the first rite, it is recommended that there be a new style of confession room, with an atmosphere of warmth and welcome. The therapeutic and counselling aspects of the sacrament are emphasised and it can be experienced as part of a healing and prayer ministry. The more leisurely approach in this new rite presupposes a change from the present practice of large numbers rushed through in slot-machine fashion.

It is obvious that the second rite can only be for special occasions, that it requires a sufficient number of confessors, and that the actual confessions should be brief. This helps penitents to see the sacrament in a community context, but it also runs the risk of a mechanical recitation of 'sins', and it leaves no opportunity for personal counselling. In time it may come to be seen as an 'interim' rite, and future development will more clearly separate private and communal celebrations, each with their appropriate ritual.

The official introduction to the new rites is at pains to declare that apart from the special circumstances justifying general absolution, penitential services are not to be confused with the sacrament itself. This reflects the rather narrow theology of Trent, with its legal categories and limited ecclesiology. But the fact that the new document already admits more than one rite leaves the door open for further development. Rather than undermine the importance of private confession and individual absolution, the variety of ways in which the sacrament of reconcilation may in future be celebrated will be an enrichment of our Christian experience of penance.

Recommended reading: Celebrating Penance. Dublin Diocesan Liturgical Commission, Veritas, Dublin, 1975. Guzie, *What a Modern Catholic Believes about Confession.* Thomas More Press, Chicago, 1974.

II COMMENTARY ON READINGS*

A. OLD TESTAMENT READINGS

1. *Gen 3:1-19.* The paradigm of all sin: wanting to be like God, to decide for ourselves what is right and wrong, to want happiness and fulfilment without reference to God's guidance on how to be truly happy.

2. *Gen 4:1-15.* This is a description not just of what happened between two people at the beginning of time, but of what is happening between people all the time. God meant us to live as brothers, to support each other, but selfishness takes over: jealousy, anger, murder. Sin begins in the heart; bloodshed is only the external final consequence.

3. *Gen 18:17-33.* God's justice does not seek its pound of flesh. His

---

*The commentary follows the order of the Readings as given in recent editions of the *Rite of Penance*, e.g. those published in Dublin by Veritas, 1976, pp. 119-227, and in Great Wakering by Mayhew-McCrimmon, 1976, pp. 126-229. Almost all the Readings assigned in the Lectionary to the Mass for Forgiveness of Sin are included in the Rite of Penance.

mercy would spare the iniquitous city of Sodom for the sake of even ten just men. As soon as we have the tiniest beginnings of repentance and conversion, he rushes in with his love and forgiveness.

4. *Ex 17:1-7.* The author of *Hebrews* and Psalm 95 both warn us not to fall into the error of the Israelites at Massah and Meribah, who provoked God by doubting his promise. They needed forty years in the desert to learn faith.

5. *Ex 20:1-21.* All sin is idolatry. To be freed from sin and selfishness, frustration and failure, we must accept God's plan, acknowledge that he is God and that all the earth is his. His law is not a burden to weigh down our hearts, but a pattern of life for freedom and happiness.

6. *Deut 6:4-9.* Devout Jews recited these verses three times a day as their principle act of piety. To put them into practice with conviction would transform our lives.

7. *Deut 9:7-19.* The history of the chosen people is a long sequence of infidelities. In so many ways they provoked him and rebelled. But time and again the prayer of Moses averted God's punishment. Prayer brings forgiveness.

8. *Deut 30:15-20.* Even after failure to keep the covenant, true repentance will always bring God's forgiveness. God leaves us free to choose between life and death, but he invites us to opt for life and happiness by following his commandments.

9. *2 Sam 12:1-9, 13.* David, the great king and the Lord's anointed, had committed adultery and murder, but when faced with his crime he admitted his guilt. Nathan's words 'Thou art the man' are addressed to each one of us. If we can repent with David: 'I have sinned against the Lord', we too can count on God's forgiveness.

10. *Neh 9:1-20.* The absurdity of sin is seen in the contrast between the never-ending goodness of God and the ingratitude of his chosen people. Over and over again they went their own way. But God is always ready to forgive, gracious and merciful, slow to anger, abounding in merciful love.

11. *Wis 1:1-16.* The truly wise man knows that there is no happiness apart from God. The Spirit of the Lord fills the earth; he is the creator of life and goodness, and does not intend the death of the sinner. To discover this truth and to amend one's life on the strength of it is true wisdom.

12. *Wis 5:1-16.* Sin has its own glamour and attractiveness, and to the sinner a godly way of life seems dull and insipid. But eventually the emptiness of the sinner's life is revealed and in a sobering moment of insight he realises how distorted was his view of reality. The righteous

live forever; they are in the care of the Lord, The real fools are those who deride them. This insight is one of the special graces of repentance.

13. *Sir 28:1-7.* There is no cheap grace. Life is all of a piece. Love of God and love of neighbour are two sides of the same coin. The sinner who harbours anger against another insulates himself against God. We must let go of our sinfulness if God's healing pardon is to reach us.

14. *Is 1:2-6, 15-18.* Israel was still going through the motions of religious observance, with its prayers and feasts. Isaiah pointed out the hypocrisy of their bloodstained praying hands; they need to mend their ways, be concerned about justice, care for the weak. Then, even though their sins be red as scarlet, God will forgive.

15. *Is 5:1-7.* This picture of the owner's concern for his vineyard is a good description of God's love for his people. He does everything possible to enable us to grow and develop, but so often we disappoint him in not producing the expected fruit.

16. *Is 43:22-28.* Throughout their history God never ceased to shower blessings on his people. But all he was offered in return was their sins. Yet if they want to repent, he is ready to forgive.

17. *Is 53:1-12.* This passage describes the perfect Servant of God who through his sufferings and death brought men to the knowledge of God. It may refer to Jeremiah, the prophet Isaiah himself, Israel, the faithful minority within the community, or the ideal people of God, but it fits most perfectly the one who bore all our sins, Jesus our Lord. There is no need to despair at not being able to make amends to God, since Jesus makes intercession for us.

18. *Is 55:1-11.* Repentance is easy when we hear God's consoling invitation to return, and the wonderful promises he makes for our future. If we let go of our sinfulness, his word can reach into our very depths to transform us. To turn from our evil ways is to be lifted up beyond what we could ever hope for.

19. *Is 58:1-11.* God, through the word of the prophet, spells out the meaning of true religion. Prayer and fasting are useless unless we stop fighting and exploitation, and reach out in love to the poor and oppressed. Only then will God hear when we call. When we change our ways he will continually guide us and make us prosper.

20. *Is 59:1-4, 9-15.* God's power is infinite and his pardon ever ready, but he will not force his love. It calls for a response, but Israel is so steeped in wickedness that it no longer even recognises the invitation. Individual sins accumulate and poison the atmosphere, so that the very structures of society are corrupted. The description could well apply to today's world of prejudice, discrimination, jungle morality.

21. *Jer 2:1-13*. The prophet accuses Israel of deserting God. It is the story of sinfulness itself. the pattern is continually repeated in personal and world history. In spite of all God's goodness, we go our own way, to seek our happiness apart from him. Even nature itself ought to be shocked at our stupidity.

22. *Jer 7:21-26*. God continually sent his prophets to assure Israel that he would be with them if only they walked in his ways. They hardened their hearts and insisted on going their own sinful way. Jeremiah's words are a warning to us; we can be even more stubborn.

23. *Ezek 11:14-21*. God always cares for his own. No matter how scattered, he will bring them together as his people. He puts a new heart into them, so that they are literally transformed. Those who turn to him and keep his commandments will be his people and he will be their God.

24. *Ezek 18:20-32*. Every man is responsible for his own conduct and his own destiny. He is judged on what he is, on what he becomes through his actions. But, whatever his sins, there is always the possibility of conversion. Turning to righteousness, his past is blotted out.

25. *Ezek 36:23-28*. So often our repentance leaves a sense of uneasiness; can we ever fully turn from our sins? This passage brings tremendous consolation: God's pardon is a healing power that touches our whole being, right down to our subconscious. God does not simply say he will no longer remember our sins, but puts his own spirit into us so that we can have his outlook and attitude, and so walk in his ways.

26. *Hos 2:16-25*. Sin is alienation, from God, from neighbour, within oneself. God's forgiveness is not simply pardon for breaking a law, but a restoration of the lost wholeness. This prophecy of Hosea describes in very personal terms the peace and harmony that will prevail: man will be once more at home and at one with God and with the whole of creation.

27. *Hos 11:1-11*. God's love and forgiveness are never-ending. Human justice would leave the sinner to his fate, but God cannot give up. No matter how often his people sin, his compassion still reaches out to them.

28. *Hos 14:2-10*. An ideal prayer for forgiveness, acknowledging as it does that it is God who takes away our iniquities, and that we have no other god but the Lord. God's love is the source of all our blessings when we turn to him in repentance.

29. *Joel 2:12-19*. In the passage immediately preceding these verses the prophet describes the plague of locusts, bringing darkness and terror, sweeping through the land like the consuming fire of God. But Joel

proclaims that it is never too late to repent. If only the people will throw themselves on God's mercy, he will rid them of this plague. But repentance must be genuine: rend your hearts, not your garments.

30. *Mic 6:1-4, 6-8.* This is one of the great passages of the Old Testament, a prophetic protest against mere formalism in religion, a perfect summary of the message of all the prophets: What does the Lord require of you but to do justice, and to love kindness, and to walk humbly with your God?

31. *Mic 7:2-7, 18-20.* A chilling description of the godlessness of Israel. Goodness seems to have disappeared from the earth. And yet God has compassion. He delights in steadfast love, casts all our sins into the depths of the sea.

32. *Zech 1:1-6.* A call to repentance and a warning to learn from the mistakes of the past. Only God's word is everlasting; he is true to his word.

B. RESPONSORIAL PSALMS

1. *Ps 12.* A cry of appeal to God; impatient but confident.

2. *Ps 24.* Prayer of hope in danger, for pardon in sin.

3. *Ps 30:1-6.* Prayer for help in trouble. Though forgotten by all we are loved by God. Only he can free us from our sins.

4. *Ps 31.* Prayer of openness and sincerity. One of the classical penitential psalms; a candid admission of sin and the consoling awareness that grace enfolds the man who trusts in God.

5. *Ps 35.* The contrast between the sinner's wickedness and God's goodness. With God is light and life.

6. *Ps 49:7-8, 14-23.* God's rejection of formalism in religious practice; he wants worship in spirit and truth.

7. *Ps 50.* One of the best-known penitential psalms, reflecting David's humble admission of guilt after his adultery and murder. God will not scorn a humble heart.

8. *Ps 72.* Since time began, good men have been troubled by the prosperity of the wicked and the sufferings of the upright; where is God's justice? But with a deeper insight the psalmist goes on to contrast the passing pleasures of the sinner with the enduring peace of God's friendship.

9. *Ps 89.* Life is so short, the human condition so fragile. It is unwise to count too much on it. True wisdom is to repent of our sins and rejoice in God's love.

10. *Ps 94.* True repentance would have us live in the spirit of this

psalm, which ought to be our daily prayer, acknowledging God as our shepherd and ruler who holds all things in his hand.

11. *Ps 118:1, 10-13, 15-16.* Perfect prayer of the repentant sinner, conscious of the joy that comes from fidelity to God's law.

12. *Ps 122.* We need God's help at all times, but particularly as we struggle to free ourselves from sinful ways.

13. *Ps 129.* Penitential psalm most familiar from its use in Christian liturgy for the dead; both a prayer for God's mercy and a confident expression of trust in the Redeemer.

14. *Ps 138:1-18, 23-24.* There is no escape from God. He sees all and knows all. A sobering thought, but also a consoling one. We have no need to hid from God; all that is necessary is to open up to him in humility and repentance.

15. *Ps 142:1-11.* A prayer of humble entreaty and confidence in God's power to save.

C. NEW TESTAMENT READINGS

1. *Rom 3:22-26.* All men, both Jew and Gentile, are sinners, but God offers free pardon to all who repent, not because anything they do can merit it, but because of what Christ has done for all of us. We can make our way from death to life in the strength of Jesus.

2. *Rom 5:6-11.* Christ died for us even when we were sinners. Now that we are reconciled with God, he can hardly fail to continue in his love and concern for us.

3. *Rom 6:2b-13.* Though we are saved by the grace of Christ, it is no cheap grace. When we commit ourselves to him, we die to the past, to our old selves, and rise to a new life centred in him. It takes an effort to live this new life, but the power of Jesus himself is available to us.

4. *Rom 6:16-23.* Freed from the slavery of sin, we now put ourselves at the disposal of God, to be used as he sees fit. To be a slave of God is true freedom, leading to eternal life.

5. *Rom 7:14-25.* Sin is disintegration and alienation; as sinners we are alienated from our true selves, and so experience the battle of warring tendencies within us. Only the grace of Christ can heal this division and have us live wholly for God.

6. *Rom 12:1-2, 9-19.* Conversion involves a turning around, a change in our way of life. Paul spells out what this means in practice: genuine care for others, living at peace with all.

7, *Rom 13:8-14.* The new life in Christ involves fidelity to the commandments, but these are simply different aspects of the basic law of Christ, to love the neighbour, and the neighbour is every man.

8. *2 Cor 5:17-21.* Once converted to Christ, we are a new creation, and we are empowered to proclaim the good news that God has made this possible for everyone who turns to him. By identifying ourselves with Christ, we grow into the same pattern of obedience.

9. *Gal 5:16-24.* Jesus gave us the only safe criterion for judging people: by their fruits. If we live by the Spirit of Christ, the fruits of the Spirit will be evident in our lives.

10. *Eph 2:1-10.* We have passed from a life of self-centredness to a new life centred on Christ in God. This was made possible not through anything that we ourselves could do, but only through God's love for us. He has made us a new creation so that we might live a new life according to his plan.

11. *Eph 4:1-3, 17-32.* The Church as a community must preserve the unity of the Spirit. This we do by our changed way of life. Bound together in Christian fellowship, we must build up the community by our kindness, generosity and patience, forgiving each other as God has forgiven us.

12. *Eph 5:1-14.* Since we are children of God now, our behaviour must reflect something of the love of our heavenly father. The light of Christ's truth shows up sinful human behaviour in its true colours; our Christian conduct must be as different from this as light from darkness.

13. *Eph 6:10-18.* Just as our conversion and salvation were by God's grace and not of our own doing, we cannot rely on our own resources to remain faithful. We need God's armour for the battle. The arms he provides are truth, integrity, the power of the Gospel, the word of God, faith and prayer.

14. *Col 3:1-10, 12-17.* Dying and rising with Christ is not just a statement of belief, but a programme for living. Christian faith and action are inseparable. We die to the old self of anger, bad temper, deceit. We live the new life of Christ which overcomes all barriers, heals all divisions. Henceforth everything we do should be in the name of Jesus.

15. *Heb 12:1-5.* In our struggle to live the life of faith, we must keep our eyes ever on Jesus, the supreme example of our faith. We may have trials, but we have not yet been called on to suffer as he did.

16. *Jas 1:22-27.* James warns against superficial conversion and hypocrisy. It is not enough to recognise the truth; we must also do the truth, denying ourselves and reaching out with practical help to those in need.

17. *Jas 2:14-26.* We are justified by faith, but we cannot be sure that it is genuine faith unless it issues in good works. Without deeds to back it up, faith is an empty shell.

18. *Jas 3:1-12.* Not all should be teachers, but every Christian preaches

by the silent sermon of his life. In this, our biggest problem is the power of speech; if we control our tongue, the rest will be easier.

19. *1 Pet 1:13-23.* To remember that our salvation cost Jesus so much should be a powerful motive to make sure that our conversion is no mere surface affair. Our love for each other must be real and from the heart.

20. *2 Pet 1:3-11.* God has given us the great gift of sharing in his own divine nature. but we cannot fully receive this gift unless we do our part by living the Christian life, with faith, goodness, self-control, patience, kindness, love.

21. *1 Jn 1:5-10; 2:1-2.* God calls us to walk in the light, but we must first acknowledge our sin. That we are sinful is no obstacle, because in Jesus our sins are taken away. The real darkness is to claim that we have no sin.

22. *1 Jn 2:3-11.* To walk in God's light we must break with sin and keep the commandments, especially the law of love. Unless we live as Christ did, we are fooling ourselves in claiming to be in the light.

23. *1 Jn 3:1-24.* Through Christ we are made children of God. To live as God's children we must break with sin and keep the commandments. Whoever keeps his commandments lives in God and God lives in him. We can be sure we are right with God when we help our neighbour.

24. *1 Jn 4:16-21.* If our lives are guided by love, we have nothing to fear. But if there is no love in our hearts and in our actions towards our neighbour, we deceive ourselves in claiming to be God's children.

25. *Rev 2:1-5.* The Lord recognises the good work of the Church at Ephesus, but complains that it is all in the past. The community has fallen away from its first fervour and so needs to repent. Conversion is never a once-for-all affair; it must be continual.

26. *Rev 3:14-22.* The Church at Laodicea was like many Christians: complacent, lukewarm, self-sufficient. They need to repent before it is too late. But for all who do repent, there is the promise of sharing in Christ's triumph.

27. *Rev 20:11-15.* A terrifying description of final judgment. Not to be taken literally, but a reminder of the reality of judgment, and of the fact that the kind of person we are in the moment of judgment depends on the kind of life we have led.

28. *Rev 21:1-8.* In this vision beyond space and time, the author describes the perfect fellowship of the people of God with their creator. Suffering, sin and death are past, and those who have been faithful to God will live with him forever.

D. GOSPEL READINGS

1. *Mt 3:1-12.* The Baptist was sent to prepare the way for Jesus. He began with a call for repentance. Sinners must turn from their ways before they can be open to the gift of new life in Christ.

2. *Mt 4:12-17.* Jesus came to bring the good news of liberation, to set people free from the slavery of sin. He began with a call to repentance.

3. *Mt 5:1-12.* Repentance means a change of heart, a new outlook. In the opening verses of the Sermon on the Mount, Jesus describes the kind of people who are destined for the kingdom of heaven. They are the humble in heart, the merciful, the singleminded, the peacemakers, not the aggressive self-seekers admired by the world.

4. *Mt 5:13-16.* Jesus reminds his followers of their lofty mission, to let their good works radiate throughout the world, so to live that people will see the power of God at work in their lives.

5. *Mt 5:17-47.* The new law preached by Jesus is not an extra commandment added to the prescriptions of the Torah, but a new dimension to the whole of morality. External obedience is not enough; conversion means a total change of heart, beginning with inner dispositions. The demands are radical; it is more than human to be able to love one's enemies, but it becomes possible when we commit our lives to Christ.

6. *Mt 9:1-8.* Jesus healed many physical ailments during his lifetime, but he showed even greater power by reaching into people's depths to heal their sins. That same power is at work today in his Church for those who open up to receive it. The paralytic admitted his need and showed his faith. We must repent if we are to experience God's forgiveness.

7. *Mt 9:9-13.* During his earthly life, Jesus spent much of his time with sinners and the outcasts of society. No matter what our sin, he will always come with his forgiveness if we let him. He called Matthew from his tax-gathering; his call can come to us at any time, we must be ready to follow.

8. *Mt 18:15-20.* Jesus intended his Church to be a community of reconciliation. We must learn to settle our differences in a brotherly spirit. Every sin involves the community, so repentance requires reconciliation with the Church. Here we have Christ's guarantee that the Church speaks in his name and with his authority.

9. *Mt 18:21-35.* This parable brings home the basic truth that love of God and love of neighbour are inseparable. If we cannot forgive our brethren we have not the dispositions necessary for our own forgiveness by God. An important aspect of the gift that is God's pardon is that we share it with others.

10. *Mt 25:31-46.* God will judge us not on our occasional acts of religious fervour, but on our basic attitude of love as manifested in the various acts of concern for the hungry, the needy, the lonely and neglected. We cannot love God and bypass our brothers in need.

11. *Mt 26:69-75.* Peter's experience in this passage is consoling on two counts. It shows that even one as close to Jesus as the leader of the Twelve could be weak enough to deny him. But we also see that he did not continue the denial, but repented immediately. Weakness and sin need not cut us off from God if we are willing to repent.

12. *Mk 12:28-34.* Life, even Christian life, can seem so complicated at times, with its many details of law and obligation. But Jesus reminds us of the constant teaching of the prophets when he tells us that everything is summed up in the one law of love. To love God and neighbour is more important than any ritual.

13. *Lk 7:36-50.* God's forgiveness is always a gift. Repentance is a necessary condition, but we cannot really merit his pardon. The sinful woman in this passage is praised by Jesus because the exuberance of her gratitude and love show how much she appreciated the gift of pardon.

14. *Lk 13:1-5.* In this passage Jesus disposes of the theory bedevilling Old Testament theology, that suffering and death are punishment for sin. He doesn't explain why disasters occur, but says that they should serve as a warning to all to be ready for death, not to postpone repentance.

15. *Lk 15:1-10.* These two parables of the lost sheep and the lost coin make the same point: there is greater joy in heaven over the repentance of one sinner than over the merits of ninety-nine pillars of the Church. God really loves to forgive people.

16. *Lk 15:11-32.* The parable of the forgiving father is the whole gospel in a nutshell. It is a perfect picture of God who respects our freedom and responsibility in allowing us to go our own way, who grieves over our mistakes, and who rushes in with his forgiveness as soon as we show the first signs of repentance.

17. *Lk 17:1-6.* Jesus warns us that whether we wish it or not, we are our brother's keeper; it is a terrible responsibility to lead another into sin. On the other hand, when our brother needs forgiveness, there must be no limit to our willingness to pardon him. God's mercy is endless.

18. *Lk 18:9-14.* As Christians, we are never in a position to look down on our fellowmen. We are all in need of God's forgiveness, which comes to us as unmerited gift. Our good works can never entitle us to come before God in search of our reward. Everything is his gift, and we must be convinced of this in order to have a right relationship with him.

19. *Lk 19:1-10.* Zacchaeus found that his life changed because of his meeting with Jesus, whom he was so anxious to see. Our encounter with the Lord in the sacrament of penance should make a change in our way of living.

20. *Lk 23:39-43.* It is never too late to repent; God's forgiveness is not limited to any special set of circumstances beyond the humble acceptance of our guilt. The good thief was probably moved by the fact that Jesus pardoned his executioners and prayed for them. The consoling words he heard from the dying lips of Jesus are an encouragement to repentance for all of us.

21. *Jn 8:1-11.* The incident of the adulterous woman highlights not only the forgiveness of Jesus, but also his delicacy and tact. Although she was presented to him as a public sinner, he would not shame her in front of her accusers, and even in private he treats her gently. It is the same Jesus we meet in the sacrament of reconciliation.

22. *Jn 8:31-36.* Sin is a slavery, but if we repent and commit our lives to the Lord we are made free. Jesus invites us to make his word our home, so that we may learn the truth and so become really free.

23. *Jn 15:1-8.* Jesus came that we might have life and have it abundantly. When we commit our lives to him we live by his life and bear his fruit. But when we cease to be nourished by his grace, we become like dry branches dropping off to be collected and burned. Repentance prunes us and enables us to become an even healthier branch of the vine. Only in the strength of Jesus can we grow and bear fruit.

24. *Jn 15:9-14.* True repentance is a movement of love in response to love. The poignancy of these words of Jesus must find an echo in a repentant heart. His death was the supreme proof of his love for his friends, and his friends are all those who keep his commandments.

25. *Jn 19:13-37.* One of the central themes of the New Testament message is that Jesus died for our sins. To conclude his account of the death of Jesus, John quotes the prophecy: 'They will look on the one whom they have pierced', meaning: 'They will see and understand'. To contemplate the death of Jesus can bring repentance and conversion.

26. *Jn 20:19-23.* When sins are forgiven in the Christian community, it is more than human pardon. It is in the power of the Holy Spirit that the Church forgives, and reconciliation with the Church both signifies and brings about reconciliation with God. When we meet Jesus in the sacrament of penance, his words: 'Peace be with you' are more than mere greeting. They are power and life and blessing. They bring us the peace that the world cannot give.

For the Sick

Brian Magee C.M.

I INTRODUCTION

The new rite of Anointing implemented from January 1st, 1974 is presented in the context of the Pastoral Care of the Sick. This highlights the understanding of anointing as a sacrament of the sick. No longer is it called Extreme Union or Last Rites. Only the later chapters of the Rite deal with the more urgent situations in which a Christian may be anointed.

The most important change in the rite is in determining the matter and form of the sacrament. The Apostolic Constitution of Pope Paul VI says: 'The sacrament of anointing the sick is administered to those who are dangerously ill by anointing them on the forehead and hands with blessed olive oil, or, according to the circumstances, with another plant oil and saying once only these words: *Per istam Sanctam Unctionem et suam piissimam misericordiam adiuvet te Dominus gratia Spiritus Sancti, ut a peccatis liberatum te salvet atque propitius allevet.*'

The teaching in James 5:14-16 is concerned with those who are sick but by no means dying. The new rite states (*Introduction,* no. 8) that those who are dangerously ill due to sickness or old age should receive the sacrament. A prudent or probable judgment about the seriousness of the illness suffices, without any scrupulosity about the decision. Cases mentioned are those of persons undergoing surgery of a major nature, old people in weak condition although not ill, and sick children if they are old enough to be comforted by the sacrament. The sacrament may be repeated in the same sickness, if the condition becomes more serious.

Anointing may be conferred upon sick people who have lost consciousness or the use of reason, if they would have requested it were they in command of their faculties. If the person is already dead, the priest is not to anoint, but pray for the dead person and console the relatives and friends.

Nn. 32-37 of the *Introduction* deal with the Church's ministry to the sick. All men and women, even non-Christian doctors and nurses, all baptised Christians, the family and friends of the sick and those who care for them, the priests and local parish community, share in Christ's healing ministry as it is continued in his Body, the Church. It is in this context that communal anointing of the sick has its place. Since all liturgical actions are not private functions but preferably should be communal celebrations with the active participation of the faithful, the rite of anointing is seen as involving the prayer of faith of the community. The anointing of the sick should normally be celebrated in the presence of the person's family and friends, actively participating. Also envisaged is a community celebration involving the anointing of several sick Christians within Mass or in a communion service. As part of a parish community's service to the sick such parish communal anointings would be suitable in Advent, Lent or retreat times.

A distinctive feature of the rite is the silent laying on of hands with the accompanying prayer of the community. The celebration of the sacrament is described as consisting 'principally in the laying on of hands by the presbyters of the church, their offering the prayer of faith, and the anointing with oil made holy by God's blessing'. The sacrament is not to be administered in a mechanical manner but be a celebration in faith. The prayer of faith is an important element for priest, recipient and worshipping community. The communal celebration should be so organised that it is seen as a gathering for prayer.

Public and private catechesis is ordered to encourage people to ask for the sacrament early in a sickness, and to teach them to receive it with faith and devotion.

What are the effects of the sacrament? Until the ninth century the extant texts of the rite speak of the bodily effects of anointing: it is a healing sacrament. The blessing of the oil was reserved to bishops, but the application was entrusted not only to priests but also the the laity who could anoint themselves, or others. It was not simply bodily health that was prayed for but total healing of body, soul and spirit. The Carolingian reform that aimed at renewal of priestly ministry suppressed lay anointing. The ritual for anointing was inserted among the rites of death-bed penance and so came to be known as the last anointing. The scholastic theologians developed their theology of the sacrament from the current practice, and so taught a spiritual effect of the sacrament, namely remission of sin. The Council of Trent however did not define this understanding, but spoke of the spiritual, physical and psychological benefits.

The present rite teaches the effects in the *Introduction* no. 6. 'This sacrament provides the sick person with the grace of the Holy Spirit by which the whole man is brought to health, trust in God is encouraged and strength is given to resist the temptations of the Evil One and anxiety about death. Thus the sick person is able not only to bear his suffering bravely, but also to fight against it. A return to physical health may even follow the reception of this sacrament if it will be beneficial to the sick person's salvation. If necessary, the sacrament also provides the sick person with the forgiveness of sins and the completion of Christian penance.'

The stress then is on the sacrament being given to a sick person, not to a sinner. In the case where the person is actually dying and should be anointed, then it would be seen as preparation for glory since it is a paschal sacrament. Chapters III-VI deal with the pastoral care of the dying. Viaticum is seen as the Last Sacrament. The order of the continuous rite is now Penance, Anointing and Viaticum.

The *Introduction* says (no. 32) that kindness shown towards the sick and works of charity and mutual help for the relief of every kind of human want should be held in special honour. The sacrament of the sick must be located within the context of an alive and active total ministry of the whole community to the suffering members of Christ. The reward of entry into the kingdom of his Father is dependant upon seeing him in the sick.

II COMMENTARY ON READINGS*

A. OLD TESTAMENT READINGS

1. *1 Kings 19:1-8. Elijah is comforted and protected on his journey.* On his journey to God Elijah is in despair and asks God to take him to himself. He is comforted and strengthened by miraculous food. The word of God and the Eucharist are to sustain us on the journey through life, and in particular in times of weakness. (n. 153)

2. *Jb 3:1-3, 11-17, 20-23. Why should the sufferer be born to see the light?* The sufferer asks Why? Why should this have happened? Where does this fit in with God's plan? It will be from Christ's words that the meaning of sickness and suffering will come. (n. 154)

3. *Jb 7:1-4, 6-11. Remember that my life is like the wind.* Like those in forced military service, in day labouring, in slavery Job sees his condition as pitiable. What is the meaning of life when you know nothing of judgment and future happiness? 'Make us know the shortness of our life that we may gain wisdom of heart' (Ps 89). Stretched on a bed of pain, we get a new perspective on life. (n. 155)

---

* The Readings are given in *Rite of Anointing and Pastoral Care of the Sick*, Dublin, Liturgical Books, 1974. Numbers given in parentheses in this commentary refer to the numbering of the readings in the Rite.

4. *Jb 7:12-21. What is man, that you make much of him?* 'Sickness, while it is closely related to man's sinful condition, cannot be considered a punishment which man suffers for his personal sins' (*Introduction*, no. 2). Job asks why God, whom he sees as a friend, should have done this to him. It was the cry of G. M. Hopkins 'Wert thou my enemy, O thou my friend, How wouldst thou worse, I wonder, than thou dost defeat, thwart me?' The whole life of Christ will be an example of the just man, sinless, yet suffering. (n. 156)

5. *Jb 19:23-27. (For the dying) I know that my redeemer lives.* The loneliness of Job, abandoned by family, friends and, apparently, God, becomes the occasion for his throwing all into an act of faith. The living God will not abandon him entirely, but will explain all in the future. In the brightness of God's light all will be revealed. (n. 157)

6. *Wis 9:9-11, 13-18. Who could know your counsel unless you had given him wisdom?* A prayer for wisdom to know the meaning of life. When sickness comes we are not able to think clearly. In suffering it will be a great blessing to have the mind of Christ, to understand the plan of God for us. (n. 158)

7. *Is 35:1-10. Strengthen the feeble hands.* A new Exodus. God who worked this wonder for his people in the past does so again. This advent hymn looks to the coming of Christ and the establishing of the kingdom. The kingdom is now, but not yet fully realised. We live in joy now in the hope of what is to come. The joy of the Lord is our strength in the sufferings of our exile. (n. 159)

8. *Is 52:13—53:12. He bore our sufferings himself.* The fourth of the Suffering Servant Songs. A sublime expression of expiatory suffering. The New Testament sees Jesus as the faithful servant who suffers for his brethren. The members of Christ's Body are called to this work of expiation with the Head. Christ's glory and triumph come out of his offering his life in atonement. The sick are to fill up what is lacking in Christ's sufferings for the salvation of the world (cf. Col 1:24; Rom 8: 19-21). This reading portrays the astonishment of those who came to realise that the diseased one was for them the source of health and blessing. How much do we owe to the prayers and intercessory work of the sick in our communities? (n. 160)

9. *Is 61:1-3. The spirit of the Lord is upon me to comfort all who mourn.* Jesus himself said that these words were fulfilled in him. He came to bring comfort and in his sufferings to give hope. No matter how afflicted anyone may be this saving word in Jesus brings comfort. The sick are anointed by God to bring the good news of the Paschal Mystery to all peoples. A true apostolate can be exercised through patient suffering. (n. 161)

B. NEW TESTAMENT READINGS

1. *Acts 3:1-10.* In the name of Jesus, arise and walk. (n. 162)
2. *Acts 3:11-16.* Faith in God has given this man perfect health. (n. 163)
3. *Acts 4:8-12.* There is no other name by which we are saved. (n. 164)

These extracts from the early life of the Church show that the apostles carried on the healing ministry of Christ. The risen Lord still works through his Church. Faith in him is needed for all healing both physical and spiritual. Faith is needed for the sacraments, they are sacraments of faith. The prayer of faith of the gathered Church in celebrating this sacrament should be inspired by these accounts of the wonderful works of the Lord.

4. *Acts 13:32-39.* The one whom God raised from the dead will never see corruption of the flesh. (n. 165)

Sickness and suffering are not the worst evils, we should fear all that would affect the soul. Sin is the great evil. God will preserve the just man despite the corruption of the flesh. Through Christ we have forgiveness even of sin.   [(n. 166)

5. *Rom 8:14-17.* If we suffer with him, we will be glorified with him.
6. *Rom 8:18-27.* We groan while we wait for the redemption of our bodies. (n. 167)
7. *Rom 8:31-35, 37-39.* Who can come between us and the love of Christ? (n. 168)

As Christ in the moment of deep agony in the garden could still express his confidence in God by crying out 'Abba', so the Spirit-filled Christian can express trust in a loving Father. In the midst of sickness we can join with Jesus in prayer to our Father, and know that we can also come to share his glory. The Christian has a great destiny, and if he suffers now it is only because he lives in a stage before the glory that awaits in the future. While all creation shares in the results of the first sin, still there is hope. For Paul the whole created physical universe will share in the triumph of Christ. Death will no longer have dominion. Just as each spring brings a sense of striving to overcome the effects of wintry death, so all creation is seen as groaning in the effort to achieve perfection. Christians themselves spread hope for the future by their confidence in the Spirit given to them. This is the first fruits of the life to come. The blessing of the first fruits implied a dedication of the whole harvest. The Christian through baptism looks forward in hope to the full harvest of eternal glory. So nothing in this life, no matter how distressing, can make a Christian forget what Christ's love has done for him.

8. *1 Cor 1:18-25.* God's weakness is stronger than man's strength.

To those who do not know the cross all human sickness is waste. There is for them nothing positive to be seen in suffering. Christ dying on the cross seemed to be at the moment of defeat, but it was also his moment of triumph to those who have faith. (n. 169)

9. *1 Cor 12:12-22, 24-27.* If one member suffers, all the members suffer with him. (n. 170)

Paul's vision of the Church as a community of sharing and service means that no one who is sick suffers alone. The prayer of the Church is prayer with and for the individual needy member. The service done to one who is ill is done to Christ. The one who suffers with Christ makes the Church fruitful in its work. There are different gifts given to each member, and the gift of suffering is, like other charisms, meant for others (cf. *Introduction,* no. 32).

10. *1 Cor 15:12-20. (For the dying)* If there is no resurrection from the dead Christ himself has not risen. (n. 171).

The fact that Christ has risen guarantees the bodily resurrection of the Christian. We are indeed the most fortunate of people, for the final fruits of Christ's victory are ours.

11. *2 Cor 4:16-18.* Though our body is being destroyed, each day it is also being renewed. (n. 172)

A sense of values, of Christian values, enables us to carry the burden of illness. The Christian who lives his faith is growing daily, even if physically he is going downhill. The effort we make in looking after the body should also be put into looking after the spiritual life. 'The role of the sick in the church is to remind others not to lose sight of the essential or higher things' (*Introduction,* no. 3).

12. *2 Cor 5:1, 6-10. (For the dying)* We have an everlasting home in heaven. (n. 173)

The Christian's true home is in heaven, and as long as it pleases the Lord we are in exile. We do our best to please the Lord, to do his will, knowing that when he calls us home his will for us then will please us.

13. *Gal 4:12-19.* My bodily sickness enabled me to bring the gospel to you. (n. 174)

Perhaps Paul's illness was the occasion that brought the Good News to the Galatians. He feels that if their difficulties are weakening their faith, he is prepared to suffer all over again for them.

14. *Phil 2:25-30.* He was sick but God took pity on him. (n. 175)

A reading for those who have not spared themselves in service of Christ in his members. They are worthy of the prayers of the community that God will restore them to health and vigour.

15. *Col 1:22-29.* In my flesh I fill up what is lacking in the sufferings of Christ for the sake of his body, the Church. (n. 176)

Paul willingly accepts suffering to help spread the Gospel. His preaching comes up against criticism, controversy and opposition. These difficulties he sees as having to be accepted if he is to be united with Christ suffering for mankind.

16. *Heb 4:14-16; 5:7-9.* We have a high priest who understands our weakness. (n. 177)

'Christ himself was sinless, yet he fulfilled what was written in Isaiah; he bore all the sufferings of his passion and understood human sorrow' (*Introduction*, no. 2). In suffering we can be closest to our Lord, because we know that he understands.   [(n. 178)

17. *Jas 5:13-16.* This prayer, made in faith, will save the sick man.

St James is dealing with something that already exists, it is not a new rite he is creating. This is not a question of charismatic healing because the presence of the presbyters represents the official authority of the local church. 'If one of you is ill': here the Greek *asthenei* does not connote a grave illness. It is the whole person who is ill: James would hardly distinguish body and soul or indeed separate sin and sickness. So the treatment is medicinal and exorcistic. The rite is for recovery of health, spiritual and physical.

The anointing with oil and prayer are the liturgical action. The anoiting is more than medicinal since it is done in the name of the Lord: it represents the healing presence of Christ. It is the prayer of faith that is brought to bear on the situation. The sick person, according to the Greek words, will be 'saved' from death and 'raised up' to life and health. The reference to forgiveness of sins shows the close connection envisaged between bodily and spiritual sickness (cf. Mk 2:3-12 and Jn 5:14).

18. *1 Pet 1:3-9.* You will rejoice even though for a short time you must suffer. (n. 179)

This baptismal exhortation reminds the early Christians that suffering may be their lot in this life. The role of martyr is to witness, so their sufferings are to witness to the faith which is theirs. It will be a faith that is purified and tested, and so worthy of the glory to be revealed.

19. *1 Jn 3:1-2.* What we shall be has not yet been disclosed. (n. 180)

God loves us; to that knowledge we hold firmly through all suffering. We know now by faith but the time will come when we shall see him as he is.

20. *Rev 21:1-7.* There will be no more death or mourning, no more crying or pain. (n. 181).

21. *Rev 22:17, 20, 21. (For the dying)* Come, Lord Jesus. (n. 182).

The thought of heaven should not be a last resort for times of near despair. Surrounded as we are by human grief, tears, and near-death we should long for the new creation, for our real home. The pleasures and cares of this world can take possession of us: there should always be time to lift our minds to heaven. If sickness makes us do this, then there is a positive value there.

C. GOSPELS

1. *Mt 8:1-4*. If you wish to do so, you can cure me.(n. 205)

2. *Mt 8:5-13*. He bore our informities. (n. 206).

3. *Mt 15:29-31*. Jesus heals large crowds.(n. 208)

4. *Mk 16:15-20*. He laid hands on the sick and they were cured.(n. 213)

5. *Lk 7:19-23*. Go tell John what you have seen. (n. 214).

6. *Jn 9:1-7*. He has not sinned; it was to let God's work show forth in him.(n. 222)

'The sacrament of anointing prolongs the concern which the Lord himself showed for the bodily and spiritual welfare of the sick, as the gospels testify, and which he asked his followers to show also' (*Introduction*, no. 5). Christ's ministry to the sick must be seen against the background of mankind's fallen condition. An understanding of original sin today lets us see sickness as something man suffers as a consequence of the sin of the world: not as the immediate result of personal sin, or as the judgment of God on a sinner. Mankind wounded by sin is in need of healing. Jesus came to establish the kingdom, to restore the lost balance, and the healing miracles are signs of that kingdom being established. The perfect reign of God has yet to be established. The miracles are signs of the kingdom 'now', by showing that Jesus offers eternal life. They are signs of the kingdom which is 'not yet', by showing man transformed as in the resurrection. The power of God entering into time is a pledge for the future glory that is to be ours.

These stories show Jesus as a man of compassion. There is concern shown and a tenderness seen in the touching and lifting up: the suffering and weak are dear to his heart. He has come as physician to heal, to restore wholeness, for these physical cures are symbols of a deeper curing. We are blind and deaf to God's call, we limp after Christ rather than follow with alacrity. This is the commentary on the blind man's cure: 'For judgment I came into this world, that those who do not see may see, and that those who see may become blind' (Jn 9:39).

7. *Mt 25:31-40*. As often as you did it to the least of my brothers, you did it to me.(n. 209)

8. *Lk 10:5-6, 8-9*. Heal the sick. (n. 215)

9. *Lk 10:25-37*. Who is my neighbour? (n. 216)

The Church's ministry to the sick is the subject of nn. 32-35 of the *Introduction* to the Rite. The service of members of the Church to those who are sick among them has always been held in high esteem. Priests have always seen this as an important part of their ministry, but all Christians are to be concerned. Medical personnel are especially dedicated to participating in Christ's love of the sick. Family and friends have also a special share in this ministry. It is important to see that this ministry involves the whole person, the ministry is for the physical and spiritual needs of the patient.

The liturgical rites for the sick: penance, communion and anointing should be seen in the context of an overall concern for the sick in the community. Communal celebrations of the Anointing of the Sick will have their full effect if they are expressions of the concern felt all the time for these members who cannot fully participate in the regular community celebrations.

We should also remember with gratitude the dedication of those who work directly for the sick. Our enthusiasms for miracles of healing which defy natural explanation should not blind us to the miracles of healing caused through the advance of medical science and the hard work of those who serve in hospitals. God's power is more regularly shown through human agents.

The charitable ministry to the sick is exampled in the story of the good Samaritan. The care and compassion shown to a sick brother or sister is care shown to Christ who said: 'I was sick and you visited me'.
[(n. 210)

10. *Mk 2:1-12*. Seeing their faith, Jesus said: Your sins are forgiven.

11. *Mk 10:46-52*. Jesus, Son of David, have mercy on me.(n. 212)

12. *Lk 11:5-13*. Ask and it will be given to you. (n. 217)

'The anointing of the sick, which includes the prayer of faith (Jas 5:15), is a sacrament of faith. This faith is important for the minister and particularly for the one who receives it. The sick man will be saved by his faith and the faith of the Church which looks back to the death and resurrection of Christ, the source of the sacrament's power, and looks ahead to the future kingdom which is pledged in the sacraments' (*Introduction*, no. 7).

The prayer of faith is best seen in the communal celebration of the sacrament. Then the community, concerned about its ailing members, gathers around them and supports them with its prayers. Especially during the silent laying on of hands can the urgent prayer of the community go out in faith for the suffering brothers and sisters. The vocalised prayer in song or words should be well chosen to suit the occasion. These readings should remind all present that Jesus looks for our faith in his healing presence in our midst.

85

13. *Mt 11:25-30.* Come to me all you who labour.(n. 207)   [(n. 211)

14. *Mk 4:35-41.* Why are you so fearful? Why do you not have faith?

'This sacrament provides the sick person with the grace of the Holy Spirit by which the whole man is brought to health, trust in God is encouraged, and strength is given to resist the temptations of the Evil One and anxiety about death' (*Introduction,* no. 6).

Sickness is a state of crisis for the individual, it carries its own fears which, if not calmed, can impede the process of healing. The comforting presence of Christ in this sacrament is to bring peace of soul. Being freed from the temptations against faith and from the powerlessness and weakness of soul, the sick person will have a positive thrust towards recovery.

Readings from the Passion (nn. 223-229)

15. *Jn 10:11-18.* The good shepherd lays down his life for his sheep.

16. The Passion readings of Holy Week.

17. *Mt 26:36-46.* If this cup cannot pass from me, then your will be done.

18. *Mk 15:33-39; 16:1-6.* The death and resurrection of the Lord.

19. *Lk 23:44-49; 24:1-6.* The death and resurrection of the Lord.

20. *Lk 24:13-35.* Was it not necessary for Christ to suffer and so to enter into his glory?

21. *Jn 20:1-9.* He saw and he believed.

'He emptied himself to death, even the death of the cross: wherefore God has exalted him' (Phil 2:7-9). Jesus, the Suffering Servant, was transformed on the Cross to the state of the Son of Man in glory. It is a journey to life through death. The Christian is inserted into that pattern. He is able to give to his dying life the same value as Jesus did: 'Always we carry with us in our body the death of Jesus, so that the life of Jesus may be seen in our body' (2 Cor 4:10-11). 'All I want to know is Christ, and the power of his resurrection, so that later I may share his actual resurrection. Meanwhile I share his sufferings by reproducing the pattern of his death—for I am not perfect yet' (cf. Phil 3:10-12).
[(n.204)

22. *Mt 5:1-12.* Rejoice and be glad for your reward is great in heaven.

23. *Lk 12:35-44.* Happy are those whom the master finds watching when he returns.(n. 218)

24. *Jn 6:35-40.* It is the will of my Father that what he has given me will not perish.(n. 220)

25. *Jn 6:54-59* He who eats this bread has eternal life.(n. 221)

'When the Christian, in his passage from this life, is strengthened by the body and blood of Christ, he has the pledge of the resurrection which the Lord promised: He who feeds on my flesh and drinks my blood has life eternal, and I will raise him up on the last day' (Jn 6:54) (*Introduction,* no. 26). 'Christ's resurrection has inaugurated the last days. To remain true to our vocation to love God, we must live here and now as though we were already in heaven. That is our destiny and our mission. Under various names God incarnate promised us life: kingdom of heaven, land of the living, perfect consolation, fulfilment of our desires, boundless mercy, the company of God. He also pointed out our way to this: detachment from self, gentleness, peacemaking, hunger and thirst for "righteousness" ' (Ladislaus Boros).

Holy Orders

Philip Gleeson O.P.

I INTRODUCTION

The rites of ordination have been revised in response to Vatican II. In 1968 the Apostolic Constitution, *Pontificalis Romani recognitio*, approved the new rituals for the ordination of deacons, priests and bishops. In 1972 certain adjustments were made in the rite for the ordination of deacons, as explained in the Apostolic Letter, *Ad Pascendum*. That same Apostolic Letter also abolished the rite of clerical tonsure, and introduced the rite for the admission of candidates for the diaconate or priesthood. In the same year, 1972, all the 'minor orders' were suppressed, and the rituals for the installation of lay readers and acolytes were introduced.

The new rites reflect the thinking of Vatican II. They take account of the picture of the ministry contained in the Constitution on the Church, and of course they also take account of the principles of liturgical reform contained in the Constitution on the Liturgy. They are revisions of the Roman rite, and as such are marked by Roman tradition. They take account of the knowledge which has been acquired about the history of the rites, and they are influenced by the comparative study of different liturgical traditions, both Eastern and Western. And, as in other areas of liturgical reform, the Apostolic Tradition of Hippolytus of Rome is never too far from mind.

We shall first look briefly at each of the various rites, and make some general comments about them. Then we shall comment on the readings which are given for the rites.

The Ordination of a Bishop

The ordination takes place after the Gospel of the Mass. The candidate for ordination is presented by priests of the diocese, a sign of the unity and cooperation which need to exist between bishop and presbyterium. The choice of candidate is approved by the whole congregation. Such approval was once a significant element in the making of a bishop. The very discreet rubric in the new ritual is at least a reminder of something

87

which may acquire fresh vigour as the reflections of Vatican II gradually become part of the life of the Church. It is a pity that mention of
approval by the congregation immediately seems to make people think
of the possibility of disapproval, whereas it might be better to think
about the positive value of letting a man know that he really has the
support and encouragement of the Christian community.

The bishop who presides at the ordination, the principal consecrator,
delivers a homily. A sample homily is included in the ritual, and it is
interesting to see what it has to say about the episcopacy. It takes its
stand, as must any treatment of orders, on the way in which the apostles
were chosen and sent out by Christ, filled with his Holy Spirit. It uses
the traditional terms to describe the task of the apostles: they were sent
to preach the Gospel, to gather the nations into one, to sanctify and to
govern. It recalls how the apostles chose others to share in their mission,
and how the laying on of hands was the gesture by which these others
were associated with the apostles' work. And it recalls how the Church
has continued the practice of appointing men to share in that work.

The sample homily also refers to the presence of Christ in the bishop
and presbyterium, and it urges people to welcome the bishop. The
bishop elect is reminded that he is being ordained to serve rather than
to be honoured, to help people rather than lord it over them, so that
even when he is governing the diocese he should model himself on
Christ the Good Shepherd rather than on the lords of the nations. He is
naturally asked to love and care for the people of his diocese, but he is
also told that his work is not exclusively the care of the Christian
people, because as successors of the apostles, bishops have a missionary
task. He is also reminded that in being ordained he is being received
into the episcopal college, and should not think of his diocese in isolation from the rest of the Church.

An interrogation follows the homily, and it underlines the most
important of the bishop's duties and responsibilities. The preaching of
the Gospel is given emphasis. Then, in the litanies, the whole assemby
prays for God's help.

The laying on of hands is the gesture which occupies the centre of
the ordination rite. The revision of the rite makes sure that this gesture
is done simply and clearly, in silence, by the principal consecrator and
then by the other bishops present, or at least by two assistant consecra-
tors. This simply gesture links the ministry of today with the ministry
of the apostles, it is a sign of sharing in the Holy Spirit, and a sign of
reception into the college of bishops.

When the laying on of hands has been completed, there is a prayer of
consecration. Significantly enough, the prayer which was given in the
previous pontifical has been dropped: it was a prayer which began by

making a rather laboured comparison between the high priests of the Old Testament and the bishops of the New. The prayer given in the revised rite is based on the simple prayer found in the Apostolic Tradition of Hippolytus of Rome, a prayer which asks that the Spirit may be given to the bishop, the Spirit which the Father gives the Son and which the Son gives the apostles.

During the prayer of consecration, the book of the Gospels is held over the head of the man being ordained, This ancient ritual is common to both East and West, and while it may look a little bizarre to us it does make the point that the bishop is ordained to preach the Gospel, and that this is his chief duty.

After the laying on of hands and the prayer of consecration, there are a number of rites which elaborate some aspects of ordination. These tend to be the more picturesque parts of the ceremony, and they come not from ancient Rome but from the Latin West outside Rome. The new ritual presents them simply as explanatory rites, ways of signifying some of the implications of the ordination which has taken place.

The bishop's head is anointed with chrism. Originally the mention of anointing was a metaphor, referring to the pouring out of the Spirit on the apostles and their successors. But then there arose the practice of interrupting the prayer of consecration and performing an anointing with oil. While the new rite retains the anointing. it no longer interrupts the prayer. Instead, the anointing follows the prayer, as a sign that the bishop participates in the priesthood of Jesus, the Anointed.

The book of the Gospels is given to the bishop. This gesture has been moved to a more prominent position than it used to occupy, and is another sign of the concern felt by the Church about the task of preaching the Gospel.

Ring, mitre and crozier are given to the bishop. The giving of the ring is accompanied by words which tell the bishop to care for the Church, the bride of Christ. There are no words to accompany the giving of the mitre; it is with some nostalgia that we say good-bye to the dreadful horns of the two testaments. The crozier, whatever its origin may have been, is presented as a sign of the pastoral office of the bishop, and is regarded as as a shepherd's crook rather than something in the nature of a sceptre.

If the newly ordained bishop is in his own cathedral, he may then preside at the celebration of the Eucharist.

The revised rite, then, keeps many of the ceremonies which gradually attached themselves to the ordination of a bishop. But it puts them together in a fairly coherent way, and prevents them from obscuring the central part of the rite, the laying on of hands and the prayer. It is noticeable that throughout the rite there is a great insistence on the preaching of the Gospel, without of course the other duties of the bishop being neglected.

The Ordination of a Priest

The ordination of a priest also takes place after the Gospel of Mass. The candidate is called forward by the deacon, and, as with the bishop, the congregation is given an opportunity to approve the choice of candidate.

A sample homily gives a picture of the priesthood. Incidentally, maybe we do need to use the word presbyter in English. At present we are using the one word, 'priest', to translate both *presbyter* and *sacerdos*. And while it may seem artificial to use 'presbyter' to translate *presbyter* and 'priest' to translate *sacerdos*, there does seem to be a need for two different words. So perhaps ICEL's translations, which do use both words, will eventually be adopted by all.

The sample homily makes the point that the whole Church shares in the priesthood of Christ, and then goes on to speak about the ministerial priesthood of bishop and presbyter. It takes its stand, as did the homily for the ordination of a bishop, on the way Christ chose the apostles, so that through them and their successors his ministry as teacher, priest, and pastor might always be made present. The bishop is seen as the successor of the apostles, the presbyter his co-worker.

The homily stresses that the priesthood in question is that of the New Testament. It is the ministry of preaching the Gospel, caring for God's people, and celebrating the liturgy, especially the Lord's sacrifice. It is good to see some of the old ideas being expressed in the vernacular, in particular the hope that the priest will believe what he reads, preach what he believes, and practise what he preaches.

Finally the man who is being ordained is urged to 'carry on the work of Christ the Head of the Church and its Pastor'. This is a role not easy to define, but it means working with the bishop to 'bring the faithful together like a unified family'. And the homily closes with a reminder that the work of representing the Head and Pastor of the Church is a service, not a title to privilege.

After an interrogation and the litanies, there is the laying on of hands by the bishop. Then, in accordance with ancient custom—the practice was there in the Rome of Hippolytus—the presbyters who are present also lay hands on the man being ordained. This is a sign that by ordination a man is received into an 'order' or group, the order of presbyters.

The prayer of consecration is a revised form of the prayer which was in the previous pontifical. It evokes the way in which God gave helpers to Moses, sons to Aaron, and companions to the apostles, and reflects that if such men needed help so too must the bishop. The prayer asks

God to renew his Spirit within the man being ordained. The prayer has been retouched so that it contains a clear reference to the work of evangelisation. It is no accident that this task is emphasised in one way or another all through the new rituals.

The rites which follow the central rite are done simply enough. The priest's hands are anointed with chrism, he is clothed with 'priestly vestments' (the formal civil dress of fifth century Rome?), and he is given bread and wine. These rites are included as explanatory rites, and it is noticeable that the accompanying words refer to the office which the priest has already received, whereas in the previous ritual the words tended to imply that it was in these secondary rites that the priest was given his various 'powers'. Not all of the previous rites have been retained. The binding of the priest's hands has been omitted, and also the second laying on of hands which took place towards the end of Mass and was associated with the sacrament of penance.

The ritual by no means tries to solve all disputed questions. But it does try to secure certain basic positions of Vatican II. One notices how it emphasises the corporate nature of the priesthood, by making it clear that being ordained means being received into the order of presbyters; and also how it gives prominence to the work of evangelisation.

The Ordination of a Deacon

Like the other ordinations, the ordination of deacons takes place after the Gospel of Mass. The candidate is called forward, the request made by 'mother Church' is put to the bishop, and the congregation gives its approval.

The sample homily speaks of the ministry of word, altar, and charity. The deacon is one who helps the bishop and presbyterium and who serves all men. It is Christ the Servant who is put forward as the example for the deacon to follow, and there is also mention of the helpers who were chosen by the apostles for the ministry of charity.

The rite which appeared in 1968 was designed to suit deacons of all kinds, permanent or en route to the priesthood, married or unmarried. But in 1972 it was decided that the rite should vary to reflect different circumstances. So, after the homily, there is a public acceptance of celibacy by those candidates who intend becoming priests and also by unmarried men who are becoming permanent deacons. This means that, as regards this detail, the 1968 ritual is followed as it stands only in the case of married men who are becoming permanent deacons.

Then, after the public acceptance of celibacy, there is a fairly simple interrogation. Since 1972 it includes a reference to the liturgy of the hours and the deacon's obligations in this respect, but it does not go into any detail about exactly how this obligation should be understood by the different kinds of deacons. The interrogation also includes a promise of obedience to the appropriate ordinary.

After the litanies, the bishop lays his hands on each candidate. Only the bishop does this; other deacons are not invited to lay on hands. In looking at the traditional texts, one has the feeling that the bishop was anxious to keep the deacon to himself. Perhaps the counsel offered by the presbyterium was something of a burden if not a plain nuisance at times, so the bishop seems to have looked to the deacon to be his executive rather than his counsellor. However, it did happen, in Rome at any rate, that the deacon became a powerful man in the diocese; the Roman archdeacon was one of the key men in that church, until Gregory the Great decided to bring the presbyterium back to prominence. One wonders how the diaconate is going to develop in our time, especially the permanent diaconate. It would change things in the Church if an order of deacons acquired a cohesiveness and sense of purpose of its own.

The prayer of consecration is a revision of the previous prayer. The Levites of the Old Testament still figure in it, but less emphasis is laid on this comparison. The seven helpers of Acts are also mentioned, but it is Christ himself who is put forward as the great example of service. The deacon's service of the sick and needy is mentioned explicitly. Indeed the picture given in the prayer is one of service in a very wide sense, both liturgical service and the ministry of charity.

Some explanatory rites follow the main part of the ordination. The deacon is clothed with stole and dalmatic, and he is given the book of the Gospels and told to believe, preach and practise what he finds in it. Then the bishop and newly ordained deacon exchange a kiss of peace, and, depending on the circumstances, any other deacons who are present may welcome the new member into their order by giving him the kiss of peace.

Clerical State and Lay Ministries

The 'clerical state' is now simply co-extensive with the orders of deacon, presbyter, and bishop. One hopes that this will help the idea of service, of ministry, to replace any ideas which may have existed about a privileged class in the Church. The rite of clerical tonsure has disappeared, but there is now a rite for the admission of candidates, in which the candidate for diaconate or priesthood expresses his willingness to go forward for ordination, and the Church accepts him as a candidate. The documents stress that this rite does not make a man a cleric, and that it should never be linked with an ordination ceremony.

The old 'minor orders' have been suppressed. It is now recognised that there is a whole variety of functions in the Church which can be performed by people who are not ordained and who do not intend to be ordained. Rites are provided for installing lay people in two such ministries, the ministries of reader and acolyte. There is also the possibility that some churches may provide rites for installing people in other ministries; that of catechist is often mentioned in this context. It is hoped that these rites will emphasise the fact that lay people have an important role to play in the Church. But some commentators fear that the ceremonies will reinforce the idea that it is necessary to be at least slightly clericalised in order to have one's place in the Church recognised; such commentators feel that it is better to let lay people fulfil the ministries without any installation ceremony, which is in fact what happens in most cases. It is at any rate unfortunate that candidates for ordination must first be installed as readers and acolytes, as if these ministries were steps up a ladder whose top rung is the episcopacy. Whatever about such reflections, the rites for the installation of readers and acolytes are simple and dignified. They bring out the importance of the ministries involved, and pray for God's blessing on the people who undertake them.

General Remarks

The new rites are not intended to be expressions of the latest theological opinions about the ministry. They are not meant to solve the various problems which exercise the exegete, the historican, the systematic theologian. They do try to retain what is of value in the tradition, and to establish certain positions which seemed important to Vatican II.

One simple but important thing is the deliberate way in which the orders of bishop, presbyter, and deacon are put alongside each other in the one publication of 1968. This marked the end of the temptation to think of priest, deacon and subdeacon on the one hand, and bishop on the other. Even the way in which the new ritual speaks about the 'ordination' of bishops is a sign that an end must be put to the era when priests and deacons were 'ordained' but bishops and kings were 'consecrated'. One notices that the newspapers now speak about the ordination of bishops, thanks no doubt to the efforts of various press officers.

In the new ritual the word 'order' is frequently used in its original senses, to designate a body of people; that is, it is used in a corporate sense. It is curious how this word gradually came to mean something which one receives rather than something into which one is received. But the original usage has been recovering lost ground for some time now. Pius XII made sure to use the word in its original meaning on a number of occasions. This way of using the word 'order' is just one of the many indications of an interest in collegiality, and indeed an interest in community in general, which is expressed in the new rituals and which characterises present ways of thinking.

The revised rites of ordination are simpler and clearer than the previous ones. In particular, they allow the laying on of hands to stand out clearly as the central gesture of the rites. It is no doubt possible to exaggerate the importance of such attempts at clarity and simplicity. But surely it is of real importance to unearth this sign, and so have a biblical gesture plainly at the centre of the celebration, thus linking the ministry of today with the ministry of the New Testament. It is important too that this gesture is common to the ordination rites of both East and West, and one recalls that Pius XII, in *Sacramentum Ordinis*, recognised the centrality of the ancient gesture. The other rites in the ordination ceremonies, while they may be more colourful and dramatic, tend to highligh one or other aspect of the ministry, and are very definitely relegated to a secondary position.

Would it be straining a point to say that the very 'undefined' nature of the central gesture fits in well with the liturgy's lack of concern about precise definitions? It is true that the prayers and secondary gestures add some precision and go some way towards distinguishing between the different orders and between people in orders and people not in orders. But the liturgy does not dwell too much on lines of demarcation. It is more interested in the common task than in the fact that there are different ways of sharing in this task. It is noticeable that a good proportion of the readings can be used for any of the three orders; and that much of what is demanded of the ordained minister is in fact demanded of every Christian.

This is one more instance of life going on without waiting to be finally defined. The ministries of bishop, presbyter and deacon do exist in the Church, whether or not we have succeeded in defining them, in distinguishing one from the other, or distinguishing them all from the ministries exercised by lay people. The search for definition and understanding is bound to continue. But there is an openness in the liturgy, like the openness of the New Testament, which looks not only to the tradition but to the future, and is an invitation to shape a future which is in continuity with the past and the present but not simply a repetition of what has gone before.

The permanent diaconate especially seems to be a ministry which is bound to develop but whose lines of development cannot be predicted. There will surely be quite a lot of variety within the order of deacons, with some deacons tending to be occupied in the administration which would otherwise prevent bishops and priests from preaching, while others work directly in the ministry of preaching.

Besides not giving precise definitions, the liturgy incorporates elements which if not contradictory are at least in tension. At times the ordained minister is seen as the sign of Christ the Head of the Church, the sign of the unique role of Christ in relation to his Church. At other times, the rites show an awareness that the minister remains a member of the Body of which Christ is the Head. It is probably true to say that in the past there has been a tendency to think of the minister as the representative of Christ the Head when he should have been reminded that he is part of the Body. But nowadays there is some inclination to allow the special role of representing Christ the Head to disappear or at least fade into the background. While the new ritual does not solve our problem, it certainly invites us to look for a solution which incorporates the different elements rather than pretend to solve it by forgetting about one of the elements.

It is understandable, even desirable, that such a tension should exist in the ritual. But it is less understandable that in several instances there are echoes of the idea that ordination is promotion to a position of privilege in the Church. All we can do is let such echoes pass us by, and pay attention to the message which comes through quite clearly: even when we see the minister as representing the Head, the Head is Christ the Servant, who forbids his followers to lord it over one another.

II COMMENTARY ON READINGS

A. OLD TESTAMENT READINGS

1. *Num 3:5-9. (For deacons)* This is the traditional comparison between the order of deacons and the tribe of Levi whose duty was the 'service of the tabernacle'. It evokes the liturgical side of the deacon's ministry.

2. *Num 11:11-12, 14-17, 24-25. (For priests)* The order of presbyters, co-workers of the bishop, is compared to the group of seventy elders who received a share in the spirit and in the burden which God had given to Moses.

3. *Is 61:1-3 (For bishops and priests)* Like the prophet, the ordained minister is given the mission of proclaiming the good news. The liturgy allows the mention of anointing to evoke both the gift of the Spirit and the chrism which is a sign of this gift in the ordination of bishops and priests.

4. *Jer 1:4-9.* The mission of all ordained ministers is to proclaim God's word to the world.

B. NEW TESTAMENT READINGS

1. *Acts 6:1-7. (For deacons)* Seven men are chosen and given responsibility for the administration of alms, the 'diakonia'. The apostles pray over them and lay hands on them. The service mentioned here is considered to be the prototype for the ministry of charity which is entrusted to the order of deacons.

2. *Acts 8:26-40. (For deacons)* Philip ('Philip the evangelist, one of the Seven [Acts 21:8]) brings the good news to the eunuch and baptises him. The order of deacons is meant to play an important role in both the missionary and liturgical activities of the Church.

3. *Acts 10:37-43.* Ministers are ordained so that, like Peter, they may bear witness to Jesus, and proclaim the good news of salvation through his name.

4. *Acts 20:17-18, 28-32, 36 (For bishops and priests)* Paul exhorts the 'overseeing elders' of Ephesus to be on their guard. The liturgy addresses this exhortation to bishops and priests, the 'pastors' who now perform this service of overseeing.

5. *Rom 12:4-8.* There is a variety of gifts in the Church. This variety should be accepted with the humility which has been urged in verse 3: 'In the light of the grace I have received I want to urge each one among you not to exaggerate his real importance. Each of you must judge himself soberly by the standard of the faith God has given him.'

6. *2 Cor 4:1-2, 5-7.* The ordained minister is the earthenware jar, the vessel of clay. It is Jesus who is Lord.

7. *2 Cor 5:14-20.* The ordained minister is the ambassador who, in the name of Christ, brings the good news of reconcilation with God.

8. *Eph 4:1-7, 11-13.* There is a variety of gifts in the Church, but it is at the service of unity.

9. *1 Tim 3:8-13. (For deacons)* The passage speaks of the qualities needed by deacons, especially married deacons. It includes a mention of women (v. 11), presumably deaconesses, which raises quite a controverted question. (It is noticeable that Eph 3:1-7 is not included as a reading suitable for the ordination of bishops and priests. It speaks about presiding elders who are married.)

10. *1 Tim 4:12-16.* This passage, which speaks about reading, preaching and teaching evokes the work common to all ordained ministers. The gesture which is mentioned, the laying on of hands, has been restored to full prominence in all three ordination rites. (Should one laugh or cry at the fact that if this passage is used at the ordination of a bishop the reference to youthfulness is supposed to be omitted?)

11. *2 Tim 1:6-14.* (For bishops) This passage mentions a laying on of

hands, and the task of witnessing to the Lord.

12. *Heb 5:1-10.* It is Christ himself who is the Priest of the New Testament. Men are ordained to be ministers of his unique priesthood.

13. *1 Pet 4:7-11.* The variety of gifts in the Church should be at the service of the community.

14. *1 Pet 5:1-4.* The ordained minister is not meant to be a dictator, but to be a shepherd who leads the flock by example, remembering that he is the servant of the 'chief shepherd'.

C. RESPONSORIAL PSALMS

1. *Ps 22.* The Lord can be trusted to guide and provide for us. The mentions of restful waters, a banquet, anointing, the overflowing cup, and dwelling in the house of the Lord, have traditionally been associated with the liturgy of the Church.

2. *Ps 83.* The joy of living close to God, in 'the house of God'. This is another psalm traditionally allowed to evoke the liturgical activities of the Church.

3. *Ps 88.* Trust in God who 'anoints' his servants.

4. *Ps 95.* The mission of proclaiming God's wonders.

5. *Ps 99.* An invitation to serve God and sing his praises. The response, Jn 15:14, evokes the friendship which Christ gives to those who serve him.

6. *Ps 109.* The unique priesthood of the Messiah.

7. *Ps 115.* The response (1 Cor 10:16) 'The blessing cup that we bless is a communion with the blood of Christ', shows that this psalm is associated with the Eucharist because of its reference to the 'cup of salvation' and 'the thanksgiving sacrifice'.

8. *Ps 116.* The psalm's exhortation to proclaim God's praise is completed by the command of Christ to proclaim the good news (Mk 16:15).

D. GOSPELS

1. *Mt 5:13-16.* The ordained minister should be like a light or sign which shows the way to the Father. So, of course, should the whole Church, and everyone in it.

2. *Mt 9:35-37.* 'The harvest is rich but the labourers are few'.

3. *Mt 10:1-5.* The mission of the apostles, who are to heal the sick and 'proclaim that the kingdom of heaven is close at hand'. (It is necessary to glance ahead to verse 7 to see the mention of proclaiming the kingdom).

4. *Mt 20:25-28*. The distinctive way in which Christ sees authority as a service, so radically different from any 'pagan' way of lording it over others.

5. *Lk 10:1-9*. The mission of the seventy-two to heal and to proclaim that the kingdom of God is very near. The harvest is rich but the labourers are few.

6. *Lk 12:35-44*. An exhortation to vigilant stewardship.

7. *Lk 22:14-20, 24-30*. Jesus' authority is expressed in service of others. In the Lord's Supper we have the memorial of his service, and the pledge of sharing in the fulness of his joy.

8. *Jn 10:11-16*. Christ is the shepherd who lays down his life for his sheep. The pastors in the Church are the ministers of this unique shepherd.

9. *Jn 12:24-26*. The service which is a following of Christ, who is the grain of wheat which dies to yield a rich harvest.

10. *Jn 15:9-17*. Love must be at the heart of obedience and service. Jesus obeys the Father and is united with him in love; those who obey Jesus are his friends rather than his servants.

11. *Jn 17:6, 14-19*. Part of the priestly prayer of Christ. Jesus dedicates himself to the Father, and prays that his disciples may share in this dedication to true worship.

12. *Jn 20:19-23*. The disciples are given the Holy Spirit and sent to bring the fulness of forgiveness and peace to the world. It has been traditional to associate this passage with the sacrament of penance, though of course it has a wider import.

13. *Jn 21:15-17*. Peter is a model for any minister, in his love of Christ and his service of Christ's flock.

Nuptial Masses

Brian Gogan, C.S.Sp. (Introduction)
Jerry Creedon, C.S.Sp. (Commentary)

I INTRODUCTION

The well being of individuals and of society as a whole is closely linked with the health of family life. Hence the importance the church attaches to the sacrament of matrimony and the family which ensues. Every effort has to be made to ensure a fruitful celebration of the sacrament which will have as its outcome a successful marriage. The measure of a successful marriage, however, is not that of this world but that of God— God's world.

The intimate partnership of married life and love has been instituted by God. It is governed by his laws. It is based on a mutual surrender in a loving alliance. This surrender takes the form of an irrevocable personal consent to the marriage covenant. Through this consent husband and wife accept each other. A relationship arises which by divine will and in the eyes of Christian faith is a lasting one. For the good of the family and its offspring and of society the continuity of this bond no longer depends on human decision alone.

Man and woman joined in matrimony 'are no longer two, but one flesh' (Mt 19:6). They render help and service to each other through an intimate union of mind, heart, body and deed. Through this union they experience the meaning of their oneness. If they are faithful it can grow deeper day by day.

This union of persons in marriage is directed not merely to the enrichment of those involved as partners but also to the generation and education of children. Happy, healthy children are the fruit of a happy, healthy marriage.

God has abundantly blessed married love. In the Old Testament God made himself present to his people through a covenant of love and fidelity. The Saviour of men and the Spouse of the Church comes into the lives of married Christians through the sacrament of matrimony. He abides with them so that just as he loved the church and handed himself over on her behalf (Eph 5:25) married partners may love each other

<p />

with undying fidelity. Authentic married love is caught up in divine love. It is enriched by Christ's redeeming power, the gift of the Spirit, and the pastoral activity of the Christian community. This love can lead married people to God as surely as any other Christian vocation.

To help them on the way to holiness, married Christians have a special sacrament. Through this sacrament they consecrate themselves to one another and to God. By reason of this sacrament they fulfil the obligations of married and family life in a Christian spirit. Everything they do in marriage, if done in the Spirit, leads to their mutual sanctification and manifests in the world the undying love of God. Their living covenant to each other reflects God's eternal covenant with man in Christ.

Married love is a deeply human one. It is directed from one person to another through an affection of the will. It finds expression in a bodily way. All the expressions of married love, the signs of friendship distinctive of marriage, have their origin in the love of God poured out in their hearts in baptism and enriched in a special way through the sacrament of marriage. This love far excels any mere sensual or erotic inclination. It is uniquely expressed and perfected in the bodily union of marriage. This bodily union is something chaste, noble and worthy. Expressed in a manner which is truly human, these actions signify and promote that mutual self-giving by which married partners enrich and support each other in thankfulness and joy.

When this love exists in mutual fidelity and is strengthened by the sacrament it remains steadfastly faithful in mind and body, in good days and in bad. It will never be profaned by adultery or divorce. If it is firmly established in the Lord, the unity of marriage will endure. It will reflect the equal personal dignity of husband and wife, a dignity acknowledged and respected in mutual love.

While in no way diminishing the importance of other aspects of marriage, true married love has as its aim to create the generation of children. Parents should regard as their proper mission the task of transmitting human life and of carefully educating those to whom it has been transmitted. They will realise that in doing this they cooperate with the love of God the creator. Together with him they bring new persons into the world who can share his life as an eternal destiny in his presence.

In bringing children into the world they will take account of both the material and spiritual conditions of the times. They will think of their own state in life. They will consult the interests of their extended family, the society in which they live and of the Church itself. Parents themselves ultimately make this judgment in the sight of God. But in their manner of acting, married partners should be aware that they cannot proceed according to whim or fancy. They must inform their conscience so that their decisions with regard to the generation of children are carried out in accordance with the mind of Christ. The divine law reveals and protects the full meaning of married love and directs it towards a truly human fulfilment.

Here one may bear in mind the teaching of *Gaudium et Spes*, paragraph 51: 'Relying on these principles, sons of the Church may not undertake methods of regulating procreation which are found blameworthy by the teaching authority of the Church in its unfolding of the divine law.' Everyone should be persuaded that human life and the task of transmitting it are not realities bound up with this world alone as they cannot be measured or perceived only in earthly terms but must always have a bearing on the eternal destiny of men.

The care of the family when it comes into being must be the primary concern of both husband and wife. Its first element is a deep communion of mind and heart between the partners. The second requirement is their painstaking cooperation in the education of the children with whom God blesses them. The active presence of the father is highly beneficial to the development of the children. The children, especially younger ones, need the care of their mother in the home. This domestic role of motherhood must be given the importance it has in the development of children. It must be safely preserved through legislation, social welfare provision and the constant pastoral teaching of the Church.

In the preservation and growth of family life first importance must be attached to constant reflection on God's word in the Scriptures, daily prayer in the home, and regular reception of the sacraments. Married people should be encouraged to take part in various movements which support married life, especially those which have a direct bearing on the welfare of the family.

The ministers of the sacrament are of course the couple getting married: the bride and the groom. It is by their action in this celebration that the sacrament is conferred on each other. The priest acts as a witness on behalf of the community together with the other witnesses.

Thematic Groupings

The rich theology, which has been summarised for us in the Constitution on the Church in the Modern World of the Second Vatican Council, paragraphs 47-52, underlies the rites of marriage in the revised ritual. The various texts selected bring out very clearly this theology. This is so in the declaration of consent. It occurs especially in the first form where the bride and groom express their consent directly to each other. It is also there in the second and third forms, though less obviously.

The prefaces of the Mass, all three of them, also reflect this theology, though the third is perhaps the one which emphasises most strongly the dignity and the value of married love: 'the love of man and woman is made holy in the sacrament of marriage and becomes the mirror of your everlasting love.' The three forms of the nuptial blessing spell out this theology in prayer. Again the third form provides perhaps the most comprehensive presentation of the doctrines combining the viewpoint of Old and New Testament in one vision. The blessings at the end of Mass also reflect this understanding of marriage. Perhaps the best way to deal with them is to choose from the options the ones most suitable to the occasion.

The following themes of celebration are suggested with appropriate selections from the readings.

1. *Love.* Here one could choose either of three gospels: Mt 22:35-40, a succinct account of the first and second commandments of God and the New Testament teaching on love; Jn 15:9-12 gives the essence of Christ's teaching on love as does Jn 15:12-16 which emphasises sacrificial love.

One could select any one of four epistles to go with these gospel readings. 1 Cor 12:21—13:8 is an obvious choice — Paul's hymn to love. The theme of love receives more theological than sacramental interpretation in the reading from Eph 5:2, 21-33 in Paul's view of married love as a sign or sacrament of Christ's love for the Church. Col 3:12-17 is a characteristic Pauline appeal for love, love which finds expression in joy and thanksgiving and praise to the Lord. The first letter of Jn 3:18-24 carries John's powerful message on the need for a love which is not mere words or talk but real and active.

Old Testament readings are also rich on the theme of love. The most obvious one is from the Song of Songs 2:8-10, 14, 16; 8:6-7 with its expression of passionate and devoted love by bride and groom. However readings from the book of Genesis either 1:26-28, 31 or Gen 2:18-24 also express in a more earthly way the basis of married love and God's will that man and wife will come together and be creative in their love for each other. As regards the responsorial psalm either no. 3 or no. 6 would seem most suitable as both emphasise God's love for us: 'the love of the Lord is everlasting' and our need to thank God for this undying love of his.

2. *Communion.* This is perhaps a slightly unusual theme for marriage but one which could appeal to younger people perhaps. It finds expression in a somewhat physical way in Mk 10:6-9 where Jesus refers to the command of God from the beginning of creation that man and wife come together in one body. Jn 17:20-26 puts it in a more spiritual,

humane way perhaps, in the prayer of our Lord for his disciples at the
Last Supper that they be one with each other. This would be an unusual passage to read in the marriage rite but one which should find,
perhaps, its happiest application in this context.

The readings from the Apostles are also rich in references to this
theme. 1 Pet 3:1-9 offers homely advice to both husbands and wives as
to how they should get along, but the underlying emphasis is on communion with each other. As one might expect, this theme is also to the
fore in the selections from the letters of John. 1 Jn 3:18-24 speaks of
love in terms of the mystical communion it can embody. It is even
more powerfully expressed in 1 Jn 4:7-12 which relates human love to
the eternal love of God.

The Old Testament reading which expresses this most powerfully is
again the Song of Songs 2:8-10, 14, 16; 8:6-7, a passionate love song.
However, one could also refer to Gen 2:18-24 with special emphasis on
the verses 'This at last is bone from my bones and flesh from my flesh!
this is to be called woman for this was taken from man.' The responsorial psalm which might be most suitable here is no. 5 'Your wife will
be like a fruitful vine in the heart of your house; your children like
shoots of the olive around your table' referring to the results of a deep
relationship between the married partners.

3. *Fidelity.* This theme might find favour with people having a less
romantic view of marriage and who look on it as a foundation for a
solid life together. The gospel readings most appropriate here are Mt
7:21, 24-25, parable of the man who built his house on the rock. The
rock here is evidently fidelity in marriage. It is also reflected in Mt
19:3-6, our Lord's teaching on the indissolubility of marriage.

It is echoed in the readings from St Paul, Rom 8:31-35, 37-39
emphasising our love for Christ as the basis of a deeply Christian life,
and therefore of a deeply Christian married life. This theme recurs in
1 Cor 6:13-15, 17-20 with its emphasis on respect for the body as the
temple of the Spirit, and therefore recognition that married fidelity is
fidelity not merely to another person but fidelity to God. 'You are not
your own property; you have been bought and paid for. That is why
you should use your body for the glory of God.'

As regards the Old Testament this theme finds some reflection in Sir
26:1-4, 13-16 where the qualities of a really good wife are described.
However, it might be necessary in the introduction to say that the same
qualities are demanded of the husband. The responsorial psalm which
might best go with this is no. 1 'They are happy whose God is the Lord'
etc. No. 4 also would suit, 'Happy the man who fears the Lord' etc.

4. *Discipleship.* Some Christians entering marriage want to see it in
terms of the living out of the gospel in a more intense way. Some of the

passages in the Lectionary express this forcibly. From among the gospels, Mt 5:1-12, the Beatitudes from the Sermon on the Mount, carries the core of this message. It's found also in Mt 5:13-16, our Lord's teaching, also from the Sermon on the Mount, on the salt of the earth, the light of the world. This theme is reflected in Rom 12:1-2, 9-18, a call to a way of life modelled 'not on the behaviour of the world around you. . . but modelled by your new mind.' It also includes an invitation to love of a very spiritual order 'love each other as much as brothers should, and have a profound respect for each other.' None of the Old Testament passages are particularly appropriate. Perhaps the reading from Tob 8:4-8 comes closest to this theme with its reference to Genesis and comment on it 'It is not good that man should be alone; let us make him a helpmate like himself. And so I do not take my sister for any lustful motive; I do it in singleness of heart.' The best responsorial psalm to take with this reading then is probably no. 2, Ps 33: 'I will bless the Lord at all times', or no. 4, Ps 111: 'Happy the man who fears the Lord, who takes delight in his command.' This theme is perhaps a little unusual, but may well appeal to people of a more profound level of Christian life.

5. *Covenant.* This theme brings out the more theological dimensions of the celebration that might appeal more to people of an intellectual bent of mind, preferably theological! It occurs in the gospel reading from Jn 2:1-11, the Marriage Feast of Cana, where the changing of the water into wine symbolises both the transformation of the old covenant into the new and the transformation of the human relationship of marriage into the sacramental mystery of Christian love. The reading from the Apostles, in this case Eph 5:2, 31-33 is particularly appropriate where Paul says of marriage: 'This mystery has many implications; but I am saying it applies to Christ in the Church.' The whole burden of his message is to recognise the sacramentality of marriage as symbolising the union between Christ and his Church, between God and his people. The obvious consequence is seen in the gift of grace which accompanies the sacrament. The somewhat mythological reading from Rev 19:1, 5-9 is also appropriate theologically speaking. Whether pastorally speaking it will be grasped by those taking part is another matter. At the same time the imagery is beautiful, 'because this is the time for the marriage of the Lamb. His bride is ready; she has been able to dress herself in dazzling white linen, because her linen is made of the good deeds of the saints. . . . Happy are those who are invited to the wedding feast of the Lamb.'

The Old Testament passages resound with this covenant theme. Tob 7:9-14 speaks of the marriage covenant as a contract according to ordinances in the law of Moses. The covenant theme is referred to most expressly in Jer 31:31-34 with the promise of the new covenant when God will write the law in our hearts. God's law is love and it is obviously deep in the hearts of those joined in the sacrament of marriage. The responsorial psalm most appropriate would seem to be no. 3, Ps 102 with its reference in the third strophe to God's justice, 'It reaches out to children's children and they keep the covenant in truth.' The refrain 'The love of the Lord is everlasting upon those who hold him in fear' also carries with it the message of God's covenant relationship with his people.

6. *The Marriage of Older People.* The selection of passages appropriate to such weddings can prove difficult. Obviously the more romantic and poetic may not be entirely appropriate, though again this is a matter of judicious enquiry. The following readings might be suggested: Mt 5:13-16 with its emphasis on authenticity in the spirit of the gospel; the reading from 1 Pet 3:1-9 which de-emphasises the visible aspects of appearance and places its greatest stress on qualities like loyalty, fidelity, and compassion. Among the Old Testament readings the fifth might be chosen from Tob 8:4-8 again with its reference to the motivation for marriage: 'I do not take my sister for any lustful motive; I do it in singleness of heart.' The responsorial psalm to go with this might well be no. 6, Ps 144 'The Lord is kind and full of compassion; slow to anger and bounding in love', emphasising God's compassion towards all his creatures.

II COMMENTARY ON READINGS

A. OLD TESTAMENT READINGS

Three of the eight readings from the Old Testament are taken from the Book of Genesis. This, I suppose, is not surprising. If Genesis is the Book of the beginnings of the story of man and his world, then we should expect it to say a good deal about marriage and about weddings. In fact its view of marriage is far more down to earth than is anything we read in the New Testament. The mystical element which is stressed in, for example, Ephesians, may be missing from the view of marriage expressed in Genesis, Tobit and Ecclesiasticus, but Genesis has, with all its matter-of-factness, a note of charm, beauty and even romance which we don't find in Paul.

1. *Gen 1:26-28, 31.* There are three main ideas expressed in this reading: (a) Man and woman are the high point of God's creation. And the sexual difference between man and woman is part of this creation. The idea of man finds its full meaning not in the male alone but in man and

woman. With this disarmingly simple statement our 'hang-ups' about sex are given the beck completely and finally to disappear.

(b) Man and woman are made in God's 'image and likeness'. Normally we tend to restrict this likeness to the spiritual and rational sides of man. Genesis makes no such restriction. The whole man, body and soul, is a reflection of, bears a resemblance to his creator.

(c) It has been pointed out that just as powerful earthly kings, to indicate their claim to dominion, put up an image of themselves in the provinces of their empire where they do not personally appear, so man is placed upon earth in God's image as God's sovereign emblem. He is therefore God's representative. But his task in carrying out this divine function is one of *responsibility*: responsibility for the creatures of the earth, responsibility for peopling the earth. At the time of Genesis this latter responsibility consisted in building a human family which was as yet in its infancy. In our days of population explosion and accompanying world hunger the responsibility may not lie in 'increasing, multiplying and filling the earth' but in striving for justice and in creating conditions within and outside the family where all men can live in dignity as real 'images' of God. Only then can man and woman look at their creation and say as God said of his: 'Indeed it is very good'.

2. *Gen 2:18-24.* Male chauvinism is a burning issue in today's world of women's lib. Male domination in church, politics and economic planning is deplored because it is a fact. Man has set himself up as the strong one, and as we know, the strong are lonely. This reading from Genesis speak to us about the aloneness of man, about his helplessness. And as the poet Rilke said: 'Love consists in this that two solitudes protect and touch and greet each other'. Solitude is here defined very realistically as helplessness, and the main point made in the reading is that one of the most vital linchpins of marital bliss consists in the remembrance by both parties of how much they need each other. There are of course traces of male chauvinism even here: most women will resent the notion of their being created from the rib of man! But forget this in order to concentrate on the statement that woman was created while man was asleep, and we hear the writer of Genesis hinting at something very beautiful, namely, woman is a mystery to man like all the other wonderful things he believes in but has not seen happen, like creation and resurrection. Finally, a very practical note is struck in the last verse of the reading: a man and a woman must break with even the closest of the old bonds if they are to make a really new beginning as man and wife. Very often if a man leaves his wife it is because in the first place he never left his mother.

3. *Gen 24:48-51, 58-67.* Here is a charming little story, which is part of the long matchmaking episode recounted in chapter 24. It is the story

of Rebecca's wedding with Isaac. Notice the qualities which Abraham's servant Eliezer looks for in the girl he sought as future wife for his master's son: she has to show a woman's readiness to help, kindness of heart and an understanding for animals.

The usual theme in Genesis of God's promise of increase to the nation and possession of land ('may your descendants gain possession of the gates of their enemies') is to be found in this passage, but the overriding notion is that of God's guidance in human affairs. But to say 'human affairs' could be misleading, because more accurately the story is an account of God's activity in human hearts where he is at work 'mysteriously directing, evening and removing resistance'. The openness of Rebecca, of her family and of Isaac to that activity is surely the point where their story of long ago and the story of today's spouses most aptly meet.

4 and 5. *Tobit 7:9-14; 8:4-8.* The story of Tobias is the story of one of the most faithful sons of Israel. He is true to his religion in exile, yet in no way intolerant towards his Gentile neighbours; he is honest to a fault and charitable to the point of risking his life. He is a man of prayer and piety. These two readings tell us about his wedding to Sarah, a woman who had been tormented by a demon which killed her seven husbands on their wedding night. Just as marriage is presented as the cure for loneliness in Genesis, so in this story, it brings peace to Sarah's troubled mind and upset body. Why? Because now God is in the marriage; somehow in this story heaven comes close to earth. The tale of Tobias and Sarah is a call to tenderness, fidelity and praying together. Perhaps its most important lesson, though, is what it tells us about love: real love doesn't bind, it sets the other free.

6. *Song 2:8-10, 14, 16; 8:6-7.* One of the aptest readings for Nuptial Masses in the Lectionary is this piece from the Song of Songs. For the Song of Songs is a love-song through and through, one of the most explicit tributes in literature to human sexuality, beauty and love. Love is here depicted for what it is, supremely tender yet 'strong as death'. It is one of the few realities which can survive death, the one force which can keep alive what the forces of death are constantly threatening to kill.

7. *Sir 26:1-4, 13-16.* Here is a very idealistic picture painted by a none too romantic sage of what he considers to be a happy marriage. True to the thinking of his time (and indeed of many in our time too) the happiness of the man is the writer's only concern. One could easily conclude from this reading that Ecclesiasticus viewed woman as simply existing for man's comfort and happiness. However, woman is at least accredited here with the power and the ability to give, and it is in creat-

ive giving that people become whole and mature. Besides, there is no explicit mention of a wife's tasks, no reminder that her role is to be fulfilled in the kitchen; Ecclesiasticus is concerned with what a good wife is, not with what she does. Goodness, cheerfulness, graciousness, modesty, chastity and beauty, these are the things that gladden a husband's heart when he finds them in his wife. Special importance is given to the virtue of being able to hold one's tongue. I doubt if anyone in our day would quarrel with this list of ingredients for a happy marriage, provided of course we do what Ecclesiasticus failed to do, make demands too on the husband.

8. *Jer 31:31-34.* This is one of the best known and dearly loved passages in the Bible. It makes two important statements about the Law or what we would call rules and regulations: firstly, it is not enough; secondly, it is not even needed to make people's lives happy and right. Jeremiah had learned this lesson through his own experience. He has been excommunicated from the Temple worship, and thereby been deprived of the normal means of reaching out to God which was through and with one's community. So he had to find his own way to God, which was the way of heart speaking to heart. The law, in his case, had not been enough, but having found this new way Jeremiah discovered that it wasn't necessary either.

The law in so far as it exists to protect individuals' rights will always be a serious consideration. But it is not enough: not enough to create the love and trust that are the very essence of a happy marriage. And where love and trust exist, there the law is not necessary.

B. NEW TESTAMENT READINGS

The readings from the New Testament come from a greater variety of sources than do those from the Old Testament. Pride of place is given to St Paul, St Matthew and St John, three very different persons yet, when they come to speak of marriage, they end up saying much the same thing. In fact there is not a real theology of marriage to be found in the New Testament. Some of the reasons for this will be given in the course of the commentaries on various readings. One very important point about the New Testament view of marriage is that in a Christian marriage there are always three: the woman, the man and Christ. Thus a mystical element is added which makes of Christian marriage something very distinctive indeed.

1. *Rom 8:31-35, 37-39.* The first of two readings from the Epistle to the Romans is taken from the central chapter of the Epistle, chapter eight, in which life inspired by belief in God's love is contrasted with life lived in fear of God's law. The first ideal put before us is forgiveness.

Belief in God's forgiveness is the starting point too in human relationships and more especially in the intimate relationship of marriage Marriages sometimes founder because a man marries not a real woman with faults, and maybe even vices as well as virtues, but his own idealisation of the woman he thinks he loves. We are reminded by St Paul that God's love for us is all the more real and enduring because he knows our weaknesses, our need for redemption, our helplessness to save ourselves. Real human love too, as distinct from infatuation, has to include forgiveness; for it accepts the other as she or he is.

The second point of this reading is much the same as that made already in the reading from the Song of Songs: the love of God is stronger than any power whatever, even death itself. No barrier can come between its power and the human heart. Now this love has become incarnate in Jesus Christ, and if Christ is part of every Christian marriage, then that same love is visible too in the love between wife and husband. And if that love endures, then through what trials soever wife and husband will triumph.

2. *Rom 12:1-2, 9-18.* The second reading is taken from that section of the Epistle to the Romans known as the 'parenetic' section: that is, the part of the Epistle which is given to practical advice, admonitions and exhortations. The advice given in this reading is directed, of course, at everyone, but it is certainly apt counsel for a woman and man on their wedding day. Paul sees Christian life in its entirety, not only those times when we pray and go to Mass, as a kind of liturgy. 'Offer your living selves as a holy sacrifice (some translate as 'relevant sacrifice'). Married life does involve sacrifice, and while neither bride nor groom should consider themselves as victims being led to the altar, neither must they expect happiness to coexist with selfishness. The sentence that follows could easily be paraphrased to read: Don't try to keep up with the Jones's! Have minds of your own, a vision, principles and values of your own, and follow them. Eminently practical advice! And there is more: Paul reminds us that love must be for real, not a pretence, not something phoney. Should we ask what the words of the wedding ceremony: 'until death do us part' mean? Is death here maybe the death of true and honest love? There must be respect. Respect comes from a Latin word meaning 'to look again', that is to acknowledge the mystery of the other and reverence it. It is the opposite of 'to suspect' which literally means 'to look under' someone ('s chair or bed!); and 'to despise' (*despicere*: 'to look down on' someone). And of course since it means 'to take a second look' (and maybe a millionth and second) at someone, it is also the opposite of writing someone off. Cheerfulness, joy even in trials, hope, a spirit of prayer (which might simply be called 'awareness'), all these are called for if love is to be real. A very practical

injunction is slipped in at the beginning of the last paragraph: 'rejoice with those who rejoice and be sad with those in sorrow', but do we find it easy to be happy over someone else's success? Am I really happy if my next door neighbour's little girl scores full marks in Maths? Do I run as quickly to tell the other neighbours as I would if the child had failed? We are counselled to make friends with the poor and to treat them as equals. Am I prepared to offer that cup of tea to an itinerant woman in the kitchen or dining room rather than at the door or in the porch or not at all. . . ? We are still on the practical level, so practical now as to be very near the bone, so near the bone in fact that Paul is beginning to sound unrealistic if not downright idealistic. Yet, Christianity is idealistic, and though the lesson ends with an exhortation to live in peace with everyone, I can easily see the married couple who take Paul's advice given here seriously, literally and in detail, getting sheer hell from their more conventional neighbours.

3. *I Cor 6:13-15, 17-20.* This comes from the section in Paul's First Letter to the Corinthians in which he sets forth his view on Christian perfection. Here he is giving his views on sex, and they are very strict views indeed. However, we should bear in mind that this letter is addressed to a rather emotionally unbalanced community. The Christians at Corinth believed not only in Christ's resurrection but in their own. As a result they seem to have adopted two extreme ethical views: one group believed that if they were risen from the dead they should live the life of angels; others thought that since they were raised from the dead they could no longer sin and could do what they like. Paul's answer here, in language that comes perilously close to Manichaeism, is that we are forbidden to do what we like (it is interesting here to note that the Community at Qumran who were Manichaean in their outlook were the only others before Paul who envisaged themselves as a Temple). Fornication, (does he mean with temple prostitutes? does his stricture include lovemaking between unmarried people who *are* in love?) Paul insists, is wrong, because it is an offence against one's own dignity as well as against the dignity of the other.

4. *1 Cor 12:31—13:8.* This is one of the most beautiful passages in the Bible. It is Paul's famous hymn to love. In the previous chapter he had been talking about various 'charisms' or gifts in Christian life, like the gift of teaching, of preaching, or prophesying. Now, he says, not everyone has all these gifts. There may in fact be people who have none of them. But one gift, and it is the greatest gift of all, which everyone is endowed with, is the gift of the power to love. Again these words are meant for everyone, but on a wedding day what more wonderful message than this could be conveyed from the altar? If I should be the most handsome, wealthy, successful, intelligent, outgoing, popular and

even dedicated guy in the country and have no genuine love for the girl I am marrying I am 'simply a gong booming or a cymbal clashing'. And I don't love her if I am not patient and kind, if I am jealous, if I am always or even often out to boost my own ego, (men are notorious egoists, and are, in my opinion, and from my own self-knowledge, incredibly vain), if I am touchy and in any way resent her. I do love her if I am ready to excuse her, to trust her, to stand by her when trials come. I love her if my first impulse is to believe her. And this kind of love, real love, never comes to an end. Not even death can kill it.

5. *Eph 5:2, 21-33.* The author's main interest in this reading is, I think, the marriage between Christ and his Church. The philosophers of the time spoke of the union of the divine spirit with matter as a sacred marriage. Ephesians transfers this terminology to the relation of Christ to his Church. And it presents the marriage of man to woman as a reflection of this union. That may account for the male chauvinism of this reading. A more likely explanation, of course, is the social thinking at the time the epistle was written when women were regarded as subject to men. Christianity did not enable those who embraced it to somersault out of their socially-conditioned mental apparatus: in fact it was far less earth-shaking in its social impact than we are sometimes led to believe.

However, the author's stress on humility brings home the important point that Christian marriage is a relation of giving and subordination; what we need to add by way of stressed supplement is the word mutual. And in fairness to Ephesians, it puts its greatest emphasis on love and on the power which love has to bring out the best in the person loved (every woman, I'm sure, would like to end up 'without spot or wrinkle'!).

6. *Col 3:12-17.* Here we have another series of practical counsels about the Christian life which apply in a special way to marriage. I have said earlier that there is no explicit, developed theology of marriage in the New Testament. And I believe that part of the reason for this lies in the 'other worldliness' of the early Christians. Paul, after all tells the Corinthians that 'the time is short. . . let those who have wives behave as though they had none'. If you don't expect the world to have a very long history, you won't waste time working out a theology of worldly realities. Interestingly, the practical instructions about the relations between members of a household which crop up again in this reading are not a Christian creation: they are also found in both pagan and Jewish writers. The christianised form, as C. F. D. Moule pointed out some time ago, is notable chiefly for its stress on the reciprocal nature of the duties: parents and masters have duties as well as children and slaves (Peake's Commentary, p. 994).

This reading is a plea for compassion, kindness, gentleness and patience. The marriage of a couple blessed with these virtues can scarcely fail to be a happy one. But our author is realistic. He knows that even though gentleness and patience are basic for human and Christian living, there can be rows. And his advice is: make peace with one another as soon as you can. We may be prodded to a more ready forgiveness if we remember how readily God forgives us. Central to his scheme of things, as usual, is love. Compassion, kindness, gentleness, patience and forgiveness, all these are metaphorically described as clothes, or more accurately, undergarments. Over them all, our author exhorts us, should be put on love. Love it is which 'holds them (i.e. the other virtues) together' and completes them. Love is the overcoat which keeps kindness, patience etc. from getting cold and damp.

Two more virtues are recommended: thankfulness and joy, one might even say lightheartedness. If we are grateful to each other and for each other we will never take one another for granted. And if we are lighthearted, if we have a sense of humour, we may not quite sing hymns all day, but we will dispel many unnecessary clouds.

7. *1 Pet 3:1-9.* The sentiments expressed in this reading are echoes of what we have heard several times already in the other New Testament readings. In fact the final paragraph is almost a word-for-word repetition of Rom 12:14-17. The author speaks of the influence which a wife can have on her husband. He seems to be against cosmetics (so were some of the Old Testament prophets, and I remember a few parish priests in Ireland who didn't go along with lipstick and rouge) but speaks with great tenderness of inner beauty which is far more important than external titivation. Notice that the wife is the centre of the writer's attention: this is probably because a Christian wife of a pagan husband stood in far greater danger where her religion was concerned than did the Christian husband of a pagan wife.

The recognition that husband and wife are 'equal heirs to the life of grace' was incompatible with domestic tyranny. And the verse: 'This will stop anything from coming in the way of your prayers' is both an indication that selfishness in the marriage relationship is a hindrance to the partners' fellowship with God and also a reminder that marriage should serve an end beyond itself, namely that fellowship with God.

8. *1 Jn 3:18-24.* The next two readings are from the great apostle of love himself, St John. The first reading is a plea for no nonsense: 'Our love is not to be just words or mere talk, but something real and active'. At the outset, therefore, John makes it clear that he is not talking about a mere feeling or sentiment but about a tenderness and a concern which show themselves in action. The charter for the Christian is presented as something very simple indeed: to believe in the name of his

Son Jesus Christ (who was the expression to the world that God's love is real and active, an incarnate, living, not an empty word) and to love one another (with that effective love described above). If this love exists between man and wife then God is with them.

9. *1 Jn 4:7-12.* The second reading from John is a description of God: God is love. If we do not know what love is, and we only know this by loving, then we literally have no notion of God; we don't know him, we can't know him. John is here, as he does in the Fourth Gospel, practically equating love with belief. Again love is a kind of awareness: awareness of the love at work in the Incarnation. It is this love of God for us, not our puny efforts to love him, that tell us what real love is. This is the only way in which God becomes visible to and alive in us: through the awareness of his love moving us to love one another. Awareness is, I believe, a kind of prayer. In *The Wasteland* T. S. Eliot deplored the terrible 'unawareness of the woman', and he interpreted that unawareness as lack of faith. Implicitly, I feel, John is doing the same thing here. Perhaps the greatest thing he does, though, is to do away with the distinction between divine love and 'merely human' love. For him even though we have never seen God, yet 'as long as we love one another God will live in us and his love will be complete in us'.

10. *Rev 19:1, 5-9.* The idea of heaven being a wedding feast is familiar to us from the Gospels, especially from the parables. Back in the Old Testament Hosea thought of Israel as the bride of Yahweh (2:19). So did Isaiah (54:1-8) and Ezekiel (16:7). We have seen how in the New Testament Epistles the figure is transferred to Christ and his Bride the Church. In the book from which this reading is taken the same notion will form the climax of the book, the New Jerusalem being the Bride of Christ (21:9f; 22:17 etc.) a symbol of her eternal union with him. In our passage however, while the Church is in mind as the bride, it seems that the members of the Church are guests and not the bride!

What can we make of this reading that will have meaning for a couple getting married today? Well, the apocalyptic writings often understood reality as taking place in heaven. What happens on earth is merely that reality in miniature. There is here a great message of hope. My marriage may have its ups and downs; it may have so many downs that I am driven to question the rightness of marriage at all. What today's reading does for me is to point to the ideal marriage which, it is implying, does not exist on earth. But, to shout for joy at it when it does take place will be the inspiration and the goal of all my present strivings.

D. GOSPELS

1. *Mt 5:1-12.* The first three readings are all taken from that great charter for Christian life, the Sermon on the Mount. There is nothing specific here concerning married people; the Sermon on the Mount is meant for all. Yet the readings have a special significance for married people and their application to the married state is not too difficult to make.

The first reading is Matthew's version of the beatitudes. Now beatitudes are not so much an exhortation to right living as promises, promises that life's circumstances are not fixed and irreversible. The fact that one grieves now in no way means that one shall always grieve. A wedding day is a day of promises. Two people promise fidelity and love. But they are not left alone and unaided in the lifelong effort to fulfil these promises. God too has made his promises. Admittedly these promises as Matthew here presents them refer directly to the hopes of Israel, but all human hopes are, indirectly, here addressed. Because people today also weep, are oppressed, are frustrated by their helplessness in the face of mass social injustice. The terms 'poor (in spirit'), those who hunger (and thirst for righteousness), the persecuted etc., are terms that set man among his neighbours in responsible love. They do not allow any pie-in-the-sky escape. They deal with the concrete realities of man among men, and not with some 'heavenly' world.

The beatitudes are a pointed reversal of popular standards which valued strength, self-sufficiency, prudence, political shrewdness (and its attendant non-involvement) rather than the stance of the beatitudes. On their wedding day the couple are reminded that their promises concern not only themselves but the whole world to which with its pain as well as its joy they are as Christians committed. And if the second part of each beatitude points towards the future ('they shall be') the first part expresses faith in a new power for the present ('Blessed are'. Admittedly the 'are' is supplied, but the sense is certainly not 'blessed will be'). In other words, the present is secretly transformed by the power of the future. Today's strivings, its stresses and strains, are transformed by that future bliss which God promises and which man and wife promise and hope for.

2. *Mt 5:13-16.* The second Gospel from the Sermon on the Mount is a plea for openness. Salt is the great preservative which is not itself preserved. The young couple are reminded that their life together must not be one of splendid isolation from those around them. Salt in the metaphorical language of the rabbis connoted wisdom. What more important virtue could be put before a couple on their wedding day! Wisdom to be patient with each other's moods, wisdom to let each other be free to

grow, wisdom to know that marriages are not made in heaven but have to be worked at patiently and lovingly in the human situation. Their lives must be a light, a light of warmth, of welcome, a light which beckons people to them but which also reminds themselves that like a lighted vehicle in the night they too are pilgrims on the way.

3. *Mt 7:21, 24-25.* The third Gospel reading is an exhortation to wisdom (see previous reading). It is the concluding statement for the whole Sermon on the Mount. The point it brings out is that wisdom is called for to heed Jesus' words because there is an urgency about life (even if we don't believe as both Jesus and Matthew may well have believed that the end of the world is near). The reading can, therefore, have a practical application. It can be a call for the ordinary wisdom which plans and makes provision. In married life one can scarcely afford the luxury of leaving things to chance.

Married life carries with it responsibilities; it also carries authority. Parents do have authority over their children. The final sentence of the third Gospel reading refers to the authority of Jesus and contrasts it with that of the Scribes. The authority of Jesus was seen to be real, authentic, not something usurped but given by the Father and earned by the Son; not something harsh and oppressive but the gentle authority which will command nothing which the person commanding is not herself and himself prepared to do.

4 and 6. *Mt 19:3-6; Mk 10:6-9.* The question of divorce was already touched upon by Matthew in the Sermon on the Mount (5:32). It comes up now in both of these readings in the context of debate. The argument used by Jesus is a well-known Jewish one: the more original, the weightier. Going back to 'the beginning' carried more weight than going back only to the Law of Moses. The argument used here by Jesus is not therefore based on any legislation but on the very law of nature. The natural thing for a man to do is to leave his parents (i.e. one way of life) and start a new life with his wife. Here we have the ideal. Whether or not it can be or even should be maintained in each concrete individual case is today the source of much debate among Christians.

It is important to note that the 'leaving' is as important for Matthew and Mark as the 'clinging'. Marriage precisely because it is a new beginning is based paradoxically upon divorce; divorce from one's primal bond to father and mother. Only when this umbilical cord is severed can I emerge as one mature enough and free enough to live and die with another my own life.

5. *Mt 22:35-40.* The case of Jesus' teaching is here put before us. The 613 laws of the Torah are reduced to two: love God, love your neighbour. It is interesting to note that to love God 'with all one's heart'

means to love him with all our inclinations. Understanding this commandment aright can save us from the spiritual schizophrenia which is so much part of our heritage. Secondly, we must love our neighbour, the husband must love his wife, the wife her husband, as ourselves, that is with the imperfections, warts and all, as Cromwell put it. If we want perfection in love, we must learn to love imperfection.

6. *See above under 4.*

7. *Jn 2:1-11.* The story of the miracle at the marriage feast of Cana is so full of aspects and meaning that I can here isolate only a few points for comment. The first point is that the marriage was the occasion on which this wonderful miracle was worked. This miracle like the parables, has to do with the ordinary world of everyday affairs, with men and women getting married. Elsewhere in the Gospels only the dire inflictions of humanity like hunger, disease and death evoke a healing word from Jesus. In this case, a petty embarrassment provoked a miracle. The miracle was worked so that people might continue to enjoy themselves.

Secondly this miracle is a sign. That is, the changing of water into wine was a symbol of the old Jewish order being replaced by the new one of Christ. It is fitting that this sign should have been given at a wedding. There too an 'old order', one's former way of life, gives place to a new way of viewing things, a new style of living. As a sign, it points to a reality in marriage which cannot be seen on one's wedding day, a reality which is hinted at by the presence of Jesus and Mary. Marriage itself is, as we have seen, a sign and symbol of the happiness of heaven.

Thirdly, the place of our Lady in this story is very striking. She is not only the one who intercedes and mediates, she is the symbol and the model of that concern, gentleness and foresight which mark the good housewife.

8. *Jn 15:9-12.* The First of these Gospel readings from the discourse at the Last Supper is saying much the same thing as the readings from 1 Jn. There is a new emphasis here though: the notion of abiding, remaining. Love, if it is real, is for ever. Besides, true love generates joy, and a joyful heart (and face) keeps love alive. Joy is one of the most frequently mentioned Christian virtues. How often does marriage mar it rather than create and increase it.

9. *Jn 15:12-16.* Here Jesus reiterates the primacy of love. But the sacrificial element of love is now presented: 'A man can have no greater love than to lay down his life for his friends'. This is clearly a reference to the costly character of Jesus' love. Further, love means not only the sharing of goods or, in the case of married love, the sharing of bed and board. It means sharing what is in and on one's mind. One does come

across wives who don't know their husband's business; and John tells us that this is the mark of a servant. The model given here for all love, and it is particularly true of married love, is the relationship between Jesus and his disciples; they are not his slaves but his friends, 'standing within the circle of mutual knowledge and love, of which Father and Son are the coincident foci' (C. K. Barrett).

10. *Jn 17:20-26*. This reading is part of the great prayer of Jesus at the Last Supper. In that prayer, which falls into four parts, Jesus prays that his approaching death may prove to be the means whereby Father and Son are mutually glorified (vv. 1-5). He prays for his disciples (vv. 6-19). He prays for later believers (vv. 20-24). He reviews the results of his mission (25f). Our reading is taken from the third section of the prayer, the final verse being brought in from section four.

Jesus prays here for unity. And this unity is to be understood from the words: 'As thou art in me, and I in thee'. The Father is active in the Son (14:10) and the Son abides in the Father, and has no meaning independently of him. They are one (10:30) not in identity, but in mutual love and consentient activity. This then is to be the characteristic of the Christian community. With all the more reason it should be the characteristic of Christian marriage. Yet, while love unites a group within itself, husband and wife within their own family circle, it can sometimes set it over against other groups, other families. Identity can be purchased at the price of openness. In verse 23 this danger is confronted and even dispelled: Jesus prays that the world may believe. In practice salvation means belonging to a redeemed community. But ideally the church as the Body of Christ is the entire universe, and since every married couple is a cell within that Body, then they too are not 'over-against' or closed to the universe: they are part of it.

III TWO SAMPLE CELEBRATIONS

A. LOVE

Introduction to the celebration. Welcome to all the family on this occasion. It's one of great significance for two people N. & N. getting married here today. For them it's a key moment in their lives. We are all gathered here to witness to their solemn promise of loving fidelity to each other. However there is someone greater than any of us here present, our risen Lord Jesus Christ. It is in his presence this promise is made and in return for this pledge to one another he will pour out in their hearts the gift of his love. Therefore it is a great day for the rest of us too. A new family will be born, a new friendship sealed, a new cell, not just in the community we live in, but in the church of Christ, the body of Christ will come to be. So let us all pray not just for a happy celebration today but for a happy life together for those about to make their promises.

Penitential Rite. God has told us in the scriptures that if I am without love, it will do me no good whatever. Let us think briefly on how we have loved. Love is patient and kind. For all the times we have failed in patience and kindness. (pause) Lord have mercy.

Love is never boastful or conceited. For all the times we have been boastful or conceited. (pause) Christ have mercy.

Love delights in the truth. For all the times we have failed to rejoice in others' success. (pause) Lord have mercy. etc.

First Reading. Song of Songs 2:8-10, 14, 16; 8:6-7. This passionate love song comes from the Bible. It includes romantic love but is also a tribute to the solidity of a love based on God's love: 'Love is strong as death — no flood can quench, no torrents drown.'

Second Reading. Eph 5:2, 21-33. God compares the love Christ has for his church to the love husband and wife have for each other. This is possible because the eternal love of God is poured into the hearts of husband and wife in the sacrament of matrimony. It makes of their union with each other a sacrament. Their union is a sign explaining to the world how Christ loves his people even until death.

Third Reading. Jn 15:9-12. At the Last Supper Christ repeatedly reminded his disciples that his main wish was for them to love one another. His promise was that in loving one another they would find joy.

Homily Note. Christ used love in marriage to explain his love for his church. Not that he meant that marriage is merely a parable for the union between Christ the bridegroom and the people of God the bride. No, the reality of Christ's love is shared by those engaged in Christian marrige. The love of God is poured out in the hearts of those who enter into Christian marriage. The love they experience for one another is in fact the eternal love of God, the love that exists between the Father and the Son. The Word made flesh, Jesus Christ our Lord, shows the same love for his church and proved it by dying on the cross.

This is the vocation of Christian marriage. Not merely to be loyal to one another, to care for one's children. It is to bear witness to a greater meaning to life: that God is, that he loves us, that he gave his Son for us and that his Son loves us with an undying love as we are called to love one another.

Undying love is a tremendous calling. As Christ's commitment to his people demanded sacrifice and patience so also married love calls for great sacrifice and great patience.. It doesn't take much imagination to be aware that difficulties arise in marriage. When we say in the ceremony 'I take you as my lawful husband or wife, for richer, for poorer, for better or worse, in sickness and in health, till death do us part,' there is an obvious recognition that what we're entering on may be a bed of roses perhaps, but the roses can have thorns.

The difficulties that arise in marriage, however, often don't come between the partners, that is from their relationship with each other, but rather from their relationship with others. Many jokes are passed about in-laws and especially mothers-in-law, and the humour is entertaining. There can be a grain of truth behind it, however, in that families can put undue pressure on a young couple to meet not their expectation for their marriage but those of their respective families. We have come here today to pray for happiness for those who are being married NN. Our coming is more than mere presence or words. It is a commitment on our part to work for their happiness. That means helping them to meet their expectations of their mariage and not ours. I'm sure that is how we all see it.

Another source of difficulty in marriage can be between the couple and the world around them. One obvious case is problems arising from financial worries. Pressure from financial causes can create difficulties in marriage. If the couple join hands, as they've joined hands today in exchanging their vows, and face the difficulties together, then this can be a source of growth for them. One doesn't grow by avoiding challenge but rather overcoming. I'm sure N. & N. recognise this. The important thing is when the problem comes they see it not as something between themselves but something which they side by side must face together.

Marriage is a call to growth. Each one of us grows individually through life as we pass through the various decades. And within that personal growth there can be tremendous growth in our relationships with each other and especially the relationship between husband and wife. If this growth takes place the marriage grows richer, the union deeper, and the covenant firmer, the witness to God's love ever brighter. This is the call God offers, God makes to N. & N. today. With his blessing and in the power of his Spirit they will answer that call.

Prayer of the Faithful. Today as N. & N. begin their married life together we all join in wishing them well, we all join in prayer on their behalf.

—That whenever we speak we may speak with love, we pray to the Lord.
—That our love may be always patient and kind, we pray to the Lord.
—That our love may always delight in the truth, the truth about ourselves and the truth about others, we pray to the Lord.
—That in our love we may be always ready to excuse, to trust, to hope, we pray to the Lord.

—That our love may endure whatever comes, we pray to the Lord.

—That our love may never come to an end, we pray to the Lord.

—For all our relatives and friends that God may pour out upon them the grace of his everlasting love, we pray to the Lord.

—For our deceased parents, grandparents and all our ancestors and relatives who have passed away, that the Lord may share the eternal joy of his kingdom with them, we pray to the Lord.

Let us pray in silence now for our own special needs and the needs of N. & N. newly married.

O God, your Son our Lord Jesus Christ loved the church and sacrificed himself for her to make her holy. Pour out your grace now on N. & N. May you make them holy so that they too may be willing to sacrifice themselves for one another. We ask this through Christ our Lord.

Invitation to the Lord's Prayer. United together in the bond of love, forming one family in Jesus Christ, we turn to our common father and pray:

Communion Prayer. (The married couple might like to supply this themselves.) Thank you, Lord, for my eyes, windows open on the wide world. I pray to you during the day, that my eyes may always open to a clear morning tomorrow. May they be ready to serve both me and my bride *or* husband, as well as my God. May my eyes be clear and straightforward, Lord. May my look be never one of disappointment, disillusionment, despair. May it know how to admire, contemplate, adore. May my eyes learn to close in order to find you more easily. May they never turn away from the world because they are afraid. May my eyes be penetrating enough to recognise your presence in the loved ones I meet as well as all others in the world around me. May they never shut on the afflictions of men. Once more today, Lord, I give you my heart, I give you my body, I give you my eyes. That in looking at all men and women, my brothers and sisters, I may see you as well as them and behind them see you as the one who beckons me on.' (Adapted from Michel Quoist, *Prayers of Life*).

Final Blessing from the Marriage Rite.

B. FIDELITY TO THE GOSPEL *(Brian Darcy, C.P.)*

Introduction to the celebration. Today we come to celebrate the joining in matrimony of two people, two Christians. This is no ordinary wedding like the wedding of a Bhuddist or Hindu, a Moslem or a Jew. It is the wedding of two Christians who commit themselves to each other to live their married life and love together in accordance with the gospel of Christ. And so we pray today that the power of Christ, his Spirit, may be given them to live their married love out in this spirit.

Penitential Rite. On a joyful occasion such as this it seems a little strange to think of penance and sinfulness. And yet every marriage is based on recognition of one's own weakness and one's need for help, not only from one's partner but also from God. So for a moment let us look at ourselves and consider our own failures to be generous. Have we shown real concern for the poor? (Pause) For all our failures, Lord have mercy.

Have we been merciful to others in though and in deed. (Pause) For all our failures, Lord have mercy.

Have we tried to find peace in our own hearts, bring peace to others? (Pause) For all our failures to bring peace, Lord have mercy.

First Reading. Tobit 8:4-9. Marriages are made in heaven. Tobias found his wife Sarah, according to the book of Tobit, by the special intervention of God. And so we could say in taking his wife 'I do so not for any lustful motive but in singleness of heart.'

Second Reading. 1 Cor 12:31–13:8. Paul's hymn to love which is ever new, ever relevant.

Third Reading. Mt 5:1-12. The teaching of Christ has a central core. Those who want to live according to his Spirit must always reflect on the central themes of his message. They come to us today in this, the refrain, of the Gospel, the beatitudes according to Matthew.

Homiletic Reflection. There are popular cartoons in the papers now. They are the little LOVE IS . . . cartoons. 'Love is holding her hand when's she's frightened'. 'Love is letting him stay quiet when he comes from work.' 'Love is warming her towel before her bath.' They're good because they don't look on love as 'moon in June' things. Love is real.

And that's what St Paul is saying too. Today N. & N. are happy, a bit nervous maybe, but happy. You are full of love for each other and it shows. That's fine. But you know each other well enough to realise that love is more than feeling good. It certainly *is* feeling good but it is also being patient, kind, helpful, understanding. It's biting your tongue when you want to squelch your partner, it's understanding that N. has her bad days, that N. his faults and that you love him with them. Love is unreasonable. You can't put conditions on your love. If you do, it is not love.

The song says, 'We've only just begun'. And so it is for you today. Your 'I do' 'really love you' is repeated day after day not in word but in action. (And it isn't a bad idea either to repeat it in words as well.) That is how the helps of the sacrament work in your lives and you become those 'Blessed'people the Gospel mentions. Today you've taken down all barriers between you. N.'s love for N. means that he has unending hope in her and she in him. When you were engaged you made countless plans for the future. Today you have more plans. And in fifty years time, if you are not making plans for your future loving life together, you are no longer in love. Love grows. Growth is only a sign of life.

Your wedding is a *feast* of love which we're all sharing. You're love for each other is telling us about God. Because God is love and all real love is his. That's why you're here with your friends. You're thanking God that you know you didn't really choose each other but that God chose you for each other. Marriages are made in heaven and your chose you for each other. Marriages are made in heaven and your marriage will be what wins heaven for you (Gospel). God is love and he has made us for himself. 'Love is man's origin, love is his constant calling, love is his final destiny.'

With N. & N. today are their friends and family. You too have been married five, ten, fifteen years. You could tell N. & N. a thing or two about love. The good times and the bad. But today think of the good times for love is 'being faithful to what you've seen in the light, when times of darkness come.'

Today you can remember the day you exchanged your wedding vows. Why not renew them today? It is a *feast* of love remember.

Finally I'm offering this Mass, and I know you'll offer it with me so that God will bless N. & N., their families, their new home and their whole life together. 'For love does not come to an end... there are three things that last: faith, hope and love. And the greatest of these is love.' Today with N. & N. we see why.

Suggested quotation: 'Marriage is not merely a sign of Christ's love, it works the same way, by work, prayer and tenderness, by listening, serving and healing, by giving life and forgiving wrong, by sorrow, pain and death... All this makes up marriage, as well as the joy and peace of a learned love, the fullness of bodily communion which is also spiritual, the fun of family life and the satisfaction of seeing children grow up loving and generous and hopeful.' (Rosemary Haughton, *The Theology of Marriage.* Cork: The Mercier Press). Two parts of the Council Documents are also excellent: Constitution on the Church in the Modern World, nn. 48-49; Decree on the Laity, n. 11.

Prayer of the Faithful. Many of us have given N. & N. wedding presents. But the greatest present we can give them is the present of our prayers. So we pray for their needs and the needs of all married people.

—That the love which N. & N. give to each other today may grow and grow to be a happy, peaceful family of love, we pray to the Lord.
Response: Lord, hear our prayer.
—That N. & N. who pledge their love in prayer before you today may

always be able to pray and share your love in the good times and bad, we pray to the Lord.

—That N. & N. will always have good health, that their children will be healthy and friends with God and that their family will always have peace of mind, we pray to the Lord.

—For the parents and families of N. & N. May they always be a source of comfort to one another and may they always be the best of friends, we pray to the Lord.

—For all those who have helped N. & N. prepare for marriage. That their lives may be filled with some of the love and happiness which N. & N. share today, we pray to the Lord.

—For all those who have difficulties with their marriage. That God may help them to sort out their differences guided always by true love, we pray to the Lord.

Each of us has our own private good wish for N. & N. We'll have a moment's silence now so that we can talk to God in our own words and ask him for that special blessing for our friends now started on their married life.

We ask Mary to share with N. & N. the peace, the happiness and the joy of her home in Nazareth. Let us share the joy of her greatest moment when the angel Gabriel came to her as we say, 'Hail Mary'.

God grant that N. & N. and all married couples may seek you and find you in each other and in their children. We ask this through Christ our Lord.

Invitation to the Lord's Prayer. Happy the peacemakers for they shall be called the Sons of God. United together in a love which brings peace we turn to our Father and say:

Communion Prayer. (The married couple might like to supply this themselves.) Lord, your providence first brought us together. Friendship ripened into love. Before your altar we have pledged ourselves to love each other as Christ loves his Church, as Jesus loved the people he preached to in Judaea many years ago. May we never forget this day of grace. May we grow, Lord, in gratitude and love. In this vision on our wedding morning, may we try to live in the light of common day, in fidelity and mutual support. We want to be ready to 'excuse, to trust, to hope, to endure whatever comes.' We thank you, Lord, for all the friends you have given us. May their friendship be always with us. May we always welcome them in our homes by our words and our actions. On this our wedding day you teach us to keep open to the needs of our community. Make us eager, Lord, to build a home modelled on the home of Nazareth. May this home bring light and warmth to the community we live in. Lord, we thank you for the gift of the Spirit poured out in our hearts in baptism, renewed and strengthened in the mission of confirmation and given us today now to deepen our union with each other. May our love for each other mature in Christ. May the Holy Spirit make our married life a way of holy living, and may old age come to us in the company of our friends.

For all the blessings of this day and for all the days that lie ahead, we thank you, Father, through Christ our Lord and in the Holy Spirit, one God forever and ever. Amen. (Adapted from The *Prayer of Husband and Wife*: Tuam Liturgical Commission, 1976.)

Final Blessing as in Marriage Rite.

Masses of the Dead

Henry Wansbrough, O.S.B.

I INTRODUCTION

The predominant spirit of the new funeral rites is one of Christian hope; the accompanying Instruction opens with the words 'the paschal mystery of Christ' and again and again the prayers return to the hope of resurrection with Christ, to the fact that the Christian has been incorporated at baptism into Christ who has destroyed death and by his resurrection renewed life. In the Instruction the participants, and especially priests, are reminded that their function is to encourage the hope of those present and their faith in the paschal mystery and the resurrection of the dead. Such is, of course, also the emphasis of the scriptural readings, and it is significant that the liturgy of the word is never to be omitted in the first type of rite (in a Church) even if there is no Mass, and that the second type of rite (in a mortuary chapel) is centred upon this liturgy of the word, which forms indeed the principal part also of the third type of rite. The biblical emphasis is, then, a feature of all the three rites. In all three, moreover, a homily is prescribed after the readings, and the celebrant is repeatedly warned that a panegyric should be avoided. The considerable variety of scripture readings provided should enable the homilist to bring out suitable aspects of the Christian hope of the resurrection.

Another notable feature of the new rite is the ceremony of farewell to the dead. The final rite after the Mass is, according to the Instruction, to be understood not as a purification of the dead (which is the function of the Mass) but as a farewell, since death involves a certain parting, though it should also be borne in mind that those who remain one in Christ cannot be totally separated even by death. The sprinkling with holy water is to be understood, then, as a reminder of that baptism which first destined the dead person to eternal life, rather than as a new washing; and the incensation is to be conceived as a salutation to the body as a temple of the Holy Spirit. The prayer, also, which accompanies this ceremony in all three rites contains features of a farewell, namely mutual comfort of those who remain behind and a looking forward to the time of meeting again in Christ at the resurrection.

Bearing in mind, perhaps, the sometimes hurried nature of the funeral rites and the possibility of tedium brought on by frequent repetition, the Instruction and the rubrics frequently stress the human sympathy which must be shown in these circumstances. The priest is a 'minister of consolation', and he is explicitly instructed to cherish and restore the family of the dead person in their grief, holding the sometimes delicate balance in striking a note which encourages their faith and hope, but does not jar on their grief. This applies also to the choice of colour for the liturgy. In the rite itself the priest is instructed to greet those present when he enters the house 'humanely'. The Church reminds him that he should also have regard for those non-Catholics who assist at the ceremonies, and for those Catholics who come to a funeral though they rarely attend the eucharist and seem to have lost the faith, 'for priests are ministers of Christ's good news to everyone'.

On the other hand, just as the homily should be an encouragement to Christian hope and not a panegyric, so there is discouragement of secular pomp, and especially of any distinction of persons which is not provided for in the liturgy.

Notes on Cremation and on the Funeral of Children

In the case of cremation the same rites may be used, and the ceremony at the graveside may even be performed in the crematorium. It is, however, to be remarked that the Church prefers burial 'because the Lord himself chose to be buried'.

For the burial of children special scriptural texts are provided, according to whether the child has been baptised and received communion or not. An important change, which goes with the uncertainty of the Church about the teaching on limbo traditional since St Augustine, is that in the case of an unbaptised child whom the parents wished to be baptised, either the home ceremony or even the other rites may be used. The admonition that the faithful are not thereby to be allowed to think that baptism is unnecessary reflects the historical genesis of the doctrine of limbo (the denial of the necessity of baptism), but does suggest that it is more important to insist on the importance of baptism than to maintain the doctrine of limbo. In the prayers prescribed for the burial of children the Church's sympathy for the bereaved is especially apparent.

II COMMENTARY ON READINGS

Before the commentary an indication is often given of a reading particularly apt for the funeral of certain categories of people.

A. OLD TESTAMENT READINGS

1. *Job 19:1, 23-27. Job's trust in his Redeemer.* In the depths of his torment, and when all seems hopeless, Job still clings to the hope of a Redeemer. He is convinced that God will play the part of his 'Avenger', the nearest relative who by Jewish law has to stand by and rescue his kinsman in need. This will be a proof of God's special care for each individual as though for a specially close relative. And Job is convinced that it is as a full human person ('from my flesh') that he will see God.

2. *Wis 3:1-9. The dead are in God's hand.* (At the death of one who died young and full of hope for the future.) What looks on the natural plane like a disaster is in fact the result of God's love for one whom he takes into his own care. Death is not an end, but is only a testing, in which someone is purified and refined so as to be fit to live with God in love.

3. *Wis 4:7-15. God takes one who is perfected.* (At the death of an adolescent or of a child.) No matter at what age someone dies, completion consists in being at rest with God. He may take the young to save them from becoming tarnished. But if he does take them it can only be that he has found them complete and pleasing to him, and wishes them to be at his side.

4. *Is 25:6-9. The Lord will destroy death.* Isaiah promises that death is only a temporary sorrow, and that a day is coming when death will be destroyed, and all the dead will rejoice in God's company. All peoples will be restored and will celebrate on God's holy mountain as at a banquet.

5. *Lam 3:17-26. Hope in silent waiting.* (When there seems no light at all.) When Jerusalem has been destroyed and everything the prophet holds dear has collapsed, he can only protest his conviction that in the end the Lord will rescue him. Now there is no hope visible, but he has chosen the Lord, and so waits in silent and patient confidence.

6. *Dan 12:1-3. The great restoration.* (At the death of a teacher). Daniel is promised that God will raise up all who are seemingly asleep in the dust, and that there will be a restoration of all the people — only after a judgment.

7. *2 Mac 12:43-45. Sacrifice for the dead.* This is the first mention in the Bible of prayer and sacrifice for the dead, and the first clear reference to individual judgment and recompense. The ancients thought of

existence after death as very shadowy, then gradually the idea of a general restoration developed, and finally the knowledge came that the individual would be rewarded for his holy life.

B. NEW TESTAMENT READINGS

1. *Acts 10:34-43. Jesus our hope of forgiveness.* (In case of doubt or hesitation.) Peter is addressing Cornelius, the first non-Jew to enter the Church. He stresses that God's call extends to all men without exception, and that all men can find forgiveness in the name and power of Christ. The glorious risen Christ is our judge, but it is he who has won us forgiveness.

2. *Rom 5:5-11. The strength of Christ's love.* Christ too went through all the agony of death, and for our sake. After this proof of God's love it would be strange if he deserted us, so to speak, half-way and did not bring us to the fruits of salvation.

3. *Rom 5:17-21. Christ's act of obedience.* (At the death of a sinner.) Sin and desertion of God need not make us give up hope, for as certain as the fact of sin, is the fact of Christ's obedience which undid it. By the very fact of being men we belong to a sinful race, but by his total obedience to God on the cross Christ has healed the consequences of sin.

4. *Rom 6:3-9. Raised to life with Christ.* By being baptised in Christ we have received his life and taken on his history as our own. Our baptism into his death means that we already share his risen life, and so, as part of him, will be raised in his resurrection.

5. *Rom 8:14-23. Heirs of God.* (Within a close family.) Our hope is founded on the fact that we have been adopted as sons, and so have a unique bond of family intimacy with the Father. From this point of view death is a release, allowing us to return to our natural place in the family. So creation is longing and yearning to be set free, and for our real position as God's sons to be made manifest. This is the joy of death.

6. *Rom 8:31-35, 37-39. The strength of God's love.* (After great sufferings.) It is absurd to suppose that God would give his Son, that Jesus would give his life, and then allow the gift to go to waste. Christ will not let go of those whom he has redeemed, for love is as strong as death. Great suffering may make it seem as though God had abandoned the sufferer, but really the sufferings are a witness to God's love, the trials by which we triumph, for by them we are privileged to share in and fill up the measure of Christ's own sufferings.

7. *Rom 14:7-9, 11-12. Alive or dead, Christ is our Lord.* (For one who has worked for others.) The context of the excerpt is the passage at the

end of his letter where Paul is encouraging his readers to have regard for other people's needs and failings. We are all members of Christ's body, so all bound to each other. The influence which we have on others works to the good or ill of all, and contributes to the building up of Christ's body. And it is according to our works in life that Christ is our Lord also when we are dead.

8. *1 Cor 15:20-28. The firstfruits of the resurrection.* The resurrection is continuous: Christ is the first, and at the end all will be presented to the Father. Meanwhile each will rise in his proper order to be with Christ in the resurrection. But times and seasons are supremely unimportant; the central pillar of the Christian hope is that since Christ is risen, death is no more than a means of joining Christ in his resurrection.

9. *1 Cor 15:51-57. Transformation in Christ.* It is death which enables us to become like God, to take on the attributes which give us a share in the divine nature and the divine state. From being weak we shall have the strength of God, from being subject to change and fluctuation we shall have the permanence and firmness of God, and from being perpetually subject to death we shall be freed from all death and decay. Death is, then, for us a transition to glory.

10. *2 Cor 5:1, 6-10. Exiled from the Lord.* (For an exile or one who has suffered or been lonely.) Our dwelling-place on earth is only a temporary tent, and our true home is in heaven. On earth we live in exile, for once we have received the Spirit of God and become members of Christ it is unnatural that we should remain here, untransformed and weak, subject to the changes, unhappiness and failures of this world. So death is something which the Christian may long for, since it is his return home to the Father.

11. *Phil 3:20-21. Conformed to Christ.* (For the handicapped.) Death is a return to our homeland where, since Christian baptism, we naturally belong. Specifically it is company and union with Christ that we are waiting for. Since baptism we are already united with him, but when death has freed us from the restrictions of this world we will be entirely transformed so that this union with him is total and extends even to our bodies. This is particularly comforting to those who have suffered some crippling disability.

12. *1 Thess 4:13-18. With Christ in his triumph.* Paul was writing to comfort and reassure new converts who realised that the Christian has conquered death, and were shattered when some of their number died before the expected coming of Christ. On the contrary, writes Paul, those who have died are at an advantage and will be the first to meet the Lord. However we understand the imagery of the last trumpet and Christ's triumphal procession (and the Church has given no official

interpretation) the crux of the idea is that the dead are in joyful company with the glorious Christ in his triumph.

13. *2 Tim 2:8-13. He is always faithful.* The message of this reading is the unshakableness of Christian hope. The hope of Paul, chained up in prison, does not waver, for faithfulness to his promises is Christ's name. He is the 'Amen' of the Father, the guarantee that all the Father has promised will be fulfilled. Death is not, then, the abandonment of hope but the means to its fulfilment: 'If we have died with Christ, then we shall live with him.'

14. *1 Jn 3:1-2. We shall see God.* Death is a veil and a mist. We cannot know the future, and can but approach it in faith. But two things John tells us, that we will see God as he really is – a sight which, unpurified as we now are, we could not bear – and that we shall be like him. We are already children of God, and to that extent share his nature and are lapped in his love. But death is the means to purification and unheard-of intimacy of union with God.

15. *1 Jn 3:14-16. To give up our lives for our brothers.* (For one who has spent his life in love.) The distinctive mark of the real Christian is love, not exactness or Church-going, and it is love which gives life and spreads both life and love around itself. If we have done this we have brought the image of God into men's lives and truly been Christ's fellow-workers, even though it has been in an unorthodox fashion, so that we will share his life in the love and life of God.

16. *Rev 14:13. Rest in the Lord.* The Apocalypse is a book of encouragement in persecution, so this verse is a promise for those who have remained faithful under trial, and have steadfastly put their trust in God, however much they were buffeted and punished by men or circumstances. All God asks of us is faith, to receive his message and stick by it. This is to 'die in the Lord' and earns the happiness of rest in him.

17. *Rev 20:11–21:1. The universe is swept away.* A reminder that everything we see and experience is totally impermanent, that the universe itself is to be swept away, which makes nonsense of all our worldly strivings and pride in our achievement. Even death and Hades are to be swept away. It is only the one seated on the throne who remains in rock-like permanence. So there is really no room for mourning, since life for each of us is but a moment before all is submitted to the one seated on the throne.

18. *Rev 21:1-7. The new heaven and new earth.* The New Testament ends with the vision of a new heaven and a new earth, an earnest of radiant happiness after the sadness and trials of this life. As the whole world is grim by comparison with this glittering vision of joy in God,

so for the individual any life, no matter how happy, is gray when compared to the rejoicing in the company of God which follows.

C. RESPONSORIAL PSALMS

1. *Ps 22.* The psalm of God as the good shepherd, whose sheep need fear no evil, for he guides them to rest.

2. *Ps 24.* A psalm of confidence. The psalmist acknowledges God's faithfulness and longs for God's forgiveness. It is the prayer of someone who has tried, but knows that he is not sinless.

3. *Ps 26.* A prayer of longing to be ever with the Lord in the land of the living.

4. *Ps 41.* A prayer in distress, yearning for the joy of the Lord, but confident in his guidance.

5. *Ps 62.* A psalm in sorrow and dryness, longing for the fresh water and the banquet of God.

6. *Ps 102.* Man's life lasts no longer than the grass, but the compassion and love of the Lord are from generation to generation.

7. *Ps 114.* God welcomes the death of his faithful ones, and for them death is a liberation.

8. *Ps 121.* A hymn of joy at the peace of God, to be sung by those going up to God's city.

9. *Ps 129.* A cry of patient longing for forgiveness, for with the Lord there is fullness of redemption.

10. *Ps 142.* A confession of sin and weakness and an appeal for God's mercy.

D. GOSPELS

1. *Mt 5:1-12. The Beatitudes.* (For several dead.) The beatitudes can be read as an invitation and as a promise. Only one who is totally blind and lacking in self-criticism could claim to have fulfilled them all, or even most of them for most of the time. But the Christian is one who has a yearning to fulfill them, who longs to receive from Christ the promises contained in them, but who also sees the joy now of fulfilling the conditions, however far he may in fact fall short of succeeding. They are a comfort and yet a matter for heart-searching about the genuineness and effectiveness of our own desires in this.

2. *Mt 11:25-30. Gentle and humble of heart.* Death strips us of all pretensions and of all importance — naked we came from the womb and naked we return to the earth — so that it is only in our simplicity that we can hope, in openness and trust in the Father. Christ was gentle and humble, and it is to those who share these qualities of his, whatever

their worldly importance or position, that he promises rest. It is to such as these that he reveals the Father, for they have the quality of childlike openness which enables them to receive the revelation and turn to him for solace.

3. *Mt 25:1-13. The ten bridesmaids.* (For one advanced in age.) This parable was no doubt originally told as a warning to be ready to meet the kingdom which had come at last but unexpectedly, in Christ's coming in his earthly ministry. The Jews claimed to be waiting for the Messiah, but many were in fact ill-prepared to receive him. Transferred to Christians the message is the same: theoretically life consists in the preparation for the final meeting with Christ in death. But we need the warning not to grow slack if the time is delayed.

4. *Mt 25:31-46. The last judgment.* The message is too well-known to need labouring, but too important to be passed over: we are judged finally not on memorable achievements, power or any other distinction, but on whether we have in practice recognised Christ in our brethren, and particularly in those in need.

5. *Mk 15:33-39; 16:1-6. The death and resurrection of Jesus.* Our hope in death is the resurrection of Christ. When we have experienced the death of those near to us we know that it is real and total. But this gospel brings home that death was real for Christ too. His death was agonising and undignified, his body was a lifeless corpse, inert and buried. Christ shared fully this experience of dying and the non-experience of death itself. And yet the Father raised him up to glorious life.

6. *Lk 7:11-17. The son of the widow at Nain.* (For an only son.) Only God can give life and so raise the dead, and the point of the story is to show that Jesus has this divine power. It shows also his great spontaneous sympathy for those distressed and in need: he was presumably just passing through this little Galilean village on the way to Jerusalem. The compassion of Christ is the compassion of God translated into human form and expressed by human means. It assures us both of the love and of the power of God.

7. *Lk 12:35-40. Welcome to a faithful servant.* A parable of watchfulness, like a number of others in the gospels, warning us that the kingdom, the judgment, the time of harvest comes suddenly and unexpectedly. So it came to the Jews and most of them were caught unawares. But this parable has in addition the promise that the master will sit his servant down to table and himself wait upon him, showing the immense affection and warm welcome which Christ offers us.

8. *Lk 23:33, 39-43. Last-minute repentance.* (For desperate cases.) Luke above all is the evangelist of forgiveness, and shows that even in the agony of death Jesus remembers others in their own death-agony.

133

These are two real criminals, justly executed, and yet Luke's lesson is that even at the last moment if a hardened sinner turns to the Lord he receives the fulness of forgiveness. Would any of the bystanders have been aware of this last-minute repentance? How many seemingly hardened sinners may make this last-minute conversion without anyone knowing it?

9. *Lk 23:44-49; 24:1-6. 'Father, into your hands. . .'* The specifice difference in Luke's account of the death of Jesus (compare gospel reading 5) is Jesus' last words, committing his spirit to the Father. He too was subject to the darkness of death; in his ignorance as man he could only entrust himself to the Father in the confidence that the Father would vindicate him. In death we can only yield ourselves unreservedly into the Father's hands, though in the knowledge that as members of Christ he will raise us up as he raised up his only Son.

10. *Lk 24:13-35. The Road to Emmaus.* One of the themes in this story which is relevant to death is the reality of the resurrection of the body. On the one hand the disciples do not at first recognise their risen Lord because he is transformed by the resurrection, suffused even in his body with the heavenly glory. On the other hand they do eventually recognise him, perhaps by his gestures, in the breaking of bread. There is continuity in the risen body, and it is the same body though transformed, which will rise again.

11. *Jn 6:37-40. Whoever believes in the Son has eternal life.* Christ's mission was to bring eternal life to those who believe in him. The believer has this life already, even on earth, the seed of immortality. He already shares God's life, so that death is only a release from the restrictions of the earthly condition, allowing the seed to blossom into eternal life. Hence there is no emptiness in death but an expansion into a fuller life.

12. *Jn 6:51-58. The Bread which gives life.* The eucharistic bread is Christ's means of giving himself and so of our being filled with his life, which he in turn draws from his Father. It is the true food which nourishes for true life. It is the pledge of immortality, for once we have received it, we have made his life our own and been taken up into his stream of life. Since the eucharist is union with him in his death and resurrection, it is a pledge that for us too death is only a preliminary to resurrection.

13. *Jn 11:17-27. The lesson of Lazarus.* For those who commit themselves to Christ death is no death, for he himself is the resurrection and life. If we are truly living in Christ and he is our life-principle, that life-principle continues. He does not say merely that resurrection and life are through him or in him, but that he *is* resurrection and life. There is

an immediacy and closeness about this which makes it impossible to fall through.

14. *Jn 11:32-45. The raising of Lazarus.* Christ's guarantee of resurrection for the dead, and his demonstration that he gives life to the dead who love him, no matter how much they are fully dead and undergoing corruption.

15. *Jn 12:23-28. Unless a wheat grain dies. . .* (For one who has given his life.) Following Christ in his suffering is the sure precondition of joining him in his glory, and a life offered in sudden martyrdom, or equally in longer service of Christ in others, is the seed of immortality. Following Christ at all must involve following him also in suffering, whether it be in loss, in deprivation, in frustration or in self-denial; but this is how we are truly conformed to Christ, so as to share with him.

16. *Jn 14:1-6. Many rooms in the Father's house.* (For the unorthodox follower of Christ.) The disciples were puzzled and frustrated by the mystery of Christ; they could not fathom him. But he stresses that the ways of God are mysterious and varied. He has many ways of bringing men to himself, many of which we may not understand; there are many rooms in his Father's house. It is not for man to limit God's mercy and to condemn those who do not conform to one pattern of searching for Christ.

17. *Jn 17:24-26. Jesus' prayer for his own.* Jesus' final prayer before he goes out to his death is for his own, that they may persevere in his love and remain always in him. He went to his death with this intention in his heart; there can be no fear for those who put their hope in him.

FUNERAL OF A BAPTISED CHILD

References are to the readings for Masses of the Dead, pages 127-134.

A. OLD TESTAMENT READINGS

1. *Is 25:6-9.* See Old Testament, no. 4.

2. *Lam 3:17-26.* See Old Testament, no. 5.

B. NEW TESTAMENT READINGS

1. *Rom 6:3-4, 8-9.* See New Testament, no. 4.

2. *Rom 14:7-9.* See New Testament, no. 7.

3. *1 Cor 15:20-23.* See New Testament, no. 8.

4. *Eph 1:3-5. God's choice.* We cannot understand why God chooses one and not another. But it is surely a mark of his special favour and

love that he should choose one so early, adopting him in a special way as his son, to live in the joy of his presence, even before he has time to be soiled by the world.

5. *1 Thess 4:13-14, 18*. See New Testament, no. 12.

6. *Rev 7:9-10, 15-17*. *'Victory to our God and to the Lamb.'* The reading suggests the vast and varied throng of those who rejoice in God's presence, and the contrast between their untarnished happiness and the trials and sorrows of this life. It envisages primarily those who come to such joy after persecution, but applies just as much to those who are spared any trials of life.

7. *Rev 21:1, 3-5*. See New Testament, no. 18.

C. RESPONSORIAL PSALMS

1. *Ps 22*. See Psalms, no. 1.

2. *Ps 24*. See Psalms, no. 2.

3. *Ps 41*. See Psalms, no. 4.

4. *Ps 148*. A thanksgiving psalm; on this earth or with Christ, young men and maidens, old men together with children praise the Lord. And their praise in heaven is purer than ours on earth.

D. GOSPELS

1. *Mt 11:25-30*. See Gospels, no. 2.

2. *Jn 6:37-40*. See Gospels, no. 11.

3. *Jn 6:51-58* – if the child has received communion. (See Gospels, no. 12.

4. *Jn 11:32-38, 40* – if the child has received communion. (See Gospels, no. 14.

FUNERAL OF AN UNBAPTISED CHILD

1. *Is 25:6-9*. See Old Testament, no. 4.

2. *Lam 3:17-26*. See Old Testament, no. 5.

Responsorial Psalm: Ps 24. See Psalms, no. 2.

Gospel: Mk 15:33-46. See Gospels, no. 5.

For Priestly or Religious Vocations

Michael Curran, M.S.C.

I INTRODUCTION

In an address delivered to the Congress of National Vocations' Directors held in Rome in December 1966, Pope Paul drew attention to the primary importance of vocation promotion for the renewal of the Church.[1] The promotion of vocations is intimately connected with the renewal of the Church. There are two aspects to this connection.

On the one hand, renewal and adaptation of inherited forms of religious life and ministry are demanded so as to foster and attract vocations. The vocation crisis is but one facet of the crisis of traditional Christianity in the modern world. It has its roots in the crisis of faith, of family life, of institution and authority. Pope John and the Council called for a sweeping *aggiornamento*, which would liberate the Christian tradition from its state of immobility and make it once again a living reality present in history. From this point of view, the vocation crisis has its roots in the past history of the Church. The aspirations of young people for personal growth, for meaningful life, for free and expansive commitment, for community prayer and participation clashed with the immobility of the institutional Church.[2]

The present state of religious life and priestly ministry, the possibilities for change and for radically new developments are best understood in the light of the history of the Church.[3] The present crisis is not the first. But it has its own cultural background in the pre-Vatican II Church. The Church is the Body of Christ, the dwelling-place of the

1. Cf. *La Documentation Catholique* 64 (1967) 7-10. The conclusions and resolutions of the Congress can be seen *ibid.*, col. 650-654. The text of Pope Paul's yearly messages on Vocation Sunday are also given in this periodical.
2. Cf. G. Lesage, *Personalism and Vocation* (Alba House, Staten Island, New York 1966); J. Toner, 'Why are the Labourers too few?', *Doctrine and Life* 23 (1973) 646-650; C. J. Peter, 'Culture and the Vocation Crisis', *Review for Religious* 28 (1969) 186-196.
3. See especially R. Hostie, *Vie et Mort des ordres religieux. Approches psychosociologiques*, (Desclee de Brouwer, Paris 1972).

Holy Spirit. We can take it that the Spirit still bestows his gifts and that where ecclesial life is healthy and positive in outlook there will be no lack of vocations necessary for the life of that particular Church. Prayer and work for vocations should grow out of the sincere desire and effort to renew the Christian life in all its dimensions, personal, familial and communitary.

Some will doubtless object that the real crisis in vocations has come from the *aggiornamento* of Pope John. Others, with better reason, will affirm that renewal is called for by the Lord himself and that it has scarcely begun. Too often the renewal has been fanciful, superficial change for change's sake.

Vocation is divine grace and human response. It is a personal and life-long commitment arising out of a deep faith in the meaing of life and in the future of the Church. Where that meaning and future are not grasped and experienced how can one respond to the call? The big obstacle to vocations is the absence of genuine renewal: a renewal that is consistent, based on faith and hope and love, open to change, built on sound theology, prayerful.

The second aspect of vocation promotion in relation to renewal of the Church was that stressed by Pope Paul. Ongoing renewal of the Church will depend on the vitality and fresh life that can only come from a continuous flow of young people into the religious life and ministry. All religious and priests should have a special interest in this promotion of vocations. It is a work that can no longer be left to chance or to the vocations' director.[4]

The dearth of vocations is not a universal phenomenon, but it is widespread enough to call for a concerted effort from all.[5] No doubt, it is best seen as a salutary crisis rather than unmitigated disaster, giving rise to despair. It is the Lord's own way of calling his Church to a deeper renewal of life and ministry in response to the needs of mankind today. There is no time for complacency either. The future of vast areas of the Church is in peril from the want of vocations. Those responsible for promoting and directing vocations should be alert to the needs and

---

4. A recent survey of the U.S. priesthood revealed that 'there has been a considerable decline in enthusiasm for vocational recruiting, a phenomenon that may be far more serious than the resignation rate': 'Text of Sociology Report in Study of U.S. Priesthood', *Social Studies* 1 (1972) 73-78. See also Sr Consolata, 'The Priest and Religious Women', *The Clergy Review* 51 (1966) 687-693.
5. There is a detailed survey of the situation in Ireland up to 1971 in *Social Studies* 1 (1972) 137-234. The decline in religious vocations in Ireland is graphically illustrated in *Focus for Action. Report by the Working Party set up by the Conference of Major Religious Superiors* (Dublin 1974), p. 67; this covers the period from 1966 to 1973.

insights of the Church, the aspirations of potential vocations and the demands of the apostolate today.[6] The possibilities, the real meaning and challenge of vocation have to be brought home to young people in such a way that their fears and their lack of knowledge may be overcome and that they may have a real opportunity of experiencing God's call to themselves.

The Lord wishes to send labourers into his harvest. He actually calls. Our task is to make this call a lived reality for those who are in reality called by God. Vocations are present in the Church. The Mass for Vocations is a great means of bringing to life this call and grace given to many, so that they may hear God's call and respond to it with faith and joy.

II COMMENTARY ON READINGS

A. OLD TESTAMENT READINGS

1. *Gen 12:1-4*. This reading stresses the relationship of vocation and faith. The living God intervenes in Abraham's life, asks him to forsake the familiar ties of his family and country, to choose instead a more blessed life in the land of promise. God's call and promise, Abraham's factual response of faith: these are the prototype of every authentic vocation.

2. *Exod 3:1-6, 9-12*. At the origin of the call of Moses there is his shattering experience of the majesty of God. But the word of God comes clearly through the experience; 'Come, I send you to Pharaoh to bring my people out of Egypt'. Moses, still terrified and reluctant, objects to the call ('who am I?' — 'why me?'), but God answers simply: 'I shall be with you'. This is a truth that the person called should never forget.

3. *1 Sam 3:1-10*. The boy Samuel is called to be a prophet by means of an unusual revelation. The Lord manifested his presence above the ark of the Covenant in the sanctuary. The old priest Eli enabled Samuel to recognise the voice of God calling him and to answer: 'Speak, Lord, your servant is listening'.

---

6. Cf. J. Newman and others, 'Attitudes of Young People towards Vocations', *Social Studies* 1 (1972) 531-550; R. Hostie, *The Discernment of Vocations*. Translated by M. Barry (Chapman, London 1973); 'Maturity and Vocation', *The Way: Supplement* 15 (1972); articles by P. J. Corish, E. McDonagh and L. Ryan in *The Furrow* 21 (1970) 280-297.

4. *1 Kings 19:16, 19-21*. The prophet Elijah is sent by God to recruit Elisha for the prophetic ministry. By throwing his cloak over him, Elijah acquires an authority over Elisha, which he cannot resist. By destroying plough and oxen Elisha formally renounces his old way of life.

5. *Is 6:1-8 (not 61:6-8 as indicated in some lectionaries)*. The vocation of Isaiah recalls that of Samuel (see third reading above). But here the revelation of the Lord Yahweh is more clearly manifest and Isaiah himself more deeply involved in the experience of his calling. He is especially struck by the holiness of God and experiences the need to be sanctified himself, purified from sin, sharing in the holiness of God. Thus sanctified he is ready to be sent as God's messenger.

6 and 7. *Jer 1:4-9; 20:7-9*. The vocation of Jeremiah, as recounted by himself, offers us a deep insight into the inner life of the person called by God. Jeremiah has a pure and deep experience of the word of God, a word that assures him of God's providential knowledge and care of him, a word more powerful than Jeremiah, a word which, planted within him, must break forth on his lips. Whatever about the prophet's own reluctance and inner conflict, whatever the dire consequences for others of the word of God, this word captivates the life of the prophet. He is servant of the word, strengthened and supported by it.

B. NEW TESTAMENT READINGS

1. *2 Cor 5:14-20*. (For priestly vocations.) St Paul says that his apostolate consists in proclaiming God's great work of reconciliation and new life through Christ. The apostle cannot be indifferent about this work of God; 'the love of Christ overwhelms us!' God needs his ambassadors to make know to all men his creative love.

2. *Phil 3:8-14*. St Paul speaks openly to his beloved Philippians about his deepest convictions and desires. He longs only for that perfection which comes from God, which is given to those who have such faith in Jesus Christ that they desire to reproduce in themselves the pattern of his death in the hope of sharing in his resurrection. Paul has been 'grasped' by Jesus Christ on the road to Damascus, he is in a race to the finish, straining forward in answer to the 'upward call' of God. Here is a wonderful witness of an ever-deepening vocation.

3. *Heb 5:1-10*. (For priestly vocations.) The enduring truth and qualities of the priestly vocation are revealed in Christ. A priest has to be called by God, not self-appointed; he is taken from among men to be mediator with God; he has to be compassionate 'because he too lives in the limitations of weakness'; he has to imitate Christ, in prayer for himself and others, in humility and learning through sufferings. Through

him Christ will continue to exercise his priesthood, being 'for all who obey him the source of eternal salvation.'

C. RESPONSORIAL PSALMS

1. *Ps 15*. The response (v. 5) expresses the point in the choice of this psalm. The person called to religious life and priesthood has the Lord as his special portion, the source of his strength, his wisdom, his joy and ultimate reward.

2. *Ps 26*. The man of faith places his trust in God at all times. His faith enlightens his path. Yet in the darkness of faith he longs for ever greater knowledge and union with God, even the vision of God face to face. 'It is your face, O Lord, that I seek' (Response, v. 8). Every priest/religious must make this quest his own.

3. *Ps 39*. The person delivered from imminent peril and distress proclaims God's merciful love and fidelity in the assembly of the people. Doing God's will with a glad and generous heart is the best response to this love and fidelity. This is Christ's own song of praise and dedication: 'Here I am, O Lord, I come to do your will' (Response: vv. 8-9). The priest/religious is called to make the response his own.

4. *Ps 83*. This psalm expresses the delight of the Jewish pilgrim at the prospect of visiting the Lord's temple in Jerusalem. The expectation sustains him on his pilgrimage. In our present context it can be applied to our life's pilgrimage to the heavenly Jerusalem. At the same time, we are already in the house of God, in his Church. The religious community is a sign of the eschatological community. The priest presides at the Eucharistic banquet in the house of God. 'They are happy, who dwell in your house, O Lord' (Response, v. 5).

D. GOSPELS

1. *Mt 9:35-38*. This passage from Matthew's Gospel bases the need for vocations on the necessity to continue the saving ministry of Christ. This ministry is described in broad outline. The compassion of Jesus goes out to the multitudes. But 'the harvest is great, the labourers are few.' So the Lord asks for prayer for vocations, for other labourers in the harvest.

2. *Mk 10:17-27*. The parallel passage in Mt 19:16-22 is the source of the doctrine of evangelical counsels ('If you wish to be perfect. . . ') in Catholic tradition. However, the accounts in Mk and Lk 18:18-23, as well as the sequel in Mt 19:23-26, show that Jesus was not teaching two complementary ways of entering the kingdom, the way of Jewish morality and the way of 'evangelical perfection.' To be 'perfect' is to be a disciple; it is a command, not simply a counsel (cf. Mt 5:48). In our

reading there is the command of radical renunciation as a condition of discipleship with Christ and entry into the kingdom: 'There is one thing you lack. Go and sell everything you own...' (cf. Lk 6:20-23). Though the passage has to do with Christian faith and the new morality rather than specifically with priestly and religious vocations, the choice of Mk in the latter context is especially suitable in view of v. 21: 'Jesus looked steadily at him and loved him.' A person is chosen out of this intimate knowledge and love Jesus has for him; he must take the radical demands of Jesus seriously in his response of faith and hope.

3. *Mt 10:28-30*. This passage is part of the apostolic discourse of Jesus to the twelve apostles. The command not to be afraid is specifically made in the context of open and fearless proclamation of the message of Christ. Heralds of the word of God should have a boundless trust in the Father's providential care even when that very proclamation of the word may entail death for them.

4. *Lk 5:1-11*. (For priestly vocations.) This passage is Luke's special version of the call of the first four disciples. Peter's vocation is thrown into special relief by the miraculous catch of fish. He is to be 'fisher of men', ready to pay out his nets far and wide in answer to the Lord's call, at his word. The renunciation of 'everything' by Peter and his companions is also thrown into sharp relief by the abundance of the catch they have made.

5. *Lk 9:57-62*. This is a collection of three sayings of Jesus which place before the would-be disciple the sacrifice and single-minded dedication demanded of him. Jesus does not trick anyone into following him, offering pie in the sky. He offers a share in his own way, a share in the sufferings and joy of working for the kingdom of God.

6. *Lk 14:25-33*. This passage like so many others in Luke's Gospel, states very clearly Jesus' demands for total dedication in his disciples. 'Great crowds' are invited to the great banquet of the kingdom of God (see parable immediately preceding). But only those who have a greater love for Jesus than for their dearest friends, only those prepared to sacrifice possessions and follow Jesus in his sufferings and death can realistically hope to be a disciple. These demands addressed to the crowds are meant for priest and religious too.

7. *Jn 1:35-51*. John's account of the call of the first disciples is full of concrete details which suggest personal reminiscence. The first disciples had originally been disciples of John the Baptist. The importance of seeing and hearing, of personal encountering with Jesus and with his disciples is underlined. Those who are called recognise him as the Messiah; but a still greater revelation is promised them.

8. *Jn 15:9-17*. This passage is a continuation of the parable of the vine and the branches. The disciples are invited to remain in the deepest communion of life, of knowledge and love and friendship with Christ and with the Father. This communion is a work of divine grace; the Son, who is loved by the Father, chooses his disciples, loves them as friends, and sends them into the world to be channels of grace for others.

III THEMATIC GROUPINGS

1. *Called.* To have a vocation is to be called by God. This call is experienced in manifold ways by those called, but in all cases it is the basis of their special relationship with God from that time on. God reveals to them his providential knowledge and love. They have a special place in the history of his people. Beyond human background and qualities this aspect of vocation, as a work of God, has to be remembered. The theme could be developed on the basis of these readings:

> Exod 3:1-6, 9-12 or Is 6:1-8.
> Ps 15:1-2, 5, 7-8, 11.
> Phil 3:8-14 or Heb 5:1-10.
> Jn 15:9-17.

2. *Faith.* Faith is a person's response to God's call. It is a faith that means a radical new departure in one's life, a conversion and renunciation of former ways of living and acting, a love of God and of Christ 'above all others', a commitment to God's will. This theme of faith could be developed through this group:

> Gen 12:1-4.
> Ps 26:1-4, 5, 8-9, 11 or Ps 39:2, 4, 7-10, 12.
> Phil 3:8-14.
> Mk 10:17-27 or Lk 5:1-11
> or Lk 9:57-62 or Lk 14:25-33.

3. *Christ.* Imitation of Christ, as man and Son of God, in his dedication to God and self-giving for all, is the ultimate objective of the disciple:

> Phil 3:8-14 or Heb 5:1-10.
> Ps 39:2, 4, 7-10, 12.
> Lk 9:57-62 or Lk 14:25-33.

4. *Heralds.* Priests and religious are called to be heralds of the Word of God through their lives and apostolates and through their proclamation of the word to all the nations of the earth:

> Jer 1:4-9.
> Ps 39:2, 4, 7-10, 12.

> 2 Cor 5:14-19.
> Mt 10:28-30 or Lk 5:1-11.

5. *Fostering.* Vocations are fostered in the Church by those who have the interest of the kingdom at heart, who pray for vocations, who encourage people to answer God's call and make the sacrifice necessary, who show in their own lives the joy of working for God's people:

> 1 Sam 3:1-10 or 1 Kings 19:16, 19-21.
> Ps 83:3-8, 11.
> 1 Cor 12:4-13, 27-31 (not indicated in the Lectionary).
> Mt 9:35-38 or Jn 1:35-51.

For Christian Unity

Patrick Lyons

I INTRODUCTION

In every celebration of Mass, during the preparation for Holy Communion, we pray for unity: 'grant us the peace and unity of your kingdom..' All four Eucharistic Prayers include a petition for unity, the Roman Canon before the Consecration and the others after — linked with the reception of the Eucharist, the sign of unity and bond of charity. As in the first Eucharistic Prayer, the intention is the unity of the Church, but the unity of the congregation gathered for the particular celebration is envisaged especially.

The Prayer of five of the Sundays of the Year (2, 5, 11, 21, 28) asks for the grace of unity for the Church or for the congregation present, and it is worth noting that there are three Masses which look to a wider horizon. The Mass for the Vigil of Pentecost prays for the unity of all mankind, as does the Mass for the Third Sunday of the Year (evidently reflecting the Readings for Year 1 — in all, a Mass with a definite unity theme), while the Prayer of Thursday of Easter Week prays for unity for all the baptised. This latter Prayer has those baptised at the Easter Vigil principally in mind, no doubt.

An intention so important as to be included in every celebration deserves to be spelled out more fully in a special Mass, so it is fitting that there should be three Masses 'For the unity of Christians' in the Roman Missal of 1970. In the previous Missal the corresponding Mass was 'For the removal of schism' (changed in 1961 to 'For the unity of the Church', the texts remaining the same). The origin of the Mass was in the Great Western Schism of the fourteenth century, and one of the parties involved, Clement VII, ruled that this Mass should be said each week. The Mass was taken over for the Roman Missal of 1570, with few emendations, and in modern times appeared somewhat anachronistic.

The Masses in the new Missal reflect present day thinking on the question of unity. Though the internal unity of the Catholic Church still needs to be prayed for, and is in fact prayed for in every Mass, the unity of all those who profess faith in Christ has come to the fore as one of the great needs of today. The Catholic Church came a little late into the modern ecumenical movement. This began early in the century with a coming together of Protestant missionary societies to deal with the problem of disunited witness which was becoming a painful source of scandal in mission territories. Catholic interest in the movement was at first officially discouraged (*Mortalium animos* of Pius XI, 1928), but was eventually approved, basically because of the threat of militant atheism, a felt need to unite in face of the common enemy (Pius XII, 1951). This much, however, without fundamental change in theological perspective nor therefore in definitive judgments — for, so long as underlying theological principles remained unaltered, cooperation with non-Catholics was intended to hasten their return to the Church, and prayer for Christian unity was prayer for the grace of this conversion on their part. It was intended as something separate, therefore, from prayer for the Church.

Perhaps even now the change in theological perspective introduced by the Vatican Council is not widely appreciated. Even more in the Constitution on the Church than in the Decree on Ecumenism (because of the order in which the documents were taken) the Council came to grips with the problem of the relationship between the Catholic Church and the other Christian Churches. It is clear from examination of the draft documents that the term 'Churches' as applied to communities of Christian separated from the Catholic Church is not used merely phenomenologically. The term had been excluded from the first two drafts of the Church document, but it was argued that withholding it from communities possessing means of grace and fostering the Christian life by their institutions could not be justified theologically. It was then included, and thus with a more than sociological value. The *relatio* for the final draft declared, in fact, that the recognition of the ecclesial nature of groups other than the one to which one belongs is the operating principle of the ecumenical movement. The word 'communities' was also used in the document out of deference for those groups which did not wish to be described as Churches.

The Council did, of course, make special claims for the Catholic Church. Having described the nature of the Church of Christ in visible, historical terms, it declared in a now famous phrase that this Church 'subsists' in the Catholic Church. This is a change from the previous draft in which it has been stated simply that the Church of Christ is the Catholic Church. As a consequence of the new formulation, it was possible to avoid any implication that the other Christian Churches are pseudo or counterfeit Churches. It meant also, and this was the main reason given in the *relatio* for the non-identification, that the relationship of persons, Catholic or otherwise, to the Church founded by Christ was not being seen in terms of member. The concept of member, which is valid and verifiable for a person in relation to a particular Church is full of difficulties when applied to an individual's status in the Church of Christ.

The Council's approach allows the fact and objective of the Church's unity to be considered in a new way. In art. 15 of the Church Constitution the objective is stated in these terms: 'All men are called to this catholic unity which prefigures and promotes universal peace'. The fact is stated thus: 'And in different ways to it belong, or are related: the Catholic faithful, others who believe in Christ, and finally all mankind, called by God's grace to salvation'. In discussing these separate categories, 'other Christians' are described as 'in some real way joined to us (the Catholic Church) in the Holy Spirit'. The Decree on Ecumenism (art. 3) states that men who believe in Christ and have been properly baptised are put in some, though imperfect, communion with the Catholic Church. It might be said, then, that praying for the unity of Christians is not all that different an idea from praying for what was described earlier as the internal unity of the Church. Whenever there is prayer for unity in the context of the Church, the true nature of that prayer includes all Christians. The perfecting of a unity that already exists imperfectly is being sought.

This much follows from considering Christians in relation to the Church of Christ and to one another. As indicated earlier, however, the Council gave recognition to the ecclesial reality of the Churches to which Christians separated from the Catholic Church belong. What this amounts to is that they are recognised as true but incomplete manifestations of the Church Christ founded. This is not a quantitative approach according to which the difference between the Catholic Church and other Churches would be found in a measurable number of ecclesial elements, nor is it the old Anglican theory of the one Church with many branches. Rather it is a qualitative judgment on the way in which the elements of Christ's Church are present in various communities. The Decree on Ecumenism recognises that 'many of the most significant elements and endowments which together go to build up and give life to the Church itself can exist outside the visible boundaries of the Catholic Church: the written word of God; the life of grace; faith, hope and charity, with the other interior gifts of the Holy Spirit, as well as visible elements' (art. 3). But the Decree points to the fact that these Churches do not possess these elements in union with the Catholic Church, through which alone the fulness of the means of salvation can be obtained. The basic defect is seen as disunity itself.

While the uniqueness of the Catholic Church is not gainsaid, the thinking behind the Decree encourages the idea of dialogue between the Churches on an equal footing. Less than two years after this Decree, which gave, in fact, special recognition to the Anglican communion, Pope Paul and Archbishop Ramsey of Canterbury met and issued a joint declaration looking forward, despite the obstacles, to a 'restoration of complete communion of faith and sacramental life'. In order to bring this about, the Anglican-Roman Catholic International Commission was set up to make a joint study of various theological and practical difficulties in the way of reunion. This Commisson has already produced agreed statements on the Eucharist, on Ministry, and on Authority. It is clear, however, that unless these deliberations have widespread support in the two Churches, and unless the documents of these qualified and duly authorised theologians are received in a trusting rather than in a carping spirit, no real progress can be made towards uniting the Churches. The whole idea of discussions presupposes such a benevolent attitude on both sides. If the right climate exists, however, the two Churches can gradually become more united in thought and practice, in a process which the Anglican co-chairman of the Commission has described as unity by stages.

In practice, then, praying for Christian unity means, for example, praying for the continued growth of the relationship between the Anglican and Roman Catholic Churches, and this in turn means praying for the success of theological discussions, and, more important, for an increase in the realisation of shared faith, an increase in hope and of fraternal charity on the part of the members of the two Churches. This direction of prayer towards particular unity schemes is as much part of prayer for Christian unity as is a general intercession for the unity of the whole body of believers.

In recent times, however, and especially since the discussion on these matters at the World Council of Churches meeting at Uppsala in 1968, the question is being asked more often whether prayer for unity should now be for the unity of mankind rather than of the Church. The reasons for this new horizon include a lessening of interest among many Christians in the Church as an international institution. There would be among such 'advanced' Christians, however, a considerable enthusiasm for the unity of the Church as embodied in a small local group. On the large scale their interest would be more aligned with the welfare of all mankind, and there are two persuasive reasons for this view. One is that modern means of communication and of travel have given a new understanding of the physical unity of the human race and of how lacking in moral unity that same community is, with millions of people in the developed countries living in affluence and caring little in practice about the deprivation suffered by those in the poorer parts of the world by reason of that same affluence. A second reason for this interest in the unity of mankind is the realisation that further polarisation of the world community could result in a war which would destroy all mankind at once. In this view, then, uniting all Christians in one world Church appears less important. However, it may be asked how realistic is the objective of world unity, whether there are any grounds for believing that the political will or the means will emerge to bring mankind together in a true community.

The sound Christian view seems to be that the unity of mankind will come only through belief in Christ, and worldwide acceptance of Christ can come only when those who believe already are united (cf. Jn 17: 21). Certainly, the Church shares in the aspiration to world unity. 'In his fatherly care for all of us, God desired that all men should form one family and deal with each other in a spirit of brotherhood,' says the Constitution on the Church in the Modern World (art. 24). But the Church concentrates on the necessary intermediate objective, its own unity. And while there is a distinction between uniting all Christians and uniting all mankind, the two aspirations are not really separate. As all men of good will are in some way related to the Church (Constitution on the Church, art. 13) 'the Church prays and likewise labours so that into the People of God, the Body of the Lord and the Temple of the Holy Spirit, may pass the fullness of the whole world' (art. 17).

It is true that the use of various theological models, in the Council's theology and since then, to describe the mystery of the Church has laid less emphasis on the 'substantialist' model, the traditional view of the Church as a visible historical society, 'as visible as the Republic of Venice' (in Bellarmine's enduring phrase), and so the future unity of the Church can be envisaged on a more spiritual, less visible level. The power of the Spirit to bring into unity the diverse elements of Christianity will be more in evidence when, instead of rigid uniformity, something of the heterogeneous character of the various communities remains. But there is among Christians at present a divergence of belief and practice which is more than a permissible pluralism, and according as human aspirations and problems assume more and more the dimensions of all mankind, the need to pray for Christian unity becomes all the more urgent, 'so that the world may believe'.

The scope of prayer for Christian unity is, then, as particular as local conditions require, whether it is dissension in a parish or a relationship with another Christian community to be fostered, and prayer for unity looks equally to the universal needs of mankind in this time of fundamental option near the end of the second millenium. A strong desire for authenticity in the Christian life and a new openness to the world would seem to be characteristic of the present time, and these, rightly or wrongly, are often contrasted with older attitudes in the Church of apparent complacency and 'siege mentality'. A real interest in prayer for Christian unity would seem a very apt demonstration of both aspects of this new spirit.

The three Masses for the Unity of Christians, showing the true liturgical outlook, have regard for needs both universal and local. There are alternative Opening Prayers in each Mass, the first Prayer in Mass A being identical with the corresponding one in the ten Solemn Intercessions of Good Friday. It is concerned with the fellowship of those who are linked by baptism; the alternative Prayer invokes the power of the Spirit to make believers witnesses of the truth before all men. Mass B has a more universal theme in the first Opening Prayer, inspired evidently by the scriptural theme of God gathering his children (Entrance Antiphon) from the nations. The alternative Prayer stresses the role of repentance in the lives of believers, so that divisions may be healed. Mass C in the first Prayer (and in the alternative) returns to the theme of the Spirit, and in a characteristically modern way asks for the outpouring of the gifts of the Spirit on God's people.

There is just one Preface for Christian Unity among the eighty of the new Missal, and, unlike many others, which are derived from the old Sacramentaries, it is new, though presumably inspired by Eph 4:4-6 and 1 Cor 12:4-6. It celebrates the unity that already exists among all those who have received the Holy Spirit. It is a very rich text, full of the poetic antitheses of the best Prefaces, too elaborate, perhaps, for full assimilation except in a really leisurely celebration. It is interesting to read it in conjunction with the very simple but telling Preface of Unity used in the Eucharistic Liturgy of Taize, and worth reproducing here: 'We give thanks to you, almighty God, for the unity of the Body of Christ, and we await with joy the day when we shall perfectly be one, that the world may know that you have sent your Son, and that he loved us as you loved him.' Here, the note of anticipation, the eschatological outlook, is more marked, and there is as well a note of Christian joy. This eschatological view is in evidence, however, in the Prayers of the Unity Masses, and it is, of course, now a characteristic of the Communion Rite in the Ordinary of the Mass.

Though not found in the Roman Missal, the effort involved in finding copies of the two Eucharistic Prayers (with Prefaces) for Reconciliation for use in a Mass for Unity would be amply repaid by the aptness and scope of the texts. These were published (with the Eucharistic Prayers for Children) for use in the Holy Year and may be used still.

II COMMENTARY ON READINGS

A. OLD TESTAMENT READINGS

1. *Deut 30:1-4.* A constant theme in the history of Israel is the future gathering into one of the scattered children of God. This passage, written probably during the exile in Babylon, puts into the mouth of Moses the promise of God to gather his own people into one, and thus into safety, provided they remember and return to the Covenant, to a life lived in God's presence, and in obedience to him. A fundamental principle of today's movement towards Christian unity is the need for all Christians to repent, and acknowledge their own sinfulness as a cause of division.

2. *Ezek 36:23-28.* The world will come to know God when his people are restored to their inheritance from their place of exile. But it all depends on God, even the inner change of heart and spirit, which will enable them to become God's people once more. Hence the importance, in the attempt to restore Christian unity, of prayer. This aspect of the movement is called 'spiritual ecumenism' in recognition of its distinct and fundamental contribution to the overall effort.

3. *Ezek 37:15-19,* 21-22, 26-28. Since the division after the death of Solomon, the unity of the people of Israel could only be achieved by bringing together the two kingdoms, referred to here as Joseph or Ephraim in the north and Judah in the south. But God promises to make his people one with a unity that will last. The intertwining of political and religious divisions is not simply a modern phenomenon but has wreaked great havoc throughout history, so it is useful to stress the note of optimism in this reading.

4. *Zeph 3:16-20.* The restoration of his people after their exile will make God exult. The suggestion of 'heaven rejoicing' evokes the Gospel idea of sinners doing penance. When 'that time' will come depends on the Lord, as the reading says, but it will also depend on man's response to God's love by conversion of life. The Decree on Ecumenism notes (art. 1) that the Lord of ages has 'in recent times begun to bestow more generously upon divided Christians remorse over their divisions and longing for unity'.

B. NEW TESTAMENT READINGS

1. *1 Cor 1:10-13.* Paul's letter was written in response to complaints about opposing factions which had arisen in the Christian community founded by him some years previously. He pinpoints the problem: the disunity which springs from putting human leaders in place of Christ. At this distance from the foundations of Christianity an ideology rather

than a human leader is more likely to usurp the place of Christ. In either case the result is sectarianism.

2. *Eph 2:19-22.* Good foundations give unvarying support under the entire extent of the building. The Apostles as a body or 'college' are a principal source to which the consciousness of the Church as a Church appeals. True growth is gauged by conformity to the plumbline of Christ's teaching. Thus height and extent, apostolicity and catholicity, lead to the unity and aptness for God's indwelling (holiness) which are the hallmarks of the Church. In this temple Gentiles are no longer aliens; the Jewish metaphor is a reminder of the overall theme of Ephesians, Jew and Gentile, all men, reconciled and united in Christ.

3. *Eph 4:1-6.* The indwelling Spirit is the single inner source of the Christian life, and as such is continually moving all members towards what promotes peace and harmony. The Spirit from whom the body of believers derive their unity is the Spirit enlivening the Body of Christ in this world, and is thus linked through the one Lord Christ with the Father, whose oneness was a cardinal belief of the Jewish faith. This shows us the strength of the idea of the Spirit as the Spirit of unity. Testing the spirits in Christianity today can be done most effectively by the use of this criterion.

4. *Eph 4:30–5:2.* Christ's love caused him to give up his life in order to draw all men to himself, and the Christian is called to love as Christ loved: thus a self-sacrificing, forgiving love that draws men together rather than divides them. Along the way to Christian unity, understanding and acceptance by others may have to be sacrificed, as it was in Christ's case, by those who imitate his unifying mission.

5. *Phil 2:1-13.* Paul's appeal for unity to the Philippians (for whom he had, in fact, a high regard) is based on what life in Christ must mean to them. Christ as a model of humility is praised in the hymn quoted. Humility in his followers will allow them to show in their lives the two fundamental aspects of unity; they will be united both in their attitudes and in their actions in relation to one another, in their sharing of conviction and of love.

6. *Col 3:9-17.* Peace in the Old Testament, and in the New, means perfection, perfect union with God. In St Paul it is clear that this union can only come about through fellowship with others so as to become the Body of Christ. Thus unity and peace are linked together in Christian thought. The more Christ's Body is built up in the world, the less room there is for distinction and division.

7. *1 Tim 2:5-8.* Christ's all-importance for those who want to have access to God is emphasised here, and the further fundamental teaching added that this access is for all men, as Christ died for all. God's plan is,

therefore, for the unity of all men, in Christ, and this gift should be asked of God in fervent prayer.

8. *I Jn 4:9-15.* John's magnificent teaching on love in the Christian life hinges on the fact that God loved us first: we have been touched by a loving God and in our turn radiate love to others. But the interdependence between faith and love is vital. To be a receptacle of God's love, and thus overflow to others, requires a faith that enables us to recognise Christ as the proof of God's love. The goal for Christians is unity of faith as well as fellowship of life.

C. RESPONSORIAL PSALMS

1. *Jer 31:10-14.* The repeated note of joy in Jeremiah's prophecy of the restoration of Israel makes this hymn useful for counteracting attitudes of pessimism. God's care for his people, his gathering them from among the nations (themes found especially in the Response), suggest the use of this Psalm with Old Testament Readings 1 and 4, New Testament Readings 6 and 8.

2. *Ps 22.* A favourite Psalm in all Christian Churches. In this animal metaphor, anointing the head with oil is not, of course, a cultic reference, but recalls the shepherd tending the cuts and scratches received by the sheep on the way to the green pastures. The wound of division among Christians is sorely in need of healing. This Psalm is especially suitable for Old Testament Readings 1, 2, 4; New Testament Readings 1 and 5.

3. *Ps 99.* Also well-known in the Christian Churches, but in another guise — as the hymn 'All people that on earth do dwell', the tune of which is named the Old Hundredth, reflecting the Hebrew numbering of the Psalms. A processional Psalm used in the Jewish Liturgy, it evokes the idea of pilgrimage, and thus also the journey of the Christian people towards the peace and unity of God's kingdom. Suitable for use with Old Testament Reading 3 and especially New Testament Reading 2.

4. *Ps 117:22-23, 25-26, 28.* Christ interpreted this Psalm as applying to himself (Mt 21:42), as did Peter subsequently (Acts 4:11). Hence its appropriateness as a response to New Testament Reading 2. Good also with New Testament Readings 1, 5, 6, 7.

5. *Ps 121:1-9.* A pilgrimage Psalm expressing joy at having arrived at Jerusalem, symbol of Jewish aspirations and achievements. The Psalm shows the close identification between the city and the Temple, God's dwelling place. The prayer for the peace of Jerusalem is a prayer for prosperity and, more spiritually, a prayer for an even greater sense of God's presence. The peace theme responds well to New Testament Reading 6. Also a good Psalm to celebrate the feeling of 'having arrived'

at a time of some ecumenical achievement, and for use with Old Testament Reading 3, and with Readings using visible images of the Church, such as New Testament Readings 2 and 6.

D. GOSPELS

1. *Mt 18:19-22.* There has been a development in the Church's understanding of Christ's presence among us. While the Encyclical *Mediator Dei* listed three presences, sacramental, ministerial and in the community itself, the Constitution on the Liturgy of Vatican II added the presence of Christ when his word is proclaimed. This greater appreciation of the many facets of Christ's presence, and especially in the proclamation of Scripture, should help to lessen the tendency to contrast the 'real presence' of Christ with a 'real absence' in other Christian communities. Many communities gather in Christ's name, and satisfy his requirements that their prayer should be effective.

2. *Lk 9:49-56.* To harmonise the dictum: 'Anyone who is not against you is for you' with the more familiar 'He who is not with me is against me' further on in St Luke's Gospel, it is enough to note that Christ allowed no neutral ground between good and evil. Failure to understand this leads to failure to recognise goodwill and to an excessive caution. Thus the exclusivism of the Jewish religion, exemplified by the attitude of the disciples towards the Samaritans and contradicted by Jesus here and in his entire ministry, reasserts itself in Christianity. Lack of cooperation between Christians contradicts Christ's message.

3. *Jn 10:11-16.* From a contrast with the hireling's attitude, which leads to a scattering and loss of the sheep, we see that it is Christ's sacrifice which saves and unites his flock, makes the scattered children of God into a people. The condition for acceptance into the flock is the same for all, both 'his own' and the other sheep, the Gentiles: that they should know him — and this comes from listening to his voice. This listening is a continuous process. But complacency can prevent his voice being heard — in the Church's authoritative guidance, in the Scriptures, in the prophetic voices of the day, in the events of life. A willingness to listen, and obey, to live in the 'now' of God's dealing with us, is crucial to the success of the movement to bring into one all those who follow Christ.

4. *Jn 11:45-52.* The power of Christ's sacrifice emerges clearly here. From the political angle his death was a matter of expedience — to make the short-term gain of averting Roman interference. In reality its consequences were incalculable, extending beyond all political boundaries, offering universal citizenship and, at the same time, intimate family membership to all who would believe in him. Through the blood

of Christ (Eph 2:13) his followers are no longer aliens but members of God's household. The power of Christ's sacrifice to unite is acknowledged and invoked in the Eucharistic Prayers. Keeping this dynamism to the forefront in the Church's consciousness is an urgent obligation on all.

5. *Jn 13:1-15.* The action which Christ asked his disciples to copy was an expression of his perfect love. The service he rendered was to be imitated so that his love might be reproduced. Christ seems to endorse here the idea of the authority of excellence. Eminence among his followers should follow from excellence of love, authenticated by service. Too easily, worldly power is substituted for spiritual authority among Christians, and then rivalry and divisions follow. The drive towards unity among Christians poses a threat to those who seek power, but vindicates the attitude of those who rival one another in imitating the unifying love of Christ.

6. *Jn 17:1-11.* (The High-Priestly Prayer of Jesus at the Last Supper is divided between this and the two following Readings, with an overlap between this and the next.)

The first section stresses Christ's unity with the Father, and because of this his power over all mankind and his concern for the disciples. All belong to the Father, and Jesus, his representative, has made himself known to the disciples so that they may find their true fulfilment in acknowledging with him their sonship of the Father. Today, Christianity is faced with the challenge of atheism in the world-view associated with the Eastern power bloc. In Western countries traditionally Christian, however, it faces the subtle challenge of an agnosticism brought about by a decline in religious consciousness. Enthusiasm for the autonomy of man threatens belief in the fatherhood of God. The various Christian traditions, with their characteristic insights, have their own light to throw on the vexing question of the challenge posed to religion by urbanised and industrialised society. A united approach is as important in dealing with this problem within the Christian world as in facing world atheism.

7. *Jn 17:11-19.* The slogan, 'Work makes free', was written on the gates of a notorious concentration camp. The specious truth contained in it was that unthinking acceptance of the regime within would make life tolerable. Christ taught (Jn 8:32) that the truth makes free, and in his prayer for the disciples he asked that they might be preserved in the truth, so that they would understand and experience the true nature of their calling: a life of fellowship reflecting that of the Father and Son. For twenty five years now in the ecumenical movement, it has been recognised that comparing and contrasting doctrinal positions 'tend to

increase disunity because each communion then stresses its own historic peculiarities'. The newer approach consists in studying together some of the great truths held in common and facing up to their implications – a dynamic approach rather than a static one, and one which recognises that the Holy Spirit continues to teach the Church.

8. *Jn 17:20-26.* The climax of Christ's prayer for his disciples brings a new vision and includes the Church of all time. The unity of the Church is, as it were, the incarnation of the shared life and love of the Father and Son. This living proof of the love that is in God will lead the world to belief. This text shows the urgency of the task undertaken by the ecumenical movement. For '. . . division openly contradicts the will of Christ, scandalises the world, and damages that most holy cause, the preaching of the Gospel to every creature' (Decree on Ecumenism, art. 1).

III THEMATIC GROUPINGS

The groupings here are based on the key ideas of the Opening Prayers, and their alternatives, of the three Mass 'For the Unity of Christians' in the Roman Missal. For suitable Responsorial Psalms see suggestions about pp. 152-153.

MASS A

1. Prayer: *Baptism, unity of faith and love.*
   Readings: Old Testament 1 (Covenant); New Testament 1 (Christ) or 8 (faith and love); Gospel 6 (sonship of Father) or 1 (presence of Christ).

2. Alternative Prayer: *Spirit, witness to all men, truth, faith and peace.*
   Readings: Old Testament 6 (witness to the world); New Testament 6 (peace); Gospel 7 (truth).

MASS B

3. Prayer: *Many nations united, obedience, one in faith and love.*
   Readings: Old Testament 1 (obedience) or 3 (nations together); New Testament 2 (Jews and Gentiles); Gospel 5 (love) or 3 (obedience).

4. Alternative Prayer: *Prayers, sorrow for sin, unity.*
   Readings: Old Testament 4 (repentance); New Testament 5 (humility, prayers); Gospel 4 (power of Christ's sacrifice).

MASS C

5. Prayer: *Spirit, truth, together.*

Readings: Old Testament 3 (together); New Testament 3 (Spirit); Gospel 2 (cooperation).

6. Alternative Prayer: *Spirit, divisions, sign to nations, believe.*

Readings: Old Testament 2 (Spirit); New Testament 4 (unite—divide); Gospel 8 (believe).

For the Evangelisation of Peoples

James Sheerin (Introduction)

Tomás Ó Curraoin (Commentary)

I INTRODUCTION

If the Church is essentially missionary, then every mission liturgy should expressly catechise, inspire and involve us in this dimension of our faith. Whether the occasion be Mission Sunday in the parish, the assembly of some mission-support group, a gathering of missionaries in retreat or recollection, or an occasional liturgy in a place of mission formation, the celebration should immerse all the participants more deeply in the saving work of Christ.

The occasion and group will suggest the particular choice of readings from the Lectionary, but whatever the time, the celebrant and organisers of any mission liturgy should ensure that the participants receive a motivation that is authentic.

The vision of mission transmitted should be truly scriptural and theological. Jesus did not patronise, or project the image of someone with a superiority complex; our attempts to deepen mission motivation should not be based on pity, patronage or any emotion which insinuates in any way the inferiority of other races. In the Incarnation we have the established pattern of all mission relationships. Jesus emptied himself and in so doing reconciled men to God and men to men. He came into the world already vibrant with God's activity. He is the revelation, the unfolding, the expression of God's love, the love that exists in the Trinity, making it One, and the love that is to be reflected and repeated in the Church. This warming love takes hold of us in reading the New Testament; it possessed St Paul and made him obsessed with Jesus. He was thrilled, obliged, to spend himself for the Gospel: 'Woe to me if I do not preach the Gospel!' (1 Cor 9:16). St Paul would have regarded any love of Christ less missionary than this as immature or decadent.

The Church has been set up by Jesus as the sign and the instrument of this saving love; 'the promulgation of the Gospel message is not something which the Church may undertake or neglect at her discretion; it is rather the function and duty imposed on her by our Lord Jesus Christ so that all may believe and achieve salvation' *(Evangelii Nuntiandi,* n. 5). 'Evangelisation is the special grace and vocation of the Church. It is her essential function. The Church exists to preach the Gospel, that is, to preach and teach the word of God so that through her the gift of grace may be given to us, sinners may be reconciled to God and the sacrifice of the Mass, the memorial of his glorious death and resurrection, may be perpetuated' *(ibid.,* n. 14).

This realisation, that Mission is as basic to the exercise of our faith as brotherly love, is the beginning of true mission awareness. It certainly takes away all temptations to complacency, vanity or triumphalism, about mission activity or involvement, especially when we reflect on the small percentage of the Church's personnel engaged in mission to those who have never possessed Christ. It also provides the true motivation for the works of compassion, justice, development and liberation in the Third World. This is particularly necessary today as it would be a pity if works for the Third World by Christians were given no deeper foundations than a guilt-complex, a vague desire to do good, or the expediency of the present world situation. In all mission activity we are living the maturity of our baptismal commitment.

II COMMENTARY ON READINGS

A. OLD TESTAMENT READINGS

1. *Is 2:1-5.* This is a very famous prophecy of the messianic-eschatological destiny of God's City (Sion) to be spiritually pre-eminent in the world; so that all peoples will be drawn upwards to Sion, to worship the true God, learn his ways, and be empowered to live according to his laws. Since all are to be guided by him, the secret of true, universal and lasting peace — among men also — is here. This hope and promise finds fulfilment in the gospel of Christ and the universal Church.

2. *Is 56:1, 6-7.* Part of 'Third Isaiah', and probably post-exilic. There is the promise of God's salvation soon to burst forth and the demand for men to prepare for it by doing right before God and to one another. The pagans will associate themselves with the Lord, by keeping his laws. They will thus rejoice in the liturgy (interior and exterior). In God's house there will be adoration in spiritual unity and truth of all peoples, bonded by love of God. Quoted by Jesus (Mk 11:17). Certainly realised in him.

3. *Is 60:1-6*. A lyrical chant, prophecy, probably dating from the early years of restoration after exile. It is addressed to the woman, spouse of God, who is in·mourning, promising a new creation of light. The Lord, his glory, will destroy earth's darkness. To this new light the exiled Jews, and the pagans will flock, with their wealth, which is meant especially to serve in public worship of Yahweh. Joy, courage, promise of light provides a scene of universal liturgy.

4. *Jon 3:10–4:11*. The contrast between the Israelite prophet's narrow nationalism — hating Assyria and wishing its destruction, displeased at their repentance and forgiveness by God — and God's boundless and universal love for his creatures, especially men, and urgent desire for their salvation, and rejoicing in their repentance. Often human prejudices, even of the men of God, have to be crushed by God's will in achieving the universal salvation of men.

5. *Zech 8:20-23*. Promise (post-exilic) that Jerusalem (city of God's presence) will be centre of the world, to which all peoples will come; it will be also its cult-centre — place of liturgical adoration of God. The pagans will attach themselves to the guidance of God's people, fervently and in great numbers, following the Jewish pilgrims, to partake in the Covenant of God with his people, and share in intercession of him. 'We have heard that God is with you' — the awakening of faith in the pagans.

B. NEW TESTAMENT READINGS

1. *Acts 1:3-8*. Introduction to Acts, and outline of its aim, as summary of the fulfilment of the last words of Jesus on earth commissioning the world mission of the apostles. It is to begin with the gift of the Holy Spirit, *the* Promise of the Old Testament, and to consist in witness (martyrdom) to Jesus, above all to his resurrection (and its consequences) even to the ends of the earth.

2. *Acts 11:19-26*. Here is the great breakthrough — the real beginning of the *pagan* missionary effort by Christians, dispersed after Stephen's martyrdom. At Antioch in Syria, *'preaching* the *Kyrios, Jesus . . .* to *Greeks'*. The highly endowed Barnabas, on behalf of the apostolic college, investigates, approves, associates the great apostle of the Gentiles with the work. Now a Church of former pagans is formed, large numbers pour in, 'believers turned to the Lord'; the 'disciples' of Jesus get their name 'christ-ians'.

3. *Acts 13:46-49*. The Jewish privilege, to be the only people of God, has given way to the universal people of God who have faith in Jesus and 'show themselves worthy of eternal life'. Their election entitled them to hear the gospel first; but God's 'salvation' and 'light' is for 'the uttermost parts of the earth'. Thus there is predestination, faith, gladness, glory, eternal life for the pagans. *Parrhesia*, or bold and un-

afraid speaking out of the truth, characterises the apostolic preaching (v. 46).

4. *Rom 10:9-18.* Again in the context of the failure of the Jews to believe in Jesus, and of the coming in of the Gentiles to the inheritance. Conditions of salvation: Jesus is Lord (Kyrios): he rose from the dead. This brings 'justification' and 'salvation' to all men, without distinction: 'everyone who invokes the Name'. But this demands mission, sending of men to evangelise; word-of-mouth proclamation of Christ. Paul at any rate claims for his own day that this has been done; no Jew has failed to hear the gospel. That is not their excuse.

5. *Eph 3:2-12.* Paul speaks here of the 'mystery' of Christ, the gospel, revealed after being hidden from eternity. Of this mystery Paul is 'minister', deacon, steward, by God's choice; and it concerns the vocation of all peoples to be 'members of the Body' of Christ, with Jews, 'partakers of the promise' fulfilled. This happens 'in the Church' into which they enter by faith — as the place in which Jesus is, and the wisdom of God is revealed.

6. *1 Tim 2:1-8.* The prayer of Christians for those in authority is to enable conditions of life (quiet, peaceable, godly, respectful) to exist, in which God's will for the salvation of all men, the coming of truth, may be realised. The one God, has established the one mediator, Jesus, as man the redeemer (ransom) of all, by his witness at a point of history to truth, to God's love. Paul has been a preacher, teacher, apostle, to all Gentiles of this gospel of salvation.

C. RESPONSORIAL PSALMS

1. *Ps 18:2-6.* The glory of God, i.e. the manifestation of his presence as creator in creation, manifested by the heavens, by days, by nights, by their being, is a type (seen by Paul in Rom 10:18; cf. no. 4 above) of all-pervading influence of the apostolic preaching of the gospel, which reveals the 'glory' of God 'to the ends of the earth'. This now happens in the voice of God's men preaching.

2. *Ps 66:2-3, 5, 7-8.* God's grace, blessing, personal favour, to his people, manifested in a bountiful harvest, will reveal to all nations his gracious ways and power to save. So the pagans will praise the true God, and live in joy in the experience of God's justice and providence.

3. *Ps 95:1-3, 7-10.* One of the psalms of God's kingship, to be established in messianic-eschatological times over the whole earth. 'The Lord reigns' as king, when all the peoples of the earth know and tell of his salvation, his glory, strength, and offer him the true liturgy. This is the 'new song', for the new creation, the new people of God.

4. *Ps 97:1-6*. Again a 'new song' to God, the king who has established his rule, displayed his power, justice, salvation, love, fidelity, to his people, and thus drawn all the nations into worship and joyous acclamation of God, 'the King, the Lord'.

5. *Ps 116*. An invitation to all the nations on earth to acknowledge and praise the true God, for his truth, fidelity, and gracious love, revealed in salvation-history to his people. The refrain is the command of Jesus to the apostles to proclaim world-wide precisely that good news (Mk 16:15).

D. GOSPELS

1. *Mt 28:16-20*. This last grandiose scene of the gospel according to Matthew occurs at a meeting place in Galilee, a mountain prearranged. Worship is now openly given to Jesus, the risen Lord, by those 'who had doubted' before. Jesus is invested with every authority for the 'building up' of the Kingdom of God on earth (cf. 2 Cor 10:8): now that the new Covenant of the Spirit has been inaugurated by his redemption and triumph. He 'therefore' invests his apostles with that same authority. Hence their commission: to instruct for discipleship the whole human race — the universal mission of the Church. This involves baptism of believers, a consecration to ('baptise into')the Blessed Trinity, and religious and moral instruction of all the members of the new era, new law. Jesus who will be physically absent after this leave-taking, will be spiritually present always, giving aid and direction to the apostolic Church until history passes away.

2. *Mk 16:15-20*. Much as in Matthew above. In Mark Jesus stresses 'proclamation' (kerygma) of 'gospel' (good news) and universality including 'every creature'. In face of the gospel proclamation everyone must take a stand, which is ultimate and eschatological: 'salvation' for those of 'faith' and 'baptism'; condemnation at the last judgment to eternal loss for unbelief. Signs which accompany and help to accredit further the gospel are exorcisms, strange languages, healings, and as in the case of Paul at Malta, escape from deadly poisonous serpents. These are only external accrediting signs to arouse unbelievers; the real miracle is the conversion and the new heart given to men of faith by the power of the Lord in glory, and by the world-wide preaching of the apostles and missionaries.

3. *Lk 24:44-53*. In Luke the culminating events take place in Jerusalem, where the Church begins. At this turning point in history the risen Jesus binds together in his own person the Old Testament promise of salvation and the future mission of the apostles. 'These' events — his death and resurrection are fulfilled 'words' of Jesus and of the Old Testament

law, prophets and writings. These spoke of the promised Messiah, his sufferings and resurrection. They 'had to be fulfilled'. Moreover it was written in God's plan, that the promised 'repentance for forgiveness of sins' is now to be preached; Jesus, the saviour, has won this. It is to be preached world-wide, by others in Christ's name. The apostles, firstly, are 'witnesses' of all the facts mentioned above, especially of Jesus. Jesus will do the one thing necessary, 'send out the Promise' – i.e. the Holy Spirit promised by the Father for the end-times. He will enlighten them further, and encourage them to witness fearlessly. 'Power from on high' will be given them. The closing verses tell summarily of his ascension (repeated more fully in Acts) and of the continuing prayer of the disciples of Jesus.

4. *Jn 11:45-52.* The great act of the raising of Lazarus precipitates the decision to kill Jesus. It is taken by the high-priest and some of the ruling body; they see the success of Jesus as arousing nationalistic desires of the people, and as endangering their state and Holy Place. It is better that he die. Political expediency chooses the lesser of two evils. But in fact the words of the high-priest are prophetic, and his decision is the chosen nation's last decision in furthering God's plan of salvation. Jesus must die, in order that the whole human race may not perish; in order to gather into the one flock of God's people, redeemed by his blood, all God's dispersed children. So unknowingly, malice and political sagacity serve the accomplishment of God's loving plan.

5. *Jn 17:11, 17-23.* From the prayer of Jesus at the last supper. Soon the disciples will be alone in the world. Jesus asks his 'Holy' Father 'to keep' them in the faith or worship of the name which unites Father and Son. In God there is Father and Son; the divine nature unites them. May faith in that name unite believers also, as it unites Father and Son in God.

May the 'Holy' Father make them holy – share in God's perfection, by the truth revealed in the 'word of God'; that, when received whole and entire, transforms men. The apostles are sent on their mission, continuing that of Jesus; for this they need sanctity like that of Jesus. Jesus as priest consecrated himself as a victim sacrificed to God, precisely that they might reproduce in themselves truly the sanctity necessary for missionaries.

Then Jesus prays for the Church of men brought to being by the apostolic ministry. They may not choose what to believe: they must be one with each other, and moreover with the Trinity, after the manner of the divine persons themselves. That will lead all men to faith in the mission of Jesus, which produces such results. And moreover, as Jesus received the 'glory' – his divinity – from the Father, he has given it, i.e. grace, created participation in divine 'glory', to believers. Thus the world of men in need of redemption will have a motive of credibility, to believe that Jesus is truly the envoy of the Father, and that the Father truly loves them as he showed by sending his Son to save the world.

For Peace and Justice

Desmond Wilson

I INTRODUCTION

We are coming to realise more and more that peace is not a quiet situation but a creative one. It is not a condition in which nothing bad or disturbing happens. It is a condition in which creative things do happen.

Therefore in our prayer for peace there is bound to be an element of longing, when we say: If only there were peace. There is bound to be an element of promise too, when we tell each other what it will be like when peace comes.

At present we are facing not only a threat to peace coming from outside, the kind of threat which people feared when Germany or Russia seemed to be swelling in pride and power, ready to devour us. When England seemed a threat to our peace, we reacted by rejecting her newspapers, her goods, her politicians and her soldiers. At present many people see a threat from within as well. For some it is the threat of organisations of armed citizens, for others it is the encroachment of public authorities into private liberties. Over all is the terrible threat of nuclear warfare if any of the powers of this world become so ambitious, or so desperate, as to feel the need of it.

Thinking about peace, then, has taken on a new urgency, in many places also a new depth. There are Christians who realise that peace is not to be had just for the praying, and not to be had either for all the negotiating in the world; there must be both. Our appeal to God must be validated by our using our own resources to create peace. Such ideas will ideally be reflected in our worship, understanding what peace really means, longing for peace, promises of peace, the commitment to working creatively for peace.

The Christian cannot stand aside from the struggle to create peace. Indeed because of his endowments and gifts, he has a special privilege of doing many good things for peace. In the liturgy of the Church the theme of peace is evident in every act of worship. In asking for the presence of Christ in the Eucharist we ask for the peace which only he can bring with him.

Peace and unity are connected; often the disturbance of our peace is caused by old unities breaking up, by attempts to create new unities which many of the people greatly fear. There has, then, to be some focus for our longing for peace, some centre which holds in spite of all the disturbance, some ultimate unchanging hope. This we find only in God.

God does not give peace against our will or in face of our resistance. He creates peace, and it is for us to bring together the elements of longing, of expectancy, of hope which will make it possible to receive God's peace, to share it with each other and to celebrate it in worship.

In our ritual prayer there are two kinds of situation provided for. One is when we are at peace, or believe we have peace as good as we can expect; our prayer asks for the preservation of peace, while there is always the underlying fear that our peace may be taken away or that it may rest on shaky foundations — we need reminders of what real peace is and we need to recall the presence of God who is our peace. The other situation is when we are at war and we ask for deliverance. We acknowledge that we have not created the conditions for God's peace in the past, we announce our willingness to make a new life, we celebrate our hope that, however dark the present, it can be redeemed.

One or other of these various themes may be uppermost in our private and public prayer at any given time. All of them are there whenever we ask for peace. Together with them there is the vitalising theme of forgiveness. It is God's forgiveness of our divisiveness, our forgiveness of each other's offensiveness, our asking pardon of God and of our fellow citizens for whatever we have done against them, whether we did it in good faith or bad.

If at present Christians accuse themselves and each other of prayer for peace which is too naive, it may be because some of the elements are forgotten. If there is truth in the accusation it may be because we Christians have lost hold of the realities of past and future. We have been too afraid to accept the reality of what our past has been, too fearful to believe in a vision of the future.

Our reflection on God's word of peace is part of our celebration of the good and the true in a world of painful change.

II COMMENTARY ON READINGS

A. OLD TESTAMENT

1. *Is 9:1-6.* The long continuing alternation between war and peace, between misery and prosperity. In their misery people are as helpless as men in the dark, where they can see neither how to work nor the fruits of their labours. They greet peace as joyfully as they greet the dawn,

and just as helplessly. In such darkness death is felt in the air and the coming of light brings reassurance. The landscape has not yet changed, but people can see their way and they know that God is still with them. Now they can work and the earth God has given will yield its fruit.

But the joy they feel is the joy of achievement, as when the harvest is safe, the victory won. There is also the symbolic destruction of all the horrors of the past, the heavy yoke, the tyrant's rod, the flags and the unhappy, bloodstained symbols of war. God who allowed the darkness and death will give the peace of achievement and the security people feel in it.

By a strange paradox it will be a child who appears as the bringer of God's peace. The men who sow and reap, who make war, who hate and fear will bow before him and he will be a prince not of war but of peace, the wise ruler who will never yield to war, nor make it, and will reign for ever.

2. *Is 32:15-20.* Man is warlike, proud in his own achievements, apt to forget that his security does not lie in weapons and wealth. It is a hard land with hard hearted people whose hardness guarantees the ever recurring cycle of violence. The hail storm which cuts like rapier and drives poor people fearful into their houses also helps to break up the hard land and makes aggressive people afraid too. It may be necessary for hearts to be broken before the Spirit can enter in.

But when he does, God's gift of peace is not the kind men win by their niggardly negotiations and bargaining. It is fruitful and generous. It is a rich harvest, which by a miracle is created even from the hardest of earth; so abundant that even the richest of human achievements seem little by comparison.

But in this peace of God, the values we have will be renewed too. Loyalty can be a warlike thing, adherence to a ruler or a party with the promise of fighting to come. In God's renewal loyalty is for peace, not war. The peace which God gives is not meant for the security of princes but for the ease and plenty of the poor. The princes have their stone walls to protect them. The poor need only the presence and the love of God.

3. *Is 57:15-19.* Here is the overwhelming forgivenss of God.

The imagery is contrast between God's way and the way of the human rulers of the earth. His name inspires reverence, not revulsion, his house is for ever, not decaying like theirs. He does not live in the heights only to descend for conquest; he lives both in the heights and in the soul of the poor. The rulers may command the poor to fall down or die, he bids them rise up and live. They will come down only to claim what is due to them, he will often forget his claims. There will be

no spite in him, but forgiveness even for those who may well betray
him again.

But God, for all his forgiving, can still emulate the rulers in severity.
Like them he will strike down those who offend, will not bestow the
royal glance of favour on them, will allow them to stray into paths
where his protection will not be available. But through it all, these
creatures are still his, even when they do not serve him well. He will be
different from the rulers in forgiving offence even in the knowledge of
future wrongdoing. He created all the people, he will redeem them all.

If God's favour were reserved for those who only do well, we should
despair. His forgiveness is our hope and peace.

B. NEW TESTAMENT READINGS

1. *Phil 4:6-9*. We often say that God as revealed in the Old Testament is
a God of wrath, as though his forgiveness and love were revealed only
from the coming of Christ. On the contrary, God's dealings with people
before Christ, as revealed in the Old Testament books, show him perpetually forgiving, forever promising, always fulfilling in spite of all our
waywardness. Even our own fault does not alienate us from him for
ever. St Paul learned the lesson of the Scriptures well; his vision of God
was enriched by his contact with those who saw Christ and by his own
intimate loving communication with God.

Here in his letter to the Philippians he gives his own witness to what
God's peace means.

God's presence is perpetual. Nothing should take away the confidence
which that brings. However terrible the labour and frightening the prospect, our worship should be in thanksgiving. In the midst of our asking
and beseeching we thank him not only for the things he has provided,
but for his being with us. This awareness of God's presence gives us
inner peace, no matter what may be going on in our world. Like all
good things, this gift of inner peace comes through and with and in
Jesus Christ, the child of promise, the prince of peace. As God promised
in the Isaiah prophecies, the peace is generous, so generous that we
could not even think adequately of it.

Because we have God among us, and because his presence is the
foundation of our peace, we should not be for ever talking about our
miseries. That would be to deny our hope, in a way to deny God and
his presence. Every word we utter is a celebration of something. If the
only words we utter are laden with doom, remembrances of past
wrongs and of future hopelessness we are not celebrating God; we are
celebrating our belief that our world is entirely and only what we make
of it. There is more to it than that, much more.

If we have hope we shall reflect upon it and talk about it. All that is true and good, all that is gracious and right must be celebrated because we owe it to God to remember and take joy in his gifts. It is not through the organisations we construct or the deals we make that peace is created. It is by what we say and do as persons before God that the rough ways are made smooth and the crooked ways straight so that God may be welcomed where he is most willing to go.

God's peace is not our creation. But our labour can open the way for it to come.

2. *Col 3:12-15.* God's generosity is not like that of a ruler who takes specially good care of his subjects. He makes it possible for his subjects to be generous in their turn, models of his own generosity. That may seem a trite saying to us now. But if we were very sensitive to God's presence in us we might pause at this passage in the letter to the Colossians, astounded by the revelation it contains. In the prayer to the Father which Jesus gave us we ask that our forgiveness of each other may be in some way comparable to his forgiveness of us. Perhaps, through saying it so often, we have become insensitive to what that means. The history of God's dealings with man shows him as condescending, gentle, patient. His invitation to us is not just: Serve me and I will treat you well; but rather: Come and learn how to be like me in all these ways.

There were times when man's ambition to be like God made him vicious, overbearing and bloody; he thought only of God's power and judgment. To be like God is to share his gift of generosity. To be like God is a gift more likely to be given to victims than to victors.

To make sure that God will share his choicest gifts, not only may we bear with one another, forgive one another, be patient and unassuming. We have also the possibility to love, to reach out to one another and by our word, our touch and our regard give a new joy to those whom God has joyfully created.

3. *Jas 3:13-18.* In Ireland we have become bitterly aware of the kind of peace we are likely to wish upon our fellow citizens, and of the methods we are likely to use to achieve it. There is a bitter jealousy between those who have power and those who have not; there is rivalry between parties and factions; there is boasting that our traditions are better than theirs, that our solutions to political and economic problems are wise and generous, other solutions mean and selfish. St James in his letter is scathing in his judgment of what we say and do. That kind of wisdom, he says, is materialistic and fit only for devils. The scriptures, written for our enlightenment, are God's word not only about what was said and done thousands of years ago, but about what we may still say and do today. Now, as then, such jealousies and rivalry bring their own

reward, 'disorder and every kind of defect'.

What is the remedy? It is not to ask for peace without opening the way for it, or to demand peace from others while creating disorder ourselves.

If we conducted our arguments about politics, economics and religion according to the guidelines of St James we should soon make a Christian revolution. Courtesy would replace attack, serenity and single-mindedness would replace deviousness. Anxiety to conquer would give way to willingness to share. The Christian revolution could begin the moment we face our opponents and ask, 'What is it you want? How can I help you achieve it?'

Perhaps within our present structures where competition is built into almost everything we do, even our learning, recreation and worship, it is too much to expect us to ask such questions with sincerity. But asking them is not giving in to anarchy or to defeat. If there is serenity and mercy, acceptance and love we can find 'the better part' together. Among us Christians there need not be victory for one and defeat for the other. There may be achievement for both.

'Peace is the seed-ground of holiness, and those who make peace will win its harvest.'

C. RESPONSORIAL PSALMS
Psalm 84: 9-14.
Psalm 121.
Psalm 71:2-3, 7-8, 12-13.

The psalms are the singing of the people who cry out in alarm, in fear, in hope. In our worship as in the whole history of God's dealings with us, there is a refrain repeated over and over, favour, betrayal, anger, forgiveness.

One of the most strengthening insights we receive from our scriptures is that there is no such thing as a purely local tyranny, or a purely local struggle towards peace. In every case it is part of the continuing alternation of good and evil, of power and sharing. With even a local tyranny the whole of God's earth is soiled. With even a local struggle towards peace the whole of creation is at least a little renewed. The psalms translate all the local struggles, the local victories and defeats, into their real world — the world of God and man constantly in dialogue.

What we engaged in is not our struggle *for* peace. . .

It is the world's struggle *towards* peace. . .

D. GOSPELS

1. *Mt 5:1-12.* A Christian revolution needs Christian revolutionaries, and a Christian revolutionary programme. In the fifth chapter of St Matthew's Gospel we read the programme. Everything overturns. The kingdom for the poor, the inheritance for those who do not push their claims, comfort for those who seem furthest from it. As for the peace-makers, they will not be seen as weaklings who want peace because they are afraid of fighting; they are God's family, whose moral power is secured in very different ways.

It is by no means simply a matter of accepting the harsh things people do to you. The programme for peace is more demanding than that. It is a strange commentary on how we have treated each other that 'peace with justice' has to be emphasised so much, as if there could be any other kind of peace on offer. Justice is only the beginning of peace, generosity makes it alive.

2. *Mt 5:38-48.* In the Old Testament writings we see the fullness of peace as God's gift, expressed by flowing streams and abundant crops. In this teaching of Christ in Matthew 5 it takes a strange turn, and a frightening one. Building defences, securely locking doors and inventing prohibitions is not a real defence. The only real defence is to make our-selves vulnerable and to challenge our opponents to deny God and strike. The reason why more people do not kill is not that our punish-ments are so severe. It is because God has spoken and said: Thou shalt not. The rash ones walk in the open with no defences except the one that counts, the presence of God, their faith in it and their confidence in the inherent good of their fellow men. Some will fall victim of their rashness; the majority will show they are right. Christ did it that way; the pacifists are among those who try to follow. What the rest of us have to do is support and encourage those who do such things and to make sure that they do not fall victim more often than they need to.

Arrangements are made by the astute. Peace is made by the good.

3. *Jn 14:23-29.*

4. *Jn 20:19-23.*

What Jesus offered was not simply success in negotiating peace. He did not promise that Christians would be more successful than others in political 'horse trading'. His peace was to be of quite a different kind. We ought not to be disappointed when Christians get up from the nego-tiating table with a miserable travesty of peace. They have no more ability for that kind of peace than anyone else.

What they have ability for in a special way is to recognise sacred moments. That is, they can through the gift of the Spirit recognise when the time has come for an act of generosity which is healing. The moment when the thought of forgiveness comes is a sacred moment. The moment when it is offered is another. The moment when people accept each other, forgiving and forgiven, is yet another. From those sacred moments a whole new life can be created. Jesus said that the peace he talked about was his to give. It was so because it resided in him, independent of everything happening in the world about him. He implied that the same was true of us. Peace is not created by manipulating outside events and people. It is by drawing on our own rich resources which God gave us in creation and enriched in redemption.

The moment when the word of God is recognised and taken to heart, when a person does not 'let my sayings pass him by' is the moment of insight which our Lord refers to in this passage from St John. It will be followed by another sacred moment when the Spirit will come to 'make all things plain'.

Nowadays we are recapturing some of the serenity of the encounters of Christ and his followers. For a long time we wished each other peace only in the most formal way. More and more the word 'peace' is appearing in the letters we write, in our greetings at Christmas, in words spoken to each other. It is a sign of the times. When we read in the Gospels, for example in John 20:19-23, that this was the greeting of Jesus to his friends we realise that in so many ways we are reaching back to the bright origins of our faith. What we are looking to is not only the purity of our doctrine.

It is also the purity of our peace.

For the Sanctification of Human Work

John Brady, S.J.

I INTRODUCTION

Most people spend the greater part of life at work. Work is the means by which we earn our livelihood, but it is more than that. It is the principal means by which we make our contribution to the building up of society, and play our part in the web of interlocking activities by which the community in which we live provides for its recurring needs and strives towards a better future. This community is in fact an ever widening circle of people which spreads from the local to the national to the international scene. When one reflects on it, many of the ordinary household goods we use every day embody the work of people thousands of miles away. Similarly a wide circle of people receive the benefits of our work. By our work, our social contribution, we are linked to our fellow-countrymen and to the world community of mankind at large. Work is one of the ways in which we are oriented dynamically towards our fellow-man. The kind of work we do is the precise way in which that orientation is given a practical expression. The way we do our work, the quality of effort we put into it, determines the quality of our social contribution. By our work we give meaning to our lives and find our place in the universe. The challenge that our work involves can help to develop our whole personality and give our lives a sense of self-fulfilment.

It has to be faced, however, that there are many unsolved problems about work. Many people find their work boring and monotonous. They experience a sense of helplessness, of inability to have any influence over the situation in which they work which leads to alienation and frustration. The problem of unemployment, of not being able to provide work for everyone who wants to work, is a pressing unsolved problem all over the world today.

So while there are positive things to be said about the value of work and its meaning, there are negative realities to be faced also. In confronting the human situation in its many-sided complexity, the Christian is stimulated to reflect on his own commitment to the task of contributing to human society, to building up the social order as a means to total human development. The Lectionary Readings on the theme 'For the Santification of Human Work' give the principal Scriptural texts which encourage our reflection.

II COMMENTARY ON READINGS

A. OLD TESTAMENT READINGS

1. *Gen 1:26−2:3.* The text links the creation of man and woman in the image and likeness of God with dominion over the rest of God's handiwork, as it were. The bibical text speaks of this dominion chiefly in the context of providing man with a source of food. However the notion can reasonably be extended to include the whole process by which man takes the material world around him into his charge, explores its potentialities and develops them. God gives the world to us in a very raw state. As the story of human civilisation unfolds, the almost unlimited possibilities it contains are gradually discovered and developed by man's ingenuity and effort. The story seems to be nowhere near its end. The material universe contains many mysteries, vast unrealised potential to meet human needs and to enrich human life. A sense of wonder at God's creation, its richness and complexity, is a natural response to contemplation of it.

2. *Gen 2:4-9, 15.* This older version of the creation story hints at the ambivalence of man in his relation to the material world. The garden contains the tree of the knowledge of good and evil. The allegory brings out the moral challenge at the centre of the effort to develop the material world. Instead of development leading to progress in human welfare, it can lead to a display of greed, hostility and an increased power of destructiveness. Our own times present us with the scandal of an enormously expensive arms race while millions are left without the essentials of a decent human life although the technology to provide it is already in existence. To try to get the potentialities of our technology brought to the service of human needs is a part of Christian concern in the modern world.

B. NEW TESTAMENT READING

1. *2 Thess 3:6-12, 16.* This text strikes a stern note. St Paul took a dim view of idleness. 'If any one will not work, let him not eat'. Work is a Christian duty, not to be passed over lightly. This text is quite relevant in our day. The welfare state seeks to protect all citizens against inabili-

ty to work due to involuntary unemployment or illness. There is a temptation, to which not a few succumb, to take unfair advantage of this effort to create a more humane society by drawing on available benefits when there is no real need to do so. This puts an unfair burden on those who work and pay taxes, and is a form of exploitation of one's fellowman.

C. RESPONSORIAL PSALMS

1. *Ps 89*. The psalm brings out the contrast between the shortness of human life and the slowly unfolding purposes of God. The world develops slowly under God's providence. Each generation makes a contribution to the totality of human wisdom, then passes on. There are many reverses and falterings in the gradually ascent of man towards a truly civilised life, which needs the help of God's grace. We pray for the gift of wisdom, for a share in the love of God for all the works of his hand, and that we may catch a glimpse of his glory in them.

2. *Ps 126*. This psalm stresses that God must be with us in all we do. We do not work in an environment totally under our control. Man proposes, God disposes. All our endeavours are fraught with uncertainty. We pray for the watchful guidance of God over our work.

D. GOSPELS

1. *Mt 6:31-34*. This extract from the Sermon on the Mount warns us against over-preoccupation with the fruits of our work, in a word, against the acquisitiveness of the consumer society. A Christian should have a measure of detachment in his attitude to material goods. His first concern is the kingdom of God and its righteousness, that is in living a life marked by justice towards all, and in responding to the love God has shown to us. The Gospel words are a healthy antidote to needless anxiety about things that can often be done without, and being so wrapped up in trivialities that we have no time for God. We need, of course, to have a responsible attitude towards life and our material needs, co-operating with God by our work in an attitude of trust.

2. *Mt 25:14-30*. The parable of the talents brings out the fact that everyone has his own gifts from God and that each of us must use to our best ability. Everyone has a contribution to make to the work of God's world. We are generally happiest when we have found a task that stretches our abilities to the full, which presents us with a challenge, yet one to which we can successfully rise. It is the best course both for our own self-actualisation and for the good of society to try to work towards a role in society in which our abilities are fully stretched. From a religious viewpoint we can have the sense of using fully the gifts God

has given us, and the opportunities his providence puts in our path. We can look forward to his consoling judgment of commendation at the end of our life if we make this the pattern of our life. Our work can be the expression of our commitment to God's world. If on the other hand we neglect our gifts, throw away our opportunities and make no worthwhile contribution to the total human effort, we are in effect rejecting God's gifts; perhaps even rejecting God himself in an absolute sense and so turning away from his call and his love.

III THEMATIC GROUPING

Theme: By our work we share in the development of God's creation, work to meet our needs in justice, and find self-fulfilment in making our contribution to the total human effort under God's provident care.

        Old Testament Reading 1.
        New Testament Reading 1.
        Responsorial Psalm 1.
        Gospel 2.

For the Starving People of the World

Michael Martin

I INTRODUCTION

Are we looking at this 'Starving People' section of the Lectionary because we feel that the hunger of half the world's population is today's greatest scandal? Or has a flood, a drought, an earthquake or a volcanic eruption caught the imagination of the media and hence of our community? Or did that hunger and oppression erupt in violence and leave us with thousands of starving and unwanted refugees? Maybe we just want to explore the treasures of the revised liturgy and prepare for Mission Sunday, World Health Day, the Lenten Fast, conventions of voluntary organisations, meetings of missionaries, overseas volunteers or development fund-raisers?

These dramatic events in the poor countries and the special occasions at home help to remind us of the 'starving peoples' of the world. We look at these people and their food: getting enough just to survive is their biggest problem; their work (for which they are usually underpaid, and are denied any real bargaining power) or their lack of work (without unemployment benefits); their education (nearly half the adult population of the world cannot read or write; their homes (wood, wattle, cardboard and tin) and the homeless (refugees, beggars) – in a word, just who they are, where they are and how they live. A fuller treatment of the food crisis would involve a detailed examination of the wider development crisis and the injustices in the present world economic system.

The poor around the world

The spectre of poverty has never been totally banished from our 'Western' societies; perhaps it will never be. From time to time surveys are published which bring home to people that in the slum areas of our cities many people are still living dangerously close to the border line of hunger – if not starvation – four million in Britain alone, according to the latest survey. The Bishops of Ireland writing on Development in 1973 remind us: 'It is true there are inequalities within our own society

176

and we must never forget that some of our people are living in poverty. But our problems are small indeed when we compare them with the problems of the developing countries ' (par. 3). 'There are many countries in the Third World today where the majority of the people go to bed hungry every night, where the majority have never learned to read or write, where a baby born today can expect to die twenty years earlier than an Irish baby' (par. 4).

It is generally acknowledged that two-thirds of the world's people are living in poverty. In Asia every country except Japan comes under this heading. Only Australia and New Zealand are regarded as reasonably affluent in the South Pacific. Amost every country in Africa has its people living in poverty, while in North and South America only the U.S.A. and Canada have most of their people living in some degree of comfort.

For every child born today to parents in the developed countries seven children are born in the poor countries, commonly called 'The Third World', and most of those seven will grow up in poverty. Poverty is still the normal condition of mankind, and those of us who live in comfort in developed societies are the exceptions. Although we in the rich countries have only 34% of the world's population we possess 90% of the world's income. We also have about 90% of the world's financial resources, and more than 90% of the world's scientists and technicians. We produce 80% of the world's protein, including 70% of its meat and we also eat it.

What is life like for the average citizen in one of the developing countries today? To begin with, he is probably not getting enough to eat. Because there is much less food available per person, his diet will include fewer calories than the 2,500 daily intake that nutritional experts consider necessary for proper health. Lack of vitamins and minerals makes him vulnerable to many diseases.

Malnutrition is the day-in day-out erosion of health that lack of food causes. There are 300 million children in the world physically or mentally handicapped because of malnutrition (U.N. Report). More than 15,000 people die of starvation every day. The horrors caused by hunger are worse than anything science-fiction depicts. The instinct for self-preservation is the strongest and most basic urge of all living things. We live in a world where many are condemned to a life of crime in order to survive..

'I didn't have any breakfast and walked around half dizzy. The daze of hunger is worse than that of alcohol. The daze of alcohol makes us sing, but the one of hunger makes us shake. I know how horrible it is to have only air in the stomach. . .' (Carolina Maria de Jasus).

'In the bad lands of Gujarat and Maharashtra last week, I talked to

people in several villages who ought, by the standards of overfed Western man, to be either dying or dead. Some nursing mothers in a village
70 miles south of Poona had eaten nothing for as much as four days at
a stretch and many in other villages were eating only every other day.
When they did eat it was no more than a single chapatty – the rough
grain pancake that is north India's staple food. No vegetables, no oil,
no milk, no sugar, in many cases not even a spoonful of chile falvour-
ing' (David Holden in *The Sunday Times*, 27 May 1973).

Since the Second World War the work of the World Health Organisation (a United Nations agency) has almost wiped out killer diseases
like bubonic plague, cholera, malaria and yellow fever, but millions of
people still suffer from other crippling diseases – leprosy, bilharzia
trachoma. Their chances of ever seeing a doctor are small because they
live in underdeveloped countries. In Africa, there are about 9,200
patients per doctor, in Southern Asia, 5,200; in the richer industrialised
countries, there are on average 750 patients per doctor. Life expectation is shorter too; in Kenya it is 40-45 years, compared with 68 for
men and 74 for women in Western Europe.

Inhabitants of developing countries are far more likely to work on
the land than those in rich countries. In India, 70% of the population is
engaged in agriculture; in England, 5%. Because of the population size
there is not enough land to go round. People may therefore decide to
try their luck in the nearest town, but many thousands of others will
have had the same idea and there are unlikely to be jobs there. Many
thousands beg for a living on the streets. Yet they know from the
radio and the cinema about the life lived in the West. Their hopes and
prospects are very low. In bitterness, they may well turn to violence as
the only way to improve their lives.

The starving people and the Christian

'We who are followers of Jesus Christ must continually try to shape our
lives by his teaching. He taught us to love one another, to feed the
hungry, to clothe the naked, to care for the sick. He said: "As you did
it to one of the least of these my brethren, you did it to me" (Mt
25:40). We know that we cannot claim to love God if we do not have
love of our fellow men. St John tells us: "If anyone has the world's
goods and sees his brother in need, yet closes his heart against him how
does God's love abide in him? Little children, let us not love in word
and speech, but in deed and truth" (1 Jn 3:17-18). (Irish Bishops on
Development, par. 10 & 11).

In the Bible poverty is a scandalous condition inimical to human
dignity and therefore contrary to the will of God. This rejection of
poverty is seen very clearly in the vocabulary used. 'Indigent', 'weak',

'bent over' and 'the wretched one driven into begging' are terms
which well express a degrading human situation, and indignation at that
situation and its causes. The first cause is the injustice of the oppressors;
poverty is caused by the inaction of others. The prophets condemn
every kind of abuse, every form of keeping the poor in poverty or of
creating new poor people. They do not merely allude to situations; they
point the finger at those who are to blame. Fraudulent commerce and
exploitation are condemned (Mic 6:10-11), as well as the hoarding of
lands (Ezek 3:9-11), the violence of the ruling classes (2 Kings 23:30,
35), slavery (Neh 5:1-5), unjust taxes (Amos 5:11-12), and unjust fun-
ctionaries (Jer 5:28). In the New Testament oppression by the rich is
also condemned, especially in Luke (6:24-25; 12:13-21; 16:19-31; 18:
18-26) and in James (2:5-9; 4:13-17; 5:16).

But it is not simply a matter of denouncing poverty. The Bible
speaks of positive and concrete measures to prevent poverty from
becoming established among the People of God. In Leviticus and Deut-
eronomy there is very detailed legislation designed to prevent the accu-
mulation of wealth and the consequent exploitation. It is said, for
example, that what remains in the fields after the harvest and the
gathering of olives and grapes should not be collected; it is for the alien,
the orphan, and the widow (Deut 24:19-21). Even more, the fields
should not be harvested to the very edge so that something remains for
the poor and the aliens (Lev 23:22). The sabbath, the day of the Lord,
has a social significance; it is a day of rest for the slave and the alien
(Ex 23:12). The triennial tithe is not to be carried to the temple; rather
it is for the alien, the orphan and the widow (Deut 14:28-29). Interest
on loans is forbidden (Lev 25:35-37). Other important measures include
the sabbath year and the jubilee year. Every seven years the fields will
be left to lie fallow 'to provide food for the poor of your people' (Ex
23:11), although it is recognised that this duty is not always fulfilled
(Lev 26:34-35). After seven years the slaves were to regain their freedom (Ex 21:2-6) and debts were to be pardoned (Deut 15:1-18). This is
also the meaning of the jubilee year of Lev 25:10-17. 'It was,' writes De
Vaux, 'a general emancipation . . . of all the inhabitants of the land.
The fields lay fallow: every man re-entered his ancestral property, i.e.
the fields and houses which had been alienated returned to their original
owners' (*Ancient Israel: Its Life and Institutions*, p. 175).

Behind these texts, we can see three principal reasons for this vigor-
ous repudiation of poverty:

1. Poverty contradicts the very meaning of the Mosaic religion. Moses
led his people out of the slavery, exploitation and alienation of Egypt
so that they might inhabit a land where they could live with human
dignity. In Moses' mission of liberation there was a close relationship

between this religion and worship on the one hand and the elimination of poverty and servitude on the other. (Ex 16:6-8; Deut 5:15; Lev 25: 42). The prophets in particular continually referred to these origins of the people, and pointed out that acceptance of poverty and injustice is to fall back into the conditions of slavery before the liberation from Egypt.

2. Poverty and injustice go against the mandate of Genesis (1:26; 2:15). Man is made in the image and likeness of God and is destined to dominate the earth. He transforms himself only by transforming nature and thus entering into relationships with other men. In this way, he becomes conscious of his dignity and his creative power and ability. He becomes more fully human.

3. Man is the sacrament of God: to oppress the poor is to offend God himself; to know God is to work for justice among men.

Hence, the mission of the future Messiah will be to proclaim justice and free the oppressed: 'good news to the poor, liberty to the captives' (Is 61:1). The God who pulled down the powerful from their thrones and exalted the lowly, who filled the hungry with good things and sent the rich away empty (Lk 1:52) will appear as the perfect fulfilment of the ideal king. The poor are blessed, are happy because the kingdom of God has begun: 'The time has come; the kingdom of God is upon you' (Mk 1:15). The kingdom of God necessarily implies the re-establishment of justice in this world. The time of hunger and poverty and slavery and exploitation and apartheid is ending, and a world of brotherhood is being created. They are blessed because the Messiah will open the eyes of the blind and give bread to the hungry. If Jesus called the poor blessed he also said that it would be very difficult for the rich to enter the kingdom of Heaven and that one cannot serve both God and money (Lk 6:13-15, 24-25). The most radical words of Jesus on the fundamental importance of the love of one's neighbour are found in Matthew's account of the last judgment (Mt 25:31-46): salvation or damnation of every man depends finally on his attitude and actions towards the poor and destitute.

The Old Testament usually placed the salvation of men within the horizon of this temporal life. The New Testament, however, gives a clear vision of man's salvation beyond history and beyond our world.

Jesus presents his mission (Lk 4:16-20) by reading from Isaiah, but the great new factor is that he makes of these despised and marginal men his 'brothers'. He makes himself one with the poor and the helpless, the hungry, the destitute, the starving people. Every man who finds himself in such a situation is the brother of Christ. Whatever is done for them is done for Christ himself. Whoever gives effective help to these 'brothers' of Jesus belongs to his kingdom; whoever leaves them in their hunger and misery excludes himself from the kingdom. For us Christians, there is a very definite and demanding message: it is Christ whom we encounter in the person of everyone who is hungry.

The document of the 1971 Synod of Bishops on 'Justice in the World' sums up the message and action of Jesus in these words:

'By this action and teaching Christ united in an indivisible way the relationship of man to God and the relationships of man to other men. Christ lived his life in the world as a total giving of himself to God for the salvation and liberation of men. In his preaching he proclaimed the fatherhood of God towards all men and the intervention of God's justice on behalf of the needy and the oppressed (Lk 6:21-23). In this way, he identified himself with his "least brethren", as he stated: "In so far as you did this to one of the least of these brothers of mine you did it to me" (Mt 25:40).'

Luke presents the community of goods in the early Church as an ideal: 'All whose faith had drawn them together held everything in common' (Acts 2:44); 'not a man of them claimed any of his possessions as his own, but everything was held in common' (Acts 4:33). They did this with a profound unity, one 'in heart and soul' (Acts 4:32). But this was not a question of erecting poverty as an ideal, but rather of seeing to it that there were no poor: 'They had never a needy person among them, because all who had property in land or houses sold it, brought the proceeds of the sale, and laid the money at the feet of the apostles; it was then distributed to any who stood in need' (Acts 4:34-35). The meaning of the community of goods is clear: to eliminate poverty because of love of the poor person.

St James (2:14-18) says that without good deeds in favour of the poor, the profession of Christian faith is useless and fails to save. He warns the faithful of the terrible fate of those who abuse riches and gives consolation to those now oppressed by the rich (5:1-6). For Paul, redemption means the establishment of brotherhood and the removal of all barriers separating men — social, cultural and racial. Faith in Christ is a life which is summed up and culminates in the love of one's neighbour. It is a love which implies the observance of justice and is put into effect through effective help to the needy (2 Cor 8:8-15). 'According to St Paul, the whole of the Christian life is summed up in faith effecting that love and service of neighbour which involve fulfilment of the demands of justice. The Christian lives under the interior law of liberty, which is a permanent call to man to turn away from self-sufficiency to confidence in God and from concern for self to a sincere love of neighbour. Thus takes place his genuine liberation and the gift of himself for the freedom of others' (Justice in the World).

II COMMENTARY ON THE READINGS

A. OLD TESTAMENT READINGS

1. *Deut 24:17-22.* Moses reviews the various laws that are to govern Israel's life in the promised land. 'Never forget that you were slaves in Egypt': poverty contradicts the very meaning of the Mosaic religion. Measures to prevent poverty are listed.

2. *Job 31:16-20, 24-25, 31-32.* Job is accused by his friends of being a sinner since God always rewards good and punishes evil. But Job is convinced of his own innocence, and knows he has been a good and upright man. This passage is from Job's final statement of his case, where he says he has never refused help to the poor, the widows, the orphans, those without clothes, strangers or travellers.

3. *Is 58:6-11.* The author of the second part of Isaiah reproaches the people who believe they have God's favour because they observe the prescribed rules of fasting, and he shows that 'to love one's neighbour' means to observe the duties of justice. The God of the Covenant rejects all religious worship that precludes the observance of justice. The ethical dimension of justice is part of the relationship between man and the God of the Covenant. Anyone who participates in ritual worship, while robbing his neighbour of his rights does not really 'know' God.

B. NEW TESTAMENT READINGS

In the Old Testament justice and the love of men play a part in the very relationship of man with God. Christian revelation so links the two that love of neighbour becomes the concrete and the only authentic fulfilment of communion with God. In the words of the Synod:

'Christian love of neighbour and justice cannot be separated. For love implies an absolute demand for justice, namely a recognition of the dignity and rights of one's neighbour. Justice attains its inner fullness only in love. Because every man is a truly visible image of the invisible God and a brother of Christ, the Christian finds in every man God himself and God's absolute demand for justice and love' (Justice in the World, 1971 Synod of Bishops).

1. *Acts 11:27-30.* The Church, the new community, was united by the same faith in 'heart and soul'. This deep union, the fruit of the Spirit of Christ, led even to a voluntary sharing of all material goods: '. . . owned everything in common; they sold their goods and possessions and shared out the proceeds among themselves according to what each one needed; . . . None of their members was ever in want. . .' (cf. Acts 2:44-45; 4:32-35). In the reading from chapter eleven famine is predicted

and the immediate response of the disciples is that each gives what he can. Brotherhood and solidarity are emphasised.

2. *2 Cor 8:1-5, 9-15.* Effective help of the needy is always the hallmark of the Christian community. Be like Jesus in our charity — giving everything. Christian poverty, an expression of love, is solidarity with the poor and is a protest against poverty.

3. *2 Cor 9:6-15.* God rewards the cheerful giver. Popular expressions like 'You will never miss what you give away' and 'The more you give the more you get' could claim a scriptural basis in this passage from Paul. Certainly giving and sharing make people thankful, and the Christian can be described as the one who gives thanks. All good things come from God.

C. RESPONSORIAL PSALMS

1. *Ps 21:23-24.* Thanksgiving, in which the community is invited to share. Worldwide worship of Yahweh is proclaimed.

2. *Ps 106:2-9.* A summons to praise God, and a prayer for Israel's prosperity. Points back to Mosaic covenant and the exodus event.

3. *Ps 111:1-9.* Another hymn of praise — because of the greatness of God's works, as seen in the historical events, e.g. manna and quail in the desert.

D. GOSPELS

1. *Mt 25:31-46.* The parable of the final judgment seems to many to summarise the essence of the Gospel message. Three points emerge: (a) the stress on communion and brotherhood as the ultimate meaning of human life. We will be definitively judged by our love for men (1 Cor 13), by our capacity to create brotherly conditions of life; (b) the insistence on a love which is manifested in concrete actions (feeding the hungry, giving drink to the thirsty, etc.). The good Samaritan in Luke 10:25-37 illustrates this point well; (c) the revelation of the human mediation necessary to reach the Lord. We find the Lord in our encounters with men, especially the poor, the hungry, the exploited. An act of love towards them is an act of love towards God.

2. *Mk 6:34-44.* The very well-known story of how Jesus fed the 5,000: 'His heart was filled with pity for them . . . so he began to teach them many things'. A comment should be made on the three or four preceding verses which point out how untimely was the arrival of all these people, yet Jesus responded to their needs as they were. Collecting the 'left-overs' (frugality?) may be more and more a Christian response in our wasteful age.

3. *Lk 14:12-14.* Do not invite the rich to your feast — invite the poor.
4. *Lk 16:19-31.* The rich man and Lazarus. Oppression by the rich is frequently condemned in Luke's Gospel. Selfishness and greed, 'luxurious living' are in conflict with the demands of the Gospel.

III THEMATIC GROUPINGS

Liturgical celebrations for 'starving peoples' need preparation. Dramatic presentations of the Exodus event, the life of Job, etc. could be very helpful. Films, slides, personal appearances from people involved in work for the hungry can set the tone for a good celebration. Here our concern is with the selection of texts and that too is important. The eleven texts given in the Lectionary are only suggestions, and those planning the liturgy (hopefully more than just the celebrant) should choose those which mean most to them.

1. *Caring Community.*
Old Testament 3 — Is 58.
Responsorial Psalm 1 — Ps 21.
New Testament 1 — Acts 11 or Acts 4.
Gospel 1 — Mt 25 or Lk 4.
These texts should be powerful in developing a sharing, caring community, open to the needs of the poor; in developing detachment from material goods, hence helping people to re-examine their own lifestyle; promoting the idea of one world, one faith, one God who detests injustice.

2. *Injustice and Hunger.*
A stronger selection on the theme of selfishness, greed and injustice as the causes of hunger might be:
Old Testament — Job 24:2-12, 14.
Responsorial Psalm 2 — Ps 106.
New Testament — Jas 5:1-6.
Gospel 4 — Lk 16.

3. *Thanks for Help.*
On the theme of thanking people for their generosity in helping the hungry:
Old Testament 2 — Job 31.
Responsorial Psalm 3 — Ps 1111.
New Testament 2 — 2 Cor 8 or 3 — 2 Cor 9.
Gospel 2 — Mk 6.

For Refugees and Exiles

Charles O'Malley

I INTRODUCTION

A migrant may be broadly defined as 'any person going to another country with the intention of settling there'. Migration has always been a fact of human history. Earliest man was a nomad. Most countries have a history of movement of people. The oldest writings contain stories of travel. The Old Testament records the wanderings and exile of God's chosen people. More recent history has seen the mass movements of peoples to the new countries – the United States, Canada, South America, Australia and New Zealand. This movement has continued down to present times.

Migratory movement is larger than ever today. Facility of travel and communication, the growth of human population, the uneven development and distribution of the world's resources, together with man's desire to travel and the current universal movement from a rural to an urban environment, are all contributory factors.

Wars and their aftermaths also uproot people. The two great wars of this century left millions homeless. The more recent conflicts in Asia, Africa and the Middle East have swelled the tide of refugees. Natural calamities, earthquakes, floods, hurricanes, droughts, famines also take their toll, destroying people's homes and forcing them to seek refuge elsewhere. Political unrest and upheavals also cause people to leave their homes and seek refuge in other countries. The number of ideological migrants (political refugees) from Eastern Europe alone numbers a million. In recent years vast numbers have been forced to leave countries such as China, Cuba, Uganda, Chile, Vietnam, Cambodia, Angola.

Most migration today is because of economic necessity – the need and urge of man to find work, to survive and to better himself and his family. This accounts for most of the thirteen million migrants in Western Europe.

Add to all these the continuing national and international migrations of South America, the legal and illegal movements of people in Central America, the thousands of students attending foreign universities, the hundreds of thousands of nomads or gypsies who belong to no single country, and one begins to grasp the magnitude and complexity of the present global migrant situation.

While suffering, misunderstanding and antagonism are often the lot of the migrant, it must be borne in mind that in God's providence migration has also brought advantages to humanity. The exile of the Israelites was a period of penance and preparation for Christ's coming. The Diaspora of the Jews after the fall of Jerusalem contributed much to the spread of Christianity in the first century. Similarly the spread of Christianity in the new-world countries came largely through migration. The Pontifical Commission for the Pastoral Care of Migrants noted that migration such as is now taking place 'is a source of reciprocal enrichment for the nations. Over and above national boundaries a more universal society is being built up and the unity of the human family is being fostered'.

The Church's concern for migrants

But migrants by their very condition are vulnerable. Barriers of differences of language, race, culture and tradition have to be overcome. They often meet with prejudice and opposition even to the denial of their fundamental rights. Recent events have shown that in cases of economic crisis they are the first to suffer.

It is for these reasons that the Church in response to the divine command to love all men and especially those in need, has shown at all times a particular concern for migrants.

In August 1953 Pope Pius XII issued the Apostolic Constitution *Exsul Familia* which is known as the 'Magna Charta for Migrants'. The Holy Family fleeing into Egypt is set out as the archetype of every refugee family. The document states that the mission of the Church is 'to offer migrants a comfort in their trials' and 'special care and unremitting aid'. It then proceeds to set out norms and procedures for the spiritual care of migrants. Particular mention is made of the *International Catholic Migration Commission* established in Geneva in 1951 'whose function is to unite and organise existing Catholic Associations and Committees, and to promote, reinforce and coordinate their projects and activities on behalf of migrants and refugees'.

In August 1969 Pope Paul VI issued the *Apostolic Letter and Instruction on the Pastoral Care of those who Migrate*. This was a revision of *Exsul Familia*. While repeating that the pastoral care of migrants had always attracted the motherly care of the Church it points out that the importance of present day migration did not escape the Fathers of the Second Vatican Council. They recommended special solicitude towards those 'who are cut off from ordinary pastoral services as in the case of migrants, exiles and refugees', and exhorted national

episcopal conferences 'to pay energetic attention to the problems confronting these persons, and to provide means for their spiritual assistance'. 'Bishops should manifest their concern for all be they natives,
strangers, or foreigners' for 'in one Spirit we were all baptised into one
body whether Jews or Gentiles, whether slaves or free' (1 Cor 12:13),
'for you are all one in Jesus Christ' (Gal 3:28).

The document identifies the hazards and difficulties amplified by
the size of present migrations. Many difficulties and sufferings arise of
which 'man is at once cause and the victim'. Among these are: tensions
due to economic inequality, differences of mentality and tradition, and
'with respect to the fundamental rights of the person every type of
discrimination, whether social or cultural, whether based on sex, race,
colour, social conditions, language or origin'. These difficulties affect
society and family, and cause problems of religion also. The Church
which is constituted 'that she might bring all men to share in Christ's
saving redemption' has therefore a special concern and competence
here. Man has certain rights as a human person and these should be
respected by all in authority. Some of these rights are enumerated −
the right to a homeland, the right to emigrate, the right to keep one's
native tongue and spiritual heritage. The denial of these rights is unjust.

Migrants must realise that they are involved in the duties of citizens
and of the community. They should accommodate themselves to their
host country, and learn to integrate in their new society. People from
undeveloped countries possessing mental powers and wealth are reminded that their leaving 'deprives their community of the material and
spiritual aid it needs'. Even though they have a right to emigrate, they
also have a duty to contribute to the progress of their home community. Developed countries are encouraged to foster the preparation and
return to the homeland of artisans and students once they have achieved
ability in their fields.

Migration gives the opportunity to the Church to promote unity
among Christians and in the case of non-Christians to be 'a sign which
points out Christ to others'. The People of God have a special duty to
migrant people 'by common cooperative effort . . . to open to all the
road . . . where each man will be loved and helped as his brother, as his
neighbour'. Migration can promote mutual understanding and cooperation, the unity of the human family, and brotherhood among peoples.

In October 1973 the Pontifical Commission for the Pastoral Care of
Migrants and Itinerant Peoples held a meeting of the presidents and
directors of the national emigrant commissions for Europe and issued
an important statement on the state and problems of present day migration, together with practical recommendations for those who work with
migrants. It points out how migratory movement in Europe has

increased enormously. Ethnic and cultural differences have multiplied. Migrants from the so-called Third World often have to live in almost subhuman conditions. Among the injustices encountered by migrants are listed the failure to recognise basic human rights, the division of families, the lack of housing, the difficulties in the way of education of migrant children, the tendency to exploit men as mere instruments of production, nationalist and racial prejudices which sometimes lead to open rejection.

A special appeal for help is made to local churches. Migrations represent an urgent call to the local Churches to become in actual fact what they are theologically. The individual churches share in the mystery of the one universal Church: each church is called on to share the burdens of others. It repeats Vatican II which says 'among all the nations of the earth there is but one People of God . . . for all the faithful scattered throughout the world are in communion with each other in the Holy Spirit'. The laity are reminded that the saving mission of the Church cannot be shouldered by the bishops and priests alone. In their work they need the cooperation in a particular way of lay people. Many questions arising from the mobility of peoples are insoluble without the cooperation of lay people. They are encouraged to help chaplains and missionaries to contact the migrants, to communicate the word of God to them, and to participate actively in the liturgy. In these areas they have opportunities that escape chaplains or missionaries. The laity occupy first place in building up and organising the earthly city in justice and charity according to God's plan.

In view of all this, the document sees emigration as 'a permanent invitation to the local Churches to open up to rediscover the meaning of the earthly pilgrimage'.

Bishops, priests, religious and laity in communion with the Pope and in the light of his teachings are asked to:

1. *Question themselves* if their acts are in harmony with what they publicly announce in their contact with each other in situations where there is indifference, segregation, racism, imposed cultural superiority etc.

2. *Commit themselves* to the full to the creation of an atmosphere favourable to migrants.

3. *Seek the way to announce Jesus Christ*, the only Saviour, within the setting of the events experienced by migrants and those who receive them.

4. *Share all research and efforts* which aim at obtaining greater justice in the condition of migrants according to the Gospel, revealing the Spirit of God which is at work in the hearts of men who are struggling to make the world a more habitable place marked by the spirit of

brotherhood in the hope of eternal life.

5. And in particular to express in practical terms in the celebration of the Eucharist, which is the sacrament of unity and life, the fact that there is only one family.

Local Churches of departure are reminded of their duty to give religious instruction and training to migrants before they go, which will enable them to live up to the values of their faith in the new environment. 'All emigrants should be educated to a genuine and complete concept of the Church'. The Churches of departure should also follow up their migrants by placing missionaries at their disposal, by giving useful information for initial contact, and by keeping in touch with those who are living abroad.

The role of the local Church of arrival is seen as very important. Migrants should be made welcome at local parish level. This can be a means of introducing them to the local ecclesial community. Two extremes to be avoided are isolation of ethnic groups, and forced assimilation. Cooperation between the authorities of the sending and receiving Churches is essential. A friendly, brotherly welcome should be extended not only to Christians not in communion with the Catholic Church but also to migrants of other faiths and beliefs.

In 1976 the International Catholic Migration Commission in response to requests from Pope Paul VI and the Pontifical Commission for Migrants presented its proposed Statute for Migrants. It sets out 'the essential rights from which migrants should benefit'. It appeals to public opinion, the press and mass media to make these rights known so that people at national and local levels would uphold them. It bases them on the universal law of love of God and of fellow creatures, and joins this to the Universal Declaration of Human Rights which declares: 'All human beings are born free and equal in dignity and rights'. The document is presented in the hope that it will be accepted by different governments and become the basis for national and international legislation and agreements.

II COMMENTARY ON READINGS

A. OLD TESTAMENT READINGS

1. *Deut 10:17-19*. Yahweh is the supreme being. He determines all standards and codes of behaviour. He is perfectly fair and just. He demands that justice be done by and for his people. But with his justice goes kindness and compassion and this brings a message of encouragement for the weak and vulnerable. These are epitomised in the orphan

and the widow. Later Christ was to identify himself with such: 'I was a stranger and you made me welcome, naked and you clothed me' (Mt 25:35-36). The Jews should know too what it means to be dependent and lonely for they have been in exile. There is a need for self examination in our attitude to strangers. Often our internal disposition is defensive and suspicious. Externally we can be cold, thoughtless and even unfriendly or unjust.

2. *Deut 24:17-22*. Here we have laid down some practical welfare directives for the care of the poor and needy in what was a primitive agricultural economy. Again and again Yahweh's concern for those 'least ones' is emphasised. We can easily translate those ancient norms into rules for modern society and apply them to our own lives e.g. invite the newcomer to our home, our club; send a worthwhile contribution to the many charities which care for emigrants, refugees and displaced persons; write to someone you know who is away from home etc. The list is endless, but the message is clear.

B. NEW TESTAMENT READINGS

1. *Rom 12:9-16*. The first part of this reading is very suitable for a mixed congregation consisting of members of the established community and emigrants. It first sets forth what real Christian charity should be, sincere, practical and based on mutual respect. It calls for perseverance of effort. It stresses the need of prayer in times of difficulty. It lays special emphasis on sharing and hospitality. It will be easy to point out practical examples of how this can be achieved in any mixed community.

The second part can well be applied to emigrants themselves. They will meet with opposition, even persecution but are to counter it with kindness. Sympathy and understanding are such wonderful virtues and they win through. Real sincerity will never be proud or condescending.

2. *Heb 11:13-16*. This reading emphasises the importance of faith and confidence in God. The great figures of the Old Testament like Abel, Enoch, Noah, Abraham, Sarah were people of outstanding faith and that faith was rewarded by God. They recognised how transitory this life is. They knew that they were only strangers and wanderers on earth, and they looked forward, as indeed all Christians should, to that better heavenly homeland. There is here a message of hope and encouragement for people like migrants who often experience opposition and insecurity. God has prepared for them a city — the heavenly Jerusalem where 'He will wipe away all tears from their eyes; there will be no more death, and no more mourning or sadness. The world of the past has gone' (Rev 21:4).

3. *Heb 13:1-3, 14-16.* This reading, like that from Romans, stresses the importance of practical charity shown in hospitality to strangers and kindness to those who are badly treated. Again a suitable reading for a mixed congregation. It goes well with the first responsorial psalm which is taken from the book of Tobit for it was Tobit's son, Tobias, who entertained Raphael the archangel without knowing it. The reading mentions the universal brotherhood of man — 'you are in one body'. It repeats again that there is no real permanence or security in this world. One can look forward to that only in the life to come. Meanwhile one can best please God by prayer and generosity to others.

C. RESPONSORIAL PSALMS

1. *Tobit 13:1-4, 6-8.* This responsorial psalm is taken from the book of Tobit. The whole of Tobit is a simple, homely story about the providence of God who is with us day by day caring for those who wander or are oppressed. It recounts how the kindness and generosity of Tobit and his son Tobias were rewarded although they had to suffer many hardships. At the end of the story Tobit, who is himself an exile in Nineveh, sings this hymn. He calls on man to praise God for his greatness, to thank him for his benefits and to repent of his sins against him.

2. *Ps 106:1, 33-36, 41-42.* These three verses are part of a long psalm which recounts the wonderful deeds of Yahweh who is man's refuge in all dangers. It is particularly suitable for emigrants or refugees because it speaks in the language of a wanderer in the desert. It sees God as one who rewards the good and gives them security — 'a city to dwell in'. He also punishes those who do evil by turning 'fruitful land into a salt waste'. The upright experience the goodness of God and rejoice and they give voice to what they feel. That is exactly what a congregation should be encouraged to do: to respond loudly and clearly 'O give thanks to the Lord for his great love is without end'.

3. *Ps 120.* The language of Psalm 120 is that of one who is at war and needs to be on his guard at all times. In many ways the emigrant or exile finds himself on the defensive. He is aware of his weakness and need for help. So he calls for the help of him who made all things. He can have confidence in knowing that the Lord is like a good sentry — he never relaxes his vigilance. He will protect him at all times and in all places guarding his 'going and coming both now and for ever'.

D. GOSPELS

1. *Mt 2:13-15, 19-23.* The significance of this reading is obvious. The holy family fleeing by night, the *Exul Familia* of the encyclical of Pope Pius XII, is the proto-type of every refugee family. The fact that

Christ chose to identify himself so closely with people away from home as to become a refugee and exile himself must be a source of encouragement to all people on the move, as well as an inspiration to all concerned with the care of migrants. One recalls the prayer composed by the Irish bishops in 1955 and recited in all churches during the years of heaviest Irish emigration. It prayed to Jesus who 'was compelled . . . to endure the hardship and poverty of emigrants'.

2. *Lk 10:25-37.* The primary significance of this Gospel reading is that it emphasises the universal law of charity binding us all — 'You must love God with all your heart . . . and your neighbour as yourself'. Christ when asked: 'Who is my neighbour', drives home his teaching in the simplest and most compelling manner — a practical everyday story of how one man showed compassion to another. The lesson to be learned will be all the more telling when one considers those who refused to help — the establishment, identifiable with the priest and the levite. Charity that was real and effective was exercised by one who was considered an alien and a heretic — the Samaritan. The application of the parable should be easy and varied, not the least important point being what the attitude of the established community should be towards new arrivals.

For Thanksgiving

Andrew Nugent, O.S.B.

I INTRODUCTION

'Thanks be to God'; 'Praise to you, Lord Jesus Christ'.

We acclaim every reading from the Lectionary with one or other of these two responses. This simple fact is highly significant. It shows that praise and thanksgiving are not marginal extras, liturgical appendices tacked on after oblations and petitions, protestations of nothingness and acts of contrition. Praise and thanksgiving are the centre and core of the liturgy. They are the Church's characteristic and unvarying response to everything that God is and does, to every word he has spoken, to every aspect of his revelation.

Christian liturgy and prayer will never be renewed until praise and thanksgiving are restored to their rightful position. All those anxious, worried little invocations, all those sonorous, mock-heroic, and occasionally preposterous protestations, all those self-denigrating and inculpatory declamations which have tended to strangle the voice of true worship — all must be bundled out to the secondary area in which they belong. Prayer, whether liturgical or personal, must concentrate primarily on what God is, and only incidentally on what man is not, or has not, or cannot. In spite of all the reforms we have witnessed, Christian prayer is still languishing (except, no doubt, among the charismatics) and simply because we have not yet remembered to put God in the central position, to adore him, to delight in his beauty and goodness, to praise and thank him with all our hearts.

If the readings for Masses 'in thanksgiving' are consigned to the back of the Lectionary, this is certainly not because thanksgiving is of lesser importance. It is because there is something tautological about the notion of a Mass 'in thanksgiving'. Every Mass is essentially and primarily a thanksgiving. 'The Lord Jesus on the night when he was betrayed took bread, and when he had given thanks, he broke it, and said, "This is my body which is for you."' (1 Cor 11:24) The very word 'Eucharist' means thanksgiving.

The various prefaces which introduce the eucharistic prayer, and the unvarying dialogue which sets the scene for the preface itself, leave us in no doubt about the emphasis and tonality of what is to follow:

Priest: Let us give thanks to the Lord our God.

People: It is right to give him thanks and praise.

This amounts to a statement of intention which governs and predetermines the entire eucharistic prayer. The priest continues, with outstretched arms:

'Father, all-powerful and ever-living God, we do well
always and everywhere to give you thanks through
Jesus Christ our Lord. . .'

Depending on the particular feast, season, or occasion, the preface goes on to specify appropriate motives for the Church's sentiments of adoration, thanksgiving, and joy. Whatever the circumstances, and whatever the motives adduced, the central thrust of this keynote prayer is always the same — to give thanks, praise, and glory to God. This is the very essence of the Mass, and of all truly Christian prayer. Petition, oblation, contrition: these important elements are certainly included; but, if they are to be authentically Christian, and not merely human reactions of fear or importunity in the face of some anonymous Deity or Force, they must stem from the specifically Christian recognition of God as Father. This means that, whatever our prayer, the radical starting point is always the realisation that we have received everything as pure gift. The first correlative of grace is gratitude.

Once again, there can be no genuine liturgical revival until these seemingly obvious, but too often forgotten truths are brought back into the forefront of Christian consciousness.

It has been necessary to sketch in these perspectives in order to present the Masses 'in thanksgiving' in their proper context. Presumably, such Masses will be chosen whenever a particular congregation wishes to thank God for some special favour received. The Mass 'in thanksgiving' is indeed the logical complement to the various Masses for specific spiritual and temporal needs. It is, however, desirable that the particular community's praise and thanksgiving should be situated within the total movement of the Church's life and worship. They must never become hermetically closed around a particular event or situation.

The joy and sorrows of individuals and of particular communities, their sufferings and their triumphs — all of this must be seen, not as so many isolated incidents, but as a participation in Christ's paschal mystery of death and resurrection, as part of the working out of God's plan of salvation, as harbingers of the coming of his kingdom. It will not perhaps be possible nor even desirable for a particular Christian community to seek to trace too exactly the precise significance within God's total providence of the specific events or circumstances which motivate their celebration of thanksgiving. They will know only that they have received tokens of God's goodness and mercy. The Mass, however, is always the expression of the whole Church's worship; it is never merely the expression of a particular assembly's reactions to a specific set of circumstances. We must try, therefore, to ensure that the congregation understands that, above and beyond the particular favour for which we want to thank God — even if it be a spiritual favour — we are joining with Christ and with the whole Church in praising and thanking God for all that he is and for his total work of creation and recreation. It is only within such perspectives that the Mass 'in thanksgiving' can assume its proper significance and most effectively deepen the Christian life and faith of the community which celebrates it.

Where priest and people, whether in intercession or in thanksgiving, concentrate too exclusively on the particular favour sought or received, there is a narrowing of perspectives, an impoverishment of understanding which may degenerate almost to the level of magical thinking. We are well aware that Christ's miracles in the Gospel were not mere cures: they were the first-fruits of the kingdom. Perhaps especially in Masses of thanksgiving, where the favour deemed to have been received will inevitably dominate people's consciousness, those responsible for the celebration must be careful not to overplay the pastoral advantage of showing God's (and their own!) relevance and effectiveness. It would be infinitely regrettable if the coming of God's kingdom should be reduced in men's understanding to a random succession of 'good turns'.

'The seventy-two came back rejoicing. "Lord." they said, "even the devils submit to us when we use your name."' Thanksgiving of a sort, and for a notable favour: this was undoubtedly the best magic the disciples had experienced. But Jesus would have them realise 'what God is offering' (Jn 4:10); he would have them recognise the Gift within the gift: 'Yes, I have given you power to tread underfoot serpents and scorpions and the whole strength of the enemy; nothing shall ever hurt you. Yet do not rejoice that the spirits submit to you; rejoice rather that your names are written in heaven' (Lk 10:17-20). This is the true spirit of the Masses 'in thanksgiving'.

II COMMENTARY ON READINGS

A. OLD TESTAMENT READINGS

1. *1 Kings 8:55-61*. King Solomon praises God for his fidelity to his covenant. 'Of all the promises of good that he made through Moses his servant, not one has failed.' God has remained close to his people. He

has brought them security and peace.

At Mass, we join with Christ in thanking God for his fidelity to the new covenant. Christ is Emmanuel, God with us. Through Christ God remains close to his people. He brings us peace. Like Solomon, let us thank God for his peace: 'Blessed be the Lord God who has granted rest to his people.' God has indeed honoured his promise in Christ: 'Come to me . . . and I will give you rest.' (Mt 11:28).

2. *Sir 50:22-24.* 'Because God was with him, Jesus went about doing good' (Acts 10:38).

Jesus was indeed 'the image of the unseen God' (Col 1:15) who 'in every way' (RSV) or 'everywhere' (Jerusalem) 'does great things.' This reading, then, is like a character-sketch of God. His characteristics are: 'to deal with us according to his mercy', 'to give us gladness of heart', 'to grant peace', 'to deliver us in our own time.'

Those who know our Lady's 'Magnificat' will recognise several ideas and phrases. This is hardly surprising: Mary knew Jesus and she knew God. May her reaction to God's wonderful goodness be ours: 'My soul magnifies the Lord, and my spirit rejoices in God my Saviour' (Lk 1:46).

3. *Is 63:7-9.* Sympathy, compassion: both words imply that one understands and relieves another's suffering by actually sharing that suffering oneself. This is what God has done for us. God-become-man is indeed the 'compassionate high priest' (Heb 2:17 *et passim*). He knows our story from the inside. The wonder of the Incarnation is mysteriously foreshadowed in this reading: 'In all their affliction he was afflicted' (RSV). 'It was neither messenger nor angel but his presence that saved them. In his love and pity he redeemed them himself' (Jerusalem).

Having become one of us, God has in turn made us members of his own family. 'Surely, they are my people.' We can best show our gratitude to God by treating others as God has treated us, by sharing their sorrows, by recognising them as brothers in Christ and sons, with him, of God our Father.

4. *Zeph 3:14-15.* Every man has his own 'old testament'. He is, like the people of Israel at the time of Zephaniah (630 BC), surrounded by enemies. These enemies may be actual people. More often, they are threats less tangible, but not less real: poverty, anxiety, ignorance, pain, the uncertainty of the future, evil in whatever form. Besides, man is his own worst enemy. It is his consciousness of his own sinfulness which makes him fear most.

This reading reassures us: 'The Lord is in your midst . . . He has cast out your enemies . . . He has taken away the judgments against you . . . You shall fear evil no more.'

To be thankful is to believe in the reality of God's saving action in our lives. In this respect we have much to learn from the people and writers of the Old Testament.

B. NEW TESTAMENT READINGS

1. *1 Cor 1:3-9*. 'I never stop thanking God.' The Russian novelist, Dostoevsky, has defined man as 'the ungrateful biped' — ingratitude on two legs. It is too true. We are much more miserable than we need to be, and simply because we fail to remember how much we have received, how much we have 'going for us', 'with God on our side' (Rom 8:31). This reading reminds us of things so big and so basic that we mostly fail to see them: 'the grace of God which was given you in Christ Jesus. . . You were enriched in him in every way. . . You are not lacking in any spiritual gift. . . God is faithful. . . He will sustain you to the end.' The lesson is clear: if we were more grateful, we would also be more hopeful — and happier.

2. *Eph 1:3-14*. The decisive factor in our lives is not our own selfishness, our own self-seeking but 'the riches of his grace which God has lavished upon us.' The inner and deepest meaning of what we are is that 'God destined us to be his sons through Jesus Christ . . . before the foundation of the world.' Let us give thanks. We are nearest to being our real selves when we live 'to the praise of his glorious grace which he freely bestowed on us in the Beloved.'

3. *Col 3:12-17*. 'Be thankful' — St Paul so instructs us no fewer than three times in this short reading. And how should we be thankful? By 'letting the word of Christ dwell in us richly.' In other words, we must show our recognition of the new life we have received by living that life with confidence and joy. If we really believe that we are 'God's chosen ones', that 'the Lord has forgiven us', that we 'were called in one body . . . to the peace of Christ' — then, surely, we must have the optimism to be patient, forgiving, considerate, full of love. Our joy, our gratitude, and our goodness to each other: these three go together. They will increase or diminish in strict proportion.

C. RESPONSORIAL PSALMS

1. *1 Chron 29:10-13*.
   'In thy hand are power and might;
   and in thy hand it is to make great
   and to give strength to all.'

It has been truly said: the more we praise God, the more we esteeem Man. 'Indeed, from his fulness we have, all of us, received' (Jn 1:16). In praising God we celebrate our own happiness and our own fulfilment.

2. *Ps 112:1-8.*
'From the rising of the sun to its setting
the name of the Lord is to be praised.'
The truth is that we do just about everything else 'from the rising of
the sun to its setting.' We seem to prefer to 'sit in the ash heap' the
psalmist refers to. What a life!
3. *Ps 137:1-5.* 'My strength of soul thou didst increase.'
Sometimes, indeed, we have no 'strength of soul', our courage is low;
we can manage so little. More than ever, we must thank God for his
'steadfast love', his 'faithfulness'. He is strong when we are weak, consistent when we are unreliable. He is always alive and active in our lives.
He will never let us go (Mt 14:31).
4. *Ps 144:2-11.* 'I will praise your name for ever and ever.'
This is exactly what we will do — because this is heaven: to praise
God for all eternity. Let us praise God more and more. In doing this,
we are certain to become more and more perfectly ourselves, 'the
perfect Man, fully mature with the fullness of Christ himself' (Eph 4:13).

D. GOSPELS
1. *Mk 5:18-20.* 'Go home to your friends, and tell them how much the
Lord has done for you.'
This, then, is the thanks God wants from us — that we share our joy
and our hope with those around us. In a world where there is so much
hardness, so much bitterness, so much discouragement, we cannot keep
the Good News of the Gospel to ourselves. Are we really grateful to
God? A measure of the sincerity of our gratitude would be how seriously we take this basic truth: men will judge our God by what they see in
us.
2. *Lk 17:11-19.* Ten said 'please' but only one said 'thank-you'. Jesus
was disappointed, not just humanly because his good turn had not been
acknowledged, but with all the sadness of God's Son, because only one
'was found to return and give praise to God'. God cannot suffer; and
yet, in Christ, God's 'reaction' to our ingratitude appears in human
form.

III THEMATIC GROUPINGS

The choice of the most suitable readings will probably depend on the
precise circumstances in which a particular congregation wishes to
celebrate thanksgiving. Equally, the actual situation may suggest a more
specific theme within the general context of thanksgiving. In that case

the two (or three) readings will be coordinated closely in function of that specific theme. If, however, no dominant theme imposes itself, it might be better to allow each reading to sound its own particular note. All the texts have been chosen in relation to the idea of thanksgiving. In practically any combination they will complement each other naturally and form a harmony. We sometimes underestimate a congregation's capacity to associate complementary aspects of a single theme. This undue pessimism can lead homilists to pass over the real and rich content of the different readings and to concentrate instead on one or two very general notions in terms of which those readings can be superficially unified. This 'lowest common denominator' approach will never deepen a congregation's understanding and appreciation of Scripture.

In the light of the remarks made above (Introduction), it seems obvious that in Masses of thanksgiving particular stess should be laid on:

(a) the fact that the Mass itself *is* thanksgiving;

(b) the insertion of the local community's thanksgiving into the whole Church's thanksgiving to God for all that he is and does;

(c) the particular portions of the Mass where the theme of thanksgiving is essentially underlined: responses to the readings, the offertory prayers over the bread and wine, the dialogue introducing the preface and the preface itself, the institution narrative, the dismissal.

It would be wholly in keeping with the spirit of the liturgy and an eloquent commentary on several of the readings chosen for these Masses if the community celebrating thanksgiving were to share its happiness by some act of charity towards those in need.

Finally, and obviously, appropriate chants should be chosen for the Entry, Offertory, Communion, and Recessional.

The Sacred Heart

Raymond Moloney, S.J.

I INTRODUCTION

Devotion to the Sacred Heart is a celebration of that love, both divine and human, which has entered human history in the person of the Word Incarnate. For a brief statement of what we celebrate in this devotion we could not do better than to turn to the new preface of the Sacred Heart in the Roman Missal: 'Lifted high on the cross, Christ gave his life for us, so much did he love us. From his wounded side flowed blood and water, the fountain of sacramental life in the Church. To his open heart the Saviour invites all men to draw water in joy from the springs of salvation.'

For a fuller statement of the object and content of this devotion we have the encyclical of Pius XII, *Haurietis aquas*. In what follows references will be made to the paragraphs of the London C.T.S. pamphlet (Do 287), which contains the text of the encyclical. Written towards the end of Pius' reign, this encyclical was already able to draw on the great advances in scriptural and theological studies generally which were to bear fruit in Pope John's council. Two points in particular were established by that encyclical which all preaching of this devotion should take into account.

Firstly, the encyclical made clear what is the object of the devotion. Devotion to the Sacred Heart is devotion to the Person of the Word Incarnate under the aspect of his love and through the symbolism of his heart opened by a lance on the cross (*Haurietis aquas*, 27, 39, 57). The encyclical also makes precise that the love symbolised by Christ's heart is threefold: his human affectivity; the created love in his human will; and, above all, the uncreated love in his divine will (27). Particularly important was the clarification by the encyclical that the divine and uncreated love in the Word Incarnate rightly belongs to the object of this devotion (27, 43, 58). Prior to the encyclical this was a point of discussion among theologians.

The second great service of this encyclical lay in the way it called this devotion back to its sources in the scriptural and mystical tradition of the Church. This was to prove a providential preparation for the liturgy of the Sacred Heart which we find in the new Missal and Lectionary. If celebrants are to avail of these new texts properly, they must first understand the biblical and patristic basis of the devotion.

As the encyclical points out (13), in searching for biblical texts on the Sacred Heart, one would look in vain for passages which make clear mention of venerating the physical heart of Jesus as the symbol of his love. That would be to read the language of later centuries back into the biblical authors. As one writer put it: 'A biblical basis for the devotion is to be found only by joining together and correlating many different texts which illumine and explain one another' (R. Gutzwiller, in *The Heart of the Saviour*, Herder & Herder 1957, p. 8). In seeking out these texts three aspects of scriptural teaching will be found particularly helpful.

First of all, our emphasis on the heart of Christ can be seen to fit in with an emphasis on the human heart generally which Scripture sees as one of the marks of the new covenant. New Testament Christianity might be summed up as a religion of the heart. This means that it is a form of faith where the value of what we do is seen to depend on what we are. Pride of place is given to the inner values from which alone power will flow into all the external aspects and structures of Christian life (cf. Mt 15:18; 12:34).

This way of speaking also underlines the fact that this inner force is especially a power for loving. In a world where charity has grown cold (Mt 24:12), Christians are called to a twofold love, love of God and of neighbour. This is part of that new heart promised to all who belong to the new covenant, a heart of flesh instead of a heart of stone (Jer 31:33; Ezek 36:25f). If all this is the vocation of all believers, it was only natural for the Church to go on to stress it in an exemplary way in the case of Christ himself.

A second source of the biblical tradition on Christ's heart will be found in the psalms. Here the references will necessarily be secondary and indirect, but yet not without a solid basis in fact. From the New Testament we can identify particular psalms as messianic. When we find that these psalms sometimes speak of the heart of the Messiah, then we have a sufficient basis for drawing on these psalms in our devotion to Christ's heart. The references in themselves are scattered and incidental, for instance: Vulgate Ps 39:7-9; 21:15; 68:21f; 15:9. But putting together the picture of the Messiah which emerges from a number of these psalms seen as a group, we have a significant, biblically based statement, which might be held to mark the first dawn of this devotion.

When we turn to the New Testament, the central text for this devotion lies in Jn 7:37-39 with its associated passages, especially Jn 19:34. It is important, however, to read Jn 7:38 according to that reading

which is preferred by Pius XII in *Haurietis aquas*. This reading marks a
return to an ancient tradition, as well as being one often favoured by
modern scholarship, e.g. The Jerusalem Bible, The New English Bible.
The reading runs as follows: If anyone is thirsty, let him come to me,
and let him drink who believes in me; as Scripture says, fountains of
living water will flow from his bosom.

The point made clear by this ancient reading is that the fountains
of living water are to flow from within Christ himself. As we know,
this was to come about in a literal way on Calvary (Jn 19:34). But for
the mystical tradition of the Church, nourished on the Scriptures, this
event was to conjure up a whole context of Old and New Testament,
full of imagery and prophecy and promise.

In the background are the words of Zechariah 12:10 and 13:1. Also
present is an allusion to the prophecy of a new temple in Ezek 47,
where we are told there will be a new stream of living water flowing
from its right side. Connected with this are the statements of the fourth
gospel on the body of Christ as the temple of the new covenant (Jn
2:21). Finally there is the vision of the Apocalypse, where the whole
city of God is watered by the stream flowing from the place of God and
the Lamb (Rev 22:1f).

What is this water flowing from the side of the temple of Christ's
body? In the context of the fourth gospel we think in the first place of
the Holy Spirit, according to the explicit statement of Jn 7:39. But
tradition has also seen a reference here to the Church and to its sacraments, through which the Holy Spirit comes to us. In the fourth gospel
Christ is the new Adam; and just as Eve was born from the side of the
first Adam, it is understandable that the new Eve, the Church, should
be born from the opened side of the Lamb. This essentially nuptial
image, made more explicit in the Apocalypse (e.g. 19:7-9; 21:9; 22:17)
underlines how this economy of salvation, flowing from the side of
Christ, is a work of the Saviour's love.

That Christ's love is part of the meaning of the opened side is confirmed by seeing here a reference to the sacraments of Baptism and
Eucharist, especially the latter. Some exegetes consider that already in
the mind of the evangelist the water and blood from the opened side
are a reference to the water of Baptism and to the cup of the Eucharist.
Certainly this is the way the text has been read in tradition and in the
liturgy.

Once the devotion has been established on a firm foundation in the
abiding truths of the New Testament, we can go on to consider the
development of the devotion and the different aspects which have been
stressed at different stages of its history. In particular we should consider those aspects of our present post-conciliar situation to which this

devotion speaks in a particularly helpful way.

There is, first of all, the image of Christ, which this devotion puts before us. Sometimes the devotion has been criticised for contradictory reasons. Some have criticised it for being too humanistic about Christ, others for exaggerating the divine in him in a kind of monophysite way. It is true that traditionally this devotion has laid special stress on the human and affective side of Christ, and this fits in very well with our contemporary concern to see Christ as fully human. However Pius XII's insistence on the divine dimension of Christ's love helps to counter exaggerations on the humanistic side.

Truth to tell, this devotion presents Christ as fully human, but not only human, as fully divine, but not only divine. To present Christ under the aspect of his love is to present him in the concrete unity of a living personality. To see him as the Sacred Heart is to see him as he is now in heaven. He is a mysterious, prophetic figure, like one of those visions seen by Daniel and Ezechiel in the Old Testament, but in his case he is transfigured by his own divinity. At the same time he retains all the human warmth which we have come to know in the New Testament. In a world made empty by secularism and cold by its lack of love and devotion, what so many need is precisely such a vision — a person of divine significance inviting us to follow the way of the beloved disciple, so that we might know Christ interiorly and belong to him from within.

A second aspect of our present situation which is relevant is our concern for a more authentic religion, one less reliant on external forms and more insistent on interior and spiritual values. This is that religion of the heart to which we have already referred. Pius XII relates this devotion to that worship in spirit and in truth of which our Lord spoke to the Samaritan woman (56). In modern times we might think of the spirit of one such as Charles de Foucauld with his stress on the interior life and his sensitive devotion to the Sacred Heart.

A religion of the heart is a religion of love. This gives us a third heading under which to consider the relevance of this devotion to our situation. The Sacred Heart is the man for others, the High Priest of self-sacrifice in the service of mankind. Today we speak much of service, compassion and reconciliation, but too often our efforts run out of that deeper inspiration which for most of us only religion can sustain. What we want is to put new heart into our efforts, a heart known by faith alone, the heart of Christ himself. He is the perfect exemplar of all such endeavours. The wound in his heart reminds us of what such work really means (Mt 25:35ff). But he is more than an example. He is a source of power, for from his heart has come the very spirit of love itself, the Holy Spirit, whose life-giving waters have come to us from the side of the victim on the cross.

As well as these traditional aspects of the devotion, which speak to us with a new eloquence after the second Vatican Council, the devotion today should take account of new developments and emphases. In the first place the devotion must be thoroughly liturgical. The new Lectionare should be of great assistance towards this end. But it is not just a question of fitting the devotion into our liturgies and calendar of celebrations. The spirit of the devotion must be liturgical also. This will mean a greater emphasis on Christ as mediator. For example, even more important than reparation *to* Christ is reparation *with* him to the Father. A more liturgical devotion will also give more attention to the resurrection of Christ. Christ shows his love for us not only in his dying but also in his rising again, in his return to his Church and in his special gift of his presence in our liturgies.

In the second place the devotion should be related to all the recent developments connected with the sacrament of Penance. In the modern Church there is taking place a great broadening and deepening of the theology and practice of penance and reconciliation. New forms of this sacrament and of the whole sacramental process connected with it are being developed. Devotion to the Sacred Heart belongs right at the centre of these developments, since the heart of Christ is the heart of mercy and forgiveness and reconciliation. In particular our concern for community and communal expressions of penance should be related to the Sacred Heart, since this Heart is the centre of the Christian community. Is it not an eloquent sign for us that the centre of a penitent people should be a heart wounded by sin?

Finally this devotion should take more account of the Holy Spirit. One of the special marks of the Church today is the growing appreciation of the place of the Holy Spirit in our lives. The fourth evangelist, however, has made it clear (at Jn 19:34, when taken with Jn 7:37-39), that there is an intimate connection between the gift of the Holy Spirit and the opening of Christ's side. The Holy Spirit is 'the Spirit of Jesus' (Acts 16:7). He is the gift of Christ's heart to the Church. Indeed it is only through the Holy Spirit within us that we can respond to Christ's love as we should. The Holy Spirit is the spirit of divine love itself. Devotion to the Sacred Heart, however, keeps before us how this love comes to us only as the water flowing from the side of Christ. In other words, we can truly receive the Spirit and grow in his gifts only in dependance on Christ and his Church and his sacraments.

In what we have set out above we have tried to give the outlines of a devotion to the Sacred Heart which takes account of the reforms of the Second Vatican Council and of the new Roman Missal and Lectionary. Like the teacher of the kingdom in the New Testament (Mt 13:52) the apostle of this devotion has to be able to bring forward both things old and things new. Different times and persons will be moved by different aspects of the devotion. The language and imagery associated with it may change. But behind all this development and variety there remains the call of the New Testament itself to a life of love in response to the mystery of love made incarnate in the person of Jesus of Nazareth. The extent to which men will be helped in their response by considering Christ's heart and opened side will vary. But there can be no doubt of this: so deeply is this imagery imbedded in the mystical tradition of the Church that it will always retain an important place in the devotion of many Christians.

II COMMENTARY ON READINGS

Readings for the Mass of the Sacred Heart are found in two special sections of the Lectionary. In the section on Votive Masses the main set of readings will be found, providing a selection out of which three readings with responsorial psalm and Alleluia verse could be chosen for any Mass in honour of the Sacred Heart. For the feast of the Sacred Heart some of these same readings are printed out again but now arranged for use according to the three-year pattern of the festive cycle. Our commentary will follow the order of readings as found among the Votive Masses towards the back of the Lectionary.

A. OLD TESTAMENT READINGS

These readings speak directly of divine love as revealed in the Old Testament. In so far as the Sacred Heart is a symbol of the Incarnate Word's divine love as well as of his human love, these readings may be taken as an indirect reference to the Sacred Heart.

1. *Ex 34:4-6, 8-9.* The divine love is tender, compassionate and forgiving, qualities which tradition has found in a special way in the heart of Christ.

2. *Deut 7:6-11.* God does not choose Israel because of the human merits of its people, but solely out of a pure act of his love. The same divine generosity will be found in Christ's love for his Church.

3. *Deut 10:12-22.* Love calls forth love. Divine love is no exception. Because of God's love for us, we too must love God and our fellow man.

4. *Is 49:13-15*. God's love for man is more constant than a mother's love for her son.

5. *Jer 31:1-4*. This passage gives us the opening verses of the great chapters of Jeremiah that look forward to a new covenant and a new form of religion to be written in the hearts of men (Jer 31:31-34). This new covenant, which the New Testament will find present in the Eucharist in a special way (1 Cor 11:25) is here seen to be due to God's 'everlasting love' for his people.

6. *Ezek 34:11-16*. One of the images in scripture closest in spirit to that of the Sacred Heart is the image of the Good Shepherd. This New Testament way of speaking of Christ (see below on Lk 15:1ff and Jn 10:11ff) has its origins in such passages of the Old Testament as this one of Ezekiel.

7. *Hos 11:1, 3-4, 8-9*. God's love for his people is as tender as a father's for his infant son. Scripture spontaneously applies to God the universal language of human affection, speaking of the feelings of God's heart. Of Hosea in general Pius XII wrote: 'Perhaps of all the saintly prophets none has described so clearly and in such passionate language as Hosea the love with which God has always pursued his people' (*Haurietis aquas*, 15).

B. NEW TESTAMENT READINGS

First Readings in Paschaltide

The book of the Apocalypse is especially associated with Paschaltide because it celebrates in so many ways the victory of the Lamb.

1. *Rev. 3:14, 20-22*. Our Lord is here understood as the Messiah coming in to share with his people the supper of the Lamb. This supper is primarily an image of the redemption. The Jews often thought of the Messiah coming like this during the celebration of the Passover. Christians have always seen the supper of the Lamb as anticipated in the Eucharist.

2. *Rev 5:6-12*. This vision of the heavenly liturgy celebrates the victory of the Lamb of God. The image of the Lamb that was immolated is close in spirit to that of the Heart of Christ pierced in sacrifice. This vision reminds us especially of Mass and Benediction, which have always had a special place in devotion to the Sacred Heart.

Second Readings

1. *Rom 5:5-11*. The proof of divine love is the fact that Christ died for sinners, not for saints. This fact is the source of reconciliation for us and of the presence of the Holy Spirit which the Heart of Christ has

poured into our hearts.

2. *Eph 1:3-10.* This passage reads like a Eucharistic Prayer. The inspired author praises God for the divine plan which has placed Christ as the centre of salvation history. Christ, the Head of the Church, is the heart of the world.

3. *Eph 3:8-12.* Traditionally in devotion to the Sacred Heart the reference in this passage to 'the infinite treasure of Christ' has been applied to the riches contained in the Heart of Christ, which are the basis of our confidence in approaching God.

4. *Eph 3:14-19.* The love of Christ for his Father and for all mankind is so far beyond our grasp that we can speak of it only under the symbol of his heart. Concering this passage Pius XII said that it shows us how the charity of Christ constitutes the summit of the Christian life (*Haurietis aquas,* 55).

5. *Phil 1:8-11.* Paul loves the Philippians 'in the heart of Christ'. Most translations lose the force of this phrase in the opening verse of the passage. The word used in Greek is one of the synonyms for 'heart'. Christ's love is to pass through us and so to draw others to itself through us.

6. *1 Jn 4:7-16.* That God is love is another way of conveying something of what we mean when we speak of Christ as the Sacred Heart.

C. RESPONSORIAL PSALMS[1]

1. *Is 12:2-6.* This psalm from the book of Isaiah is that referred to in the title of Pius XII's encyclical, *Haurietis aquas.* The theme fits in especially with Jn 7:37-39. and with Jn 19:34 (see below).

2. *Ps 22.* This psalm is probably the greatest favourite in the whole psalter. It celebrates the goodness of God as the Shepherd of Israel (see above on Ezekiel 34:11-16). Christians have always related it in a special way to God's love for us in the Eucharist. Cf. Mk 6:34-44 (Lectionary, page 68).

3. *Ps 24.* A prayer for true repentance, this psalm celebrates the constancy of God's love. God's love is the ground of our hope for forgiveness.

4. *Ps 32.* A psalm of joy and praise, these verses speak of God's heart and of our hearts. The Introit of the Mass of the Sacred Heart was formerly taken from this psalm.

[1] The responsorial psalms in the Lectionary are chosen for their references to God's love for his people. If one wanted psalms referring to the heart of the Messiah, one could turn to Lectionary, Wednesday of Holy Week, for Ps 68, or to Lectionary, Easter Monday, for Ps 15.

5. *Ps 33.* A prayer of hope in times of trial, this psalm was quoted by St John Fisher on the scaffold.

6. *Ps 102.* A sensitive prayer of thanksgiving, this psalm celebrates the infinitude of divine compassion in wiping away our sins.

D. GOSPELS

1. *Mt 11:25-30.* Here we catch a glimpse of both the divine and the human in Christ's love: that divine love by which he knows and loves his Father from all eternity, and that divine and human love by which he looks on all who labour and are burdened.

2. *Lk 15:1-10.* Pius XII cites Gregory the Great for the thought that in the parables on the mercy of God, such as those in this passage, the very heart of God himself is made manifest (*Haurietis aquas,* 30).

3. *Lk 15:1-3, 11-32.* The Father of the prodigal shows us what divine love is, while the sons show us what human sin is. The parable brings home to us how closed we are to God's love.

4. *Jn 10:11-18.* This passage brings out not only the love of Christ as the Good Shepherd but also the sovereign freedom of his heart in accepting his Father's will.

5. *Jn 15:1-8.* The parable of the vine expresses our Lord's desire that love and union should reign among his followers. This is one of the fundamental 'thoughts of his heart' (Ps 32).

6. *Jn 15:9-17.* The acid test of true devotion to the Sacred Heart will be found in the love we have one for another. Citing this text, Pius XII said, 'In truth it was his own love, more than the violence of his executioners, that nailed our divine Redeemer to the cross' (Haurietis aquas, 38).

7. *Jn 17:20-26.* One of the deepest designs of Christ's heart is the Eucharist. This chapter of John's gospel gives us some insight into the mind and heart of Christ as he prays in the last supper and in the Mass for unity. Only through, with and in the heart of Christ (cf. Phil 1:8), will we come to that love and union which he plans for us.

8. *Jn 19:31-37.* When read in the light of Jn 7:37-39, this scene gives us our principal New Testament basis for devotion to the Sacred Heart. St Augustine points out how Christ's side is not just pierced but *opened.* This is a sign to us how the divine life, coming to us through the sacraments especially, is to be seen as the gift of Christ's love to his bride the Church.